Becoming a Critical Thinker

Becoming a Critical Thinker

Sandra Egege

BLOOMSBURY ACADEMIC
LONDON • NEW YORK • OXFORD • NEW DELHI • SYDNEY

BLOOMSBURY ACADEMIC
Bloomsbury Publishing Plc
50 Bedford Square, London, WC1B 3DP, UK
1385 Broadway, New York, NY 10018, USA
29 Earlsfort Terrace, Dublin 2, Ireland

First published in by RED GLOBE PRESS 2021
Reprinted by Bloomsbury Academic

A catalogue record for this book is available from the British Library.

A catalog record for this book is available from the Library of Congress.

ISBN: PB: 978-1-3520-1133-3
ePDF: 978-1-3520-1134-0
eBook: 978-1-3503-1464-1

Series: Bloomsbury Study Skills

To find out more about our authors and books visit
www.bloomsbury.com and sign up for our newsletters.

Contents

Foreword

This book is intended to take anyone interested in becoming a better critical thinker through the various steps and techniques you need to apply a critical approach to your thinking processes. Applying a critical approach will improve your ability to demonstrate critical thinking in your written and oral communication, your academic work or your daily work/life interactions. To assist with understanding the relevance and importance of critical thinking to academic study specifically, and everyday life more broadly, the discussions about critical thinking are placed within an *epistemological framework* or context. An understanding of epistemology helps us understand why certain claims get accepted as knowledge and others don't. It reveals the constitutive relationship between belief and knowledge, and knowledge creation and critical thinking. What we believe informs our actions, which is why it is important those beliefs are based on reliable knowledge. Critical thinking helps us evaluate knowledge claims for reliability.

Critical thinking is not just about applying a useful set of skills to a problem, an idea or a piece of text. It is a rigorous process of self-reflective thinking that develops over time and with practice. But it is worth the effort. Developing a critical thinking capacity helps us engage in constructive debate on social issues, contribute productively in the workplace, and make more informed decisions in our daily lives. By becoming a critical thinker, we can be a more thoughtful and confidant contributor to our society.

Where possible, I have used real life examples to illustrate a critical thinking point. This is why many of them are drawn from current affairs, political events and news items as they have appeared in the recent media.

Dr Sandra Egege
Flinders University, 2020

Glossary

Analysis	dividing a text or argument into its constituent parts in order to understand its meaning and intent and how this is conveyed
A posteriori	something only knowable on the basis of experience; empiricism
A priori	something that can be known by reason alone, independent of experience, like maths or logic; rationalism
Argument	a claim that is put forward and justified by other related claims (called premises)
Assumption	a concept, idea or point of view that is assumed (implicit) or stated (explicit) as accepted fact; often acts as a basis for argument
Claim	a statement in an argument; a premise; a conclusion; an assumption
(being) Critical	the process of examining something against a set standard, objective or set of criteria to see if it meets the requirements
Critiquing	evaluating an object (text) against a standard to ascertain strengths and weaknesses, positives and negatives; critically assessing the value of an object
Deduction	process of logical inference which follows rules of validity; deducing a specific outcome from given, logically related statements; deductive arguments are truth preserving
Epistemology	study of knowledge; how we know what we know (criteria) and how we know that we know it (evidential reliability)
Evaluation	assessing the worth of something against set criteria
Evidence	facts, data or other information used to justify or support a claim
Fallacy	common linguistic mistake in logic or reasoning resulting in unjustified conclusion or inference
Generalisation	a claim drawn from a specific set of examples that is (supposedly) applicable to all similar instances of the same kind
Hypothesis	a possible explanation of a phenomenon or event that is put forward, should be susceptible to testing
Induction	process of inference from evidence leading to generalisation or prediction; inference to the best explanation

Inference	a claim or conclusion drawn from evidence; what is inferred
Justification	reasons put forward to support a claim or action
Knowledge	claims drawn from evidence through a process of inference (induction or deduction) that conform to reality; claims that are justified and accepted as true; statements of fact
Logic	method of reasoning using accepted rules of inference; can be formal or informal
Logical connectives	words that illustrate logical relationships between ideas such as 'if…then…'; 'or'; 'and'; 'not'
Methodology	used to describe the framework that informs primary research; quantitative or qualitative research models
Ontology	what our understanding of reality is and of what it consists; our worldview; sometimes a synonym for metaphysics
Phenomenology	the study of subjective existence, how things appear to our consciousness or conscious experience; being in the world
Position	the point of view taken by the author on an issue
Premise	statement that directly supports the conclusion of an argument; more than one premise may be contained in the same sentence
Proposition	a thought or statement contained in a sentence, often formulated as 'it is claimed that…'
Reasoning	logical process of working out connections between facts and ideas leading to solution or inference; uses logical connectives like 'if…then…'
Reviewing	process of critically evaluating a piece of research, program or text; often leads to recommendations for improvement
Statement	a claim that can be true or false; may be more than one statement in a sentence
Synthesis	the result of pulling together common themes, ideas, trends, usually as part of literature review

CHAPTER

1

Why Critical Thinking Matters: Research, Knowledge and Epistemology

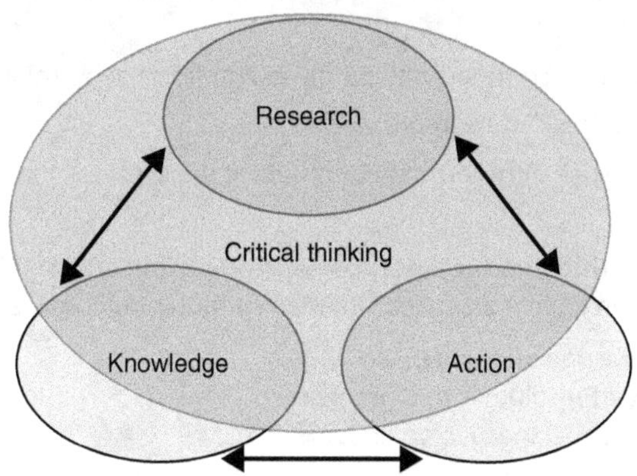

Why critical thinking matters

Have you ever asked yourself why critical thinking is valued? What is it about critical thinking that makes it such a desirable attribute?

The answer is both simple and complex. First, we don't have complete knowledge – there is a lot about our world that we still don't know or don't understand. The history of knowledge has also shown us that what we think we know can sometimes turn out to be false. Secondly, there are a lot of problems in the world, big and small, that need solving. While we want to find the right solutions to those problems, we don't always know what the right solutions are and there may be more than one solution to choose from, depending on the context. How do we know which is the best?

It is not easy for humans to find out the truth about the world, to discover what reliable knowledge is and to work out what a possible solution might be. The world is a complex system of inter-related parts. Make a change here and it may have negative consequences there. What works in one situation may not work in another. To complicate matters even more, human thinking is fallible; we know we can make mistakes. How things appear is not always the way they are. We are prone to all sorts of influences on our thinking that can affect our perception and our objectivity and these influences can have an impact on the kinds of conclusions we reach. We need to be careful and cautious. We need a rigorous thinking process that will enable us to overcome our limitations and minimise our mistakes in order to come to the most reliable conclusions we can – basically to make our thinking better. **This process is critical thinking.**

The importance of critical thinking

Assumptions

- There is good and bad thinking – some thinking practices are better than others.
- Good thinking practices produce better, more reliable outcomes.
- We want to develop good thinking practices because we want the best outcomes.
- Critical thinking is considered to be the exemplar of good thinking practice.
- Thinking practices can be improved.

Conclusion – We can all become (better) critical thinkers.

We use critical thinking for a purpose – we apply our critical thinking skills to an issue, a problem, an idea or a situation to reach a better outcome, such as:

- Increased knowledge and understanding
- A possible or better solution to a problem
- A new or broader perspective on an issue
- A change of belief or practice
- Confirmation of an old idea or current practice.

So what is the critical thinking process?

While there is a lot of debate and disagreement about what critical thinking is, there are a few accepted definitions available that share key characteristics (Facione, 1990; Paul and Elder 2001, 2010). The following definition attempts to capture those features while directing the process of critical thinking towards its purposes, whether that is within the university, at work or in a broader community context.

Critical thinking is the process of analysing, evaluating and critiquing information in order to ***increase our understanding and knowledge of reality***. It includes the capacity to reason well in order to come to an objectively justifiable conclusion about something. It is the skill or ability to assess and evaluate the way information is presented, to draw out the relevant or reliable claims and to ***use reasoning and logic to justify well-founded conclusions*** based on the information or knowledge distilled from this critical process. It is to ***come to the best conclusion or decision we can***, based on what we currently know.

The following chapters will set out how we can become (better) critical thinkers. Applying critical thinking skills to the problems we encounter can help us to come to well-informed and well-thought out conclusions, decisions and solutions. If our actions are based on reliable information and inference rather than on ill-informed or even false beliefs, then we are likely to achieve better outcomes. Our actions will resonate with the way the world is.

A first step in becoming a critical thinker is in understanding where our knowledge or information comes from.

- What is the process of knowledge creation?
- What is a fact?
- What makes something (a fact) a reliable piece of information?
- How does a fact become knowledge?
- Why should we accept some statements of facts but not others?
- How do we know that we know? Can we believe our senses?

Research

Let's start within the university context. What is unique about a university is that it is both a repository of knowledge and a place where knowledge is created. At a university, not only do you have access to knowledge on a range of topics but you can have access to a range of knowledgeable people – academics who are experts in their chosen field. They have become experts not just by knowing a lot but by **adding to the knowledge in their field**. They have undertaken **research** and discovered new and interesting things.

Research is the systematic exploration of a topic undertaken in order to increase **knowledge and understanding**. The research process is used to establish or confirm facts, reaffirm the results of previous work, solve new or existing problems and support and/or develop new theories, ideas and approaches.

We conduct research to increase our knowledge base, to explore new ideas and to see if old ways still hold. We conduct research because we know things change and old ideas may no longer work or be relevant. Research is not conducted haphazardly; it needs to be thorough and targeted towards what it is attempting to find out. The outcomes can contribute to knowledge of all kinds – of the physical world (including the laws governing that world), space, human behaviour, health, culture and society.

The process of research

Research is usually driven by what are called '**hypotheses**', statements or propositions that one sets out to find evidence for (to verify or confirm) or against (to falsify). These could also be in the form of **research questions** – i.e. *why do birds fly in formation?* Once data or evidence has been gathered relevant to that research question, then a possible answer (hypothesis) is generated that could then be tested – i.e. *birds fly (change their position of flight or flap their wings) to give themselves the best aerodynamic advantage.*

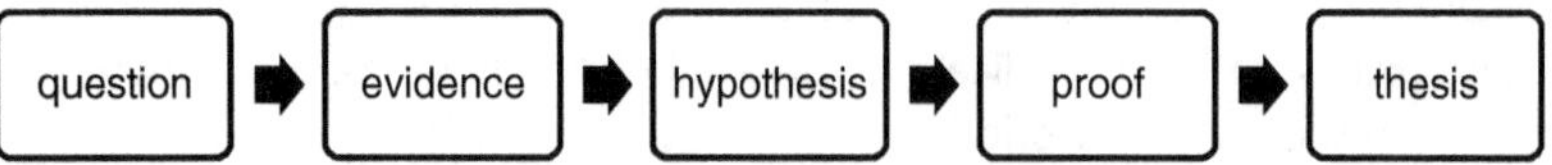

Research is curiosity or needs driven; it is a systematic exploration and investigation into some phenomenon to find out something about it. If all goes well, what we find out through this process ends up becoming accepted as fact or knowledge or a legitimate alternative perspective. The hypothesis becomes the '**thesis**', which is then put forward as a **knowledge claim**. If it stands up to rigorous scrutiny, it gets adopted as '**fact**' or '**theory**' and becomes part of our knowledge base; for example, *birds fly in formation to conserve energy and maximise aerodynamic effect* (*Nature* 505, 399–402. 2014, doi:10.1038/nature12939).

While research in the humanities is not always about discovering facts, it is guided by similar principles – to increase knowledge and understanding of the object under investigation. The difference is that the object may be a text, an author or artist, a theory or an approach. Nevertheless, any new claims, interpretations or approaches will still need to be supported by evidence and rigorously argued for if they are to become a part of the discipline's curriculum.

Understanding the **process of knowledge creation** will help us to think critically about claims to knowledge.

What is knowledge?

In any field of study, there is an accumulated body of facts and theories that is generally accepted, which constitutes the **knowledge** base of that field. We rely on these well-accepted facts and theories to support the claims we make about particular aspects of the world we live in. This knowledge informs our decisions and determines our actions. It is used as the foundation for our beliefs and our claims to expertise. However, this body of knowledge didn't just sit around waiting to be discovered. Research isn't just about collecting all the facts and data on a given topic. A great deal of time and effort has gone into establishing that body of knowledge. It has emerged from a long history of hypothesising and testing and inferring and verifying and arguing and justifying, often against rival positions. To draw any conclusions or to posit **knowledge claims**, our research has to satisfy strict criteria.

Knowledge = justified true belief

*Propositional knowledge involves making a knowledge claim about something. In order to count as knowledge, the claim must satisfy certain strict criteria.

- Someone must believe it (knowledge must be *known* by someone).
- It must be true (it is a fact about the world as far as we know).
- It must be justified (there should be convincing reasons for believing it to be true).

[*A proposition is a meaning or thought contained in a sentence. A statement is a verbalised proposition. Propositional knowledge is often called 'knowledge that…' to distinguish it from 'knowing how…']

The **justified true belief** definition of knowledge holds that the truth of the statement is proportional to the strength of the justification (Egege and Kutieleh, 2013; Sievers, 2001). If we want to evaluate a claim, to find out whether or not it is true, then we need to think about why we would believe it. What is the evidence for it? How is it justified? The most important criterion for a knowledge claim is the **justification** – the evidence, proof or reasons for supporting a claim. The stronger or more convincing the evidence or reasons, the more likely it is that the claim is true or is likely to be true, as far as we know.

To justify a claim, the **evidence or reasons** need to be reliable; they need to be relevant; they need to be sufficient. They need to be convincing.

EXAMPLE 1

Propositional statement – *There is life on Mars.*

Does this statement count as knowledge? Does it satisfy the criteria set out above? Let's say that John believes it to be true (many people believe in alien life, especially as a possibility and even as a probability). Let's imagine further that it is actually true and there is life on Mars (it is a fact about Mars). So the claim satisfies the first two criteria set out above. What about some reasons for believing it to be true? At this point in time, we do not have good reasons to justify the claim. We don't know if it is true and we haven't *proved* it to be true. We don't have any evidence. This means it can't (yet) count as knowledge *even if it were true*. As such, it remains a hypothetical claim or opinion (there *may* be life on Mars).

EXAMPLE 2

Propositional statement – *Water boils at 100°C.*

Does this statement count as knowledge? Does it satisfy the criteria set out above? A lot of people believe it to be true. Let's imagine further that it is actually true, water boils at 100°C (it is a fact about water on Earth). So the claim satisfies the first two criteria set out above. What about some reasons for believing it to be true?

- We are taught this as a fact at school.
- It has been laboratory tested and measured (first in 1705).

- Thermometers are calibrated using the fixed freezing and boiling points of water in the Celsius (centigrade) scale, 0–100.
- If we were to boil water, it is likely it will boil at 100°C (we can test it).

It looks like there are convincing reasons to believe the statement to be true. This means we can claim that this is something we know – it counts as knowledge.

Knowledge claims or statements

Your first task in becoming a critical thinker is to be able to separate factual statements (claims) from other kinds of statements. We need to be able to identify which statements are knowledge claims and which are not. If we can't do this, we won't be able to evaluate or critique the text properly. We need to know which statements the author is putting forward as facts for us to accept.

Any text or article will have a lot more in it than just information, knowledge claims or statements of fact. It will have the author's opinion, some discussion that might include someone else's opinion, some background information, some specific information relating to the topic like data and possibly an argument supporting a conclusion or point of view. We discuss these in more detail in later chapters. Other kinds of sentences can be questions, exclamations, commands, opinions, expressions of feeling and recommendations or prescriptive statements.

To be **a critical thinker**, you need to be able to identify knowledge claims from other kinds of statements or claims.

Exercise 1

Look at these statements. Can you tell what type of statements they are? Which ones are knowledge claims or facts? (clue: *which ones can be true or false?)*

1. Keep off the grass
2. Today was hot
3. Tony has three sisters
4. Water is a combination of hydrogen and oxygen
5. (I think) chocolate is delicious
6. Marijuana should be legalised

Justification

Once we have identified factual statements or knowledge claims, we are in a position to evaluate them. Just because something is written as if it is a fact about something or someone, doesn't mean it is true or is something we know. If you are unsure of a claim, you should always ask for **evidence** to support or justify it. Ask 'How do you know that? What makes you think/believe it is true?' If there is no justification or reason given to support a claim, it should be treated as an opinion or someone's belief. The exceptions are when something is common knowledge or it is a logical consequence of the way a statement is worded. In some pieces of writing, the authors do not provide evidence to back up their claims; these are often opinion pieces like a blog or personal webpage. Hypothetically, any statement of fact or a knowledge claim could be shown to be true or false depending on available evidence. This is the case for all bodies of knowledge in every discipline.

EXAMPLE 3

Humanities

These statements are written as fact. They can be shown to be true or false.

- Christopher Marlowe was the real author of Shakespeare's plays.
- Darwin's theory of evolution inspired many of Thomas Hardy's themes.
- Shakespeare is the greatest playwright of all time.
- A concrete object must have weight and mass.
- The Mahabharata is the longest poem ever written.

Academic writing should always support its claims with evidence. The evidence will come from reliable sources that are then **referenced** so you can check the source.

While we want to question some claims and while it is good to make sure we have good reason to believe certain claims, it is also essential to accept certain statements as fact. As we mentioned above, there is a large, well-established reliable body of knowledge across a broad range of fields that we accept and which we use to justify certain beliefs or argue for certain positions. In our world we are cognisant of many different things and this knowledge is reliable in a range of situations. Ships float and planes fly, most of the time. Antibiotics fight bacterial infections and doctors can now transplant livers, faces and hands successfully. Think of our knowledge of mathematics and harmonics, neurology and psychology. We have developed computers, drones, artificial intelligence (AI), the internet and email – all products of human knowledge. As such, there are many established knowledge claims we accept as true unless or until they are shown to be false.

Scepticism is a healthy approach to new and novel claims but **cynicism** of all knowledge is unfounded. It is important we get the balance right.

There are, however, other types of claims that are more contentious, especially ones that appear to overturn currently accepted beliefs or which are new and untested. We want (or should want) proof of their truth before we accept them or believe them. Are we justified in believing them? Think about why some can be accepted as true and why others may need additional evidence or clarification.

First think if a statement can be accepted at face value or whether it requires **justification.**

**Recent research has shown that Altavista and Google are reliable for checking factual information.*

Exercise 2

Look at the knowledge claims below. They are all statements of fact that could be shown to be true or false. Which of these statements can you accept and which would require further proof?

1. Water boils at 100°C.
2. This is a sentence.
3. $\sqrt{81} = 9$
4. The Earth revolves around the sun.
5. Macron was elected as the President of France in 2017.
6. When it rains, plants grow.
7. WWI ended in 1918.
8. The sun casts longer shadows as the afternoon moves into evening.
9. A vegan diet is healthier than a diet that includes eating meat.
10. Climate patterns are changing.
11. Washing your hands reduces the risk of spreading infection.
12. Koalas don't drink water.
13. Ramadan is a Muslim fast.
14. Scientists have identified the gene responsible for obesity.
15. Religion helps people cope with misfortune.
16. There is less crime now than there was 100 years ago.

What counts as proof or evidence?

In order to assess knowledge claims or other statements of fact, to see if they have grounds to be accepted, we need to be able to recognise the kind of evidence that would support them or prove them to be false. Each type of statement will require a certain kind of evidence. For example, the statement that 'it is raining' can be proven by observation. However, the statement that 'a water molecule is composed of two hydrogen atoms and one oxygen atom' cannot be proven by observation. A laboratory with special electrolysis equipment and some prior knowledge of atoms would be needed.

We also need to understand how much or little evidence is needed to prove or disprove a claim. Think of each statement as an hypothesis. How would you set about testing its truth or falsehood? What evidence would support it and what would prove it false? What would count as enough evidence to make it acceptable?

Exercise 3

Compare the statement to the accompanying evidence. Is it enough to prove the fact?

1. A vegan diet is healthier than a diet that includes eating animal proteins.
   - Diets that include a large proportion of fruits and vegetables have been shown to be healthier than diets that include relatively few of these foods.
2. Climate patterns are changing.
   - Scientists have detected recent increases in levels of CO^2, a green house gas which traps heat in the atmosphere.
3. Scientists have identified the gene responsible for obesity.
   - Studies have identified variants in several genes that may contribute to weight gain and body fat distribution.
4. Religion helps people cope with misfortune.
   - Many Bible stories demonstrate how God *comforts* His people in *times of sorrow. The Bible gave me comfort when I was depressed.*

How do you rank the quality of the evidence given? Is it enough to justify the claim? What type of evidence is it? Is it reliable? Are some types of evidence more reliable than others (scientific experiments and statistical data are considered more reliable than personal testimony but in some cases statistical data is not relevant and personal testimony is)? Think about what additional evidence you might need to show that these statements might be true? What might make them false?

Statement 16 – *There is less crime now than there was 100 years ago.*
What kind of evidence would we accept as supporting (or not) this statement? How would we compare today to 100 years ago? Would it be a comparison of numbers of prisoners in gaol over the years per capita? Would it be crime rates? Would it be all types of crimes or just a few? Some acts were criminal then (i.e. homosexuality, homelessness) that are not now; some acts are a crime now (i.e. heroin and marijuana possession; child exploitation) that were not a crime then. Would we look at the whole world or focus on just one country? What evidence would show the claim to be false? Proving whether Statement 16 is true or false will be complicated and will require us to clarify what we mean by terms like 'less' and 'crime'. Less crime where?

Knowledge and epistemology

The reason it is important to look at the evidence for a claim and to see whether it is justified or not is because we want to make sure that what we believe about the world really is true or is as reliable as it can be. Remember: knowledge = *justified* true belief. But even when there are strong grounds to believe something, it may turn out not to be true in some circumstances.

Does water always boil at 100°C?

It turns out that there are some circumstances when water DOES NOT boil at 100°C (or freeze at 0°C). These are when:

- Air pressure changes (up a mountain)
- It is not distilled water (dissolved impurities)
- Objects are added to the water (i.e. metal chips)
- There is dissolved air in the water
- The container is changed (glass, metal, ceramic)
- The surface of the container is treated or coated
- The heating method is changed (slow/fast; using fire/oil)

This situation alerts us to an important fact about the world we live in: **context matters.** Some claims are true, that is, they are a fact about the world in certain circumscribed conditions. While generalisations are not false – they apply most of the time, in most situations – there can be exceptions, depending on the context. The world is full of complex inter-relations. What acts one way in a laboratory may act differently in an uncontrolled environment. We also need to understand how simple facts rely on other simple facts or knowledge, rather like building blocks.

Finding out about the world is not easy. Researching to establish the truth of a claim requires applying rigorous procedures, checks by other experts and repetition to make sure the findings are right. We know we have made mistakes in the past and that we can (and do) still make mistakes. Applying critical thinking skills helps to minimise the risk of mistakes.

Epistemology – How do we know ***what*** we know (what is the evidence?) and how do we know ***that*** we know (could we be mistaken?)?

It has been known for a long time that there are multiple barriers to thinking and seeing clearly, and to thinking and seeing objectively. Plato (500 BCE) famously described our reality is like being in a cave where we only see shadows and reflections of the outside world from which we draw inferences about that world. We need tools to get out of the cave so we can see clearly.

Barriers to knowledge and thinking critically

- What appears to be the case is not always the case (appearance/reality distinction)
- Our perceptual apparatus is limited and easily tricked (we need tools to improve it)
- It is hard to be objective (we see things from our own perspective)
- We select information based on our prior beliefs and biases
- We are prone to logical fallacies

So where does this leave our knowledge claim? It turns out that we can still claim that *water boils at 100°C* (it is a fact about pure water) as long as we state under what conditions; i.e. in optimal circumstances. For it to hold true, we have to **qualify** our claim – ***x is true if and when.***

The next few chapters address some of the known barriers to knowledge and thinking critically. Understanding what the barriers are and how we can minimise their impact will help us develop our critical thinking capacity so we can become better critical thinkers.

Chapter summary

- Critical thinking is the process of analysing, evaluating and critiquing information in order to increase our understanding and knowledge of reality.
- Research is the systematic exploration of a topic undertaken in order to increase knowledge. The research process is used to establish or confirm facts, reaffirm the results of previous work, solve new or existing problems, support and/or develop new theories.
- Understanding the process of knowledge creation will help us to think critically about claims to knowledge.
- To be a critical thinker, you need to be able to identify knowledge claims from other statements or claims.
- Think if a statement can be accepted at face value or whether it requires justification. What would count as justification?

Answers to Exercises 1–3

Exercise 1

Which ones are knowledge claims or statements of fact (*Which ones can be true or false?*)?

- Only 3 and 4 are statements of fact (Tony has three sisters, and water is a combination of hydrogen and oxygen) that can be proven to be true or false.
- 1 (Keep off the grass) is a command.
- 5 (Chocolate is delicious) is an opinion and assumed to be true for the person expressing it.
- 6 (Marijuana should be legalised) is a prescriptive statement.
- While 2 could be said to express a fact, 'hot' is a relative term, so will depend on comparison between norms. What is hot here may not be hot somewhere else.

Exercise 2

Which of these statements can you accept and which require further proof?

Once we have identified a statement of fact or knowledge claim, we need to decide if we can accept it at face value or if it demands further proof or supporting evidence.

- *Common knowledge* – Statements 1, 4, 7 (Water boils at 100°C; The Earth revolves around the sun; WWI ended in 1918) can be accepted without additional evidence because we know them to be true or they count as common knowledge. Statements 5, 12 & 13 (Macron was elected as the President of France in 2017; Koalas don't drink water; Ramadan is a Muslim fast) could be less common knowledge but we can easily find out if they are true or not by looking them up in an encyclopedia or by searching Google. Common knowledge rarely needs additional proof but it may need a reference. Statement 11 (Washing your hands reduces the risk of spreading infection) could fall under this category too as we have known about washing hands and bacteria for a long time, but there was a time when this was not known.
- *A priori knowledge* – Statements 2 & 3 (This is a sentence; $\sqrt{81} = 9$) are what are called *a priori* because they can be worked out without needing additional information. Maths and logic fall under this category. If you apply the right rule, in this case linguistic (2) or mathematical (3), you can check if the statement is right or wrong, true or false.
- *Observation* – Statements 6 & 8 (When it rains, plants grow; The sun casts longer shadows as the afternoon moves into evening) can easily be proven true or false by observation (theoretically so could Statement 12 if in Australia). We learn a lot about our world from observation – gravity, the seasons, our physical environment, our potential and limitations, other people. Observations generally don't need additional evidence (i.e. counting how many people are in a room) but there are limitations, which will be discussed in Chapters 2 and 3.
- *Empirical data* – This leaves statements 9, 10, & 14–16 (A vegan diet is healthier than a diet that includes eating meat; Climate patterns are changing; Scientists have identified the gene responsible for obesity; Religion helps people cope with misfortune; There is less crime now than there was 100 years ago). These last few may or may not be true. They are not known *a priori*, (we can't work them out), they don't count as common knowledge yet, and they can't be known by observation alone. These statements would need to be proven before we accept them as knowledge. We would need to see what empirical evidence was available to support them. What research has been conducted and what have researchers discovered?

Exercise 3

Analysis

For each of the statements 1–4, the evidence presented appears relevant to the claim. Let's assume it is also reliable (we know the source and believe it to be true). Is it sufficient?

- For statement 1 (A vegan diet is healthier than a diet that includes eating meat), the evidence provides grounds for an increase in fruit and vegetables but there is no evidence that this needs to exclude animal proteins, or that (all) animal proteins are unhealthy. We need this additional evidence before we can accept the claim as true.
- Statement 2 (Climate patterns are changing) is interesting. It could be offering an explanation about why the climate is changing or it could be arguing *that* the climate is changing. We need to know that heating the atmosphere will cause changes to climate patterns and that the CO_2 produced will heat it enough to cause the changes.
- Statement 3 (Scientists have identified the gene responsible for obesity) requires a lot more justification to link a gene variation for fat distribution to a gene responsible for obesity before this can be accepted as true. Genes rarely work in isolation and what triggers their 'expression' is complex.
- Statement 4 (Religion helps people cope with misfortune) uses anecdotal evidence which is both difficult to disprove or to generalise to the whole population. However, as a statement of belief – e.g. some people have found religion helps them cope with misfortune – it cannot be proven true or false. It is true for them if they say it is true.

CHAPTER

2

Overcoming Barriers – Cognitive Biases

How do we know that x is true?

In Chapter 1, we examined what it takes for something to become knowledge. It had to be true; it had to be believed and it had to be justified. It had to satisfy very specific criteria. The criteria depend on the kind of knowledge or fact it is. The claim 'it is raining' can be verified or falsified by looking outside. Here we are using our powers of observation to see if the statement accords with reality. It is also something we can check for ourselves. But if the claim was 'it is raining in Rome' and we do not live in Rome, then we cannot check it ourselves. We will need to rely on some other way to verify the claim. We need additional evidence for our belief. Ultimately, we want (and need) to get it right; we don't want our decisions to be based on erroneous information or false beliefs.

> We want to be sure, as much as we can, that what we ***think*** is the case really ***is*** the case.

True or false beliefs?

Unfortunately, it is not always easy to know if we are right or wrong in our beliefs and practices. We know from history that we have made mistakes and been wrong in the past. We know we can still be wrong. We can be wrong as a society and we can be wrong as individuals. **We can believe things that are false.** Why does this matter? Some false beliefs are trivial and have little or no consequences. Some false beliefs may even be beneficial in certain circumstances (i.e. believing one is invincible in war). Some, however, are not trivial or beneficial and can lead to very negative consequences.

- The false belief that cholera was an airborne disease led to 600 deaths in 1854 in London.
- The false belief that some races are inferior to others has led to genocide, systemic injustice, intergenerational poverty and ill health for millions of people.

- Children with HIV/AIDS were banned from kindergartens and public pools because it was falsely believed AIDS could spread through saliva, touch or close contact.
- Some cancer patients have relied on the false efficacy of non-traditional alternative therapies which failed to halt the spread of disease.

No doubt you can think of other examples. As students, researchers, future policymakers and members of society, it is better for you to believe things that are true or likely to be true, rather than false. Doing so will lead to better outcomes for everyone. But to be able to do that, you need to be aware of the barriers to good thinking and how to overcome them.

The human brain and its shortcomings

Alarmingly slapdash in its approach to the truth, your brain manipulates, distorts, and censors evidence to fashion a more palatable version of reality for itself. Capricious and easily distracted, it is swayed by emotions that cloud your judgement and unconscious impulses that exert a hidden influence over your will. Prone to wild irrationalities, stubbornly close-minded, it finds evidence for its pre-established beliefs where none exists and blinds itself to counter evidence with the help of strategically selective powers of reason and memory. Blinkered by self-love, it indulges in ego-inflating vanities and self-serving fictions while at the same time succumbing to unsavoury stereotypes and prejudices about others.

'How Your Brain Distorts and Deceives.' Cordelia Fine, *W.W. Norton,* 2008

Exercise 1

Past false beliefs

Look at the following statements. These were once accepted as true, as facts about our world. They are now considered to be false. Think why it was that people believed them to be true. What kind of evidence do you think was used to support them (but think what evidence proved them to be false)? Why do we no longer accept these claims as true?

1. The Earth is stationary and is orbited by the Sun.
2. Metals can be turned into gold (alchemy).
3. Witches exist, have magical powers and can change into animal forms (therianthropy).
4. Anglo-Saxons are more intelligent than Africans.
5. Animals are mechanistic and do not feel pain, so don't need anaesthetic.
6. A collection of 60 diaries written by Hitler were discovered in 1980s.

Barriers to knowledge – false beliefs, fake news and personal bias

Today, most of us can see why the beliefs (above) are false. Our worldview (ontology) has changed with increased understanding and additional knowledge. However, we are still prone to false beliefs. There has been a lot of concern in recent times about

fake news stories, stories that are being deliberately fabricated and spread by sections of the established media and Facebook/social media to serve a political purpose, much like war time propaganda. These stories are accepted as true by large numbers of the population. At the same time, genuine or true stories are being labelled as fake news (Chapter 6 discusses how to check information sources for reliability). As critical thinkers, we need to be aware of this trend and, through the use of careful critical analysis, combat it where we can.

We are all susceptible to holding **false beliefs.**

Why is it we prefer to believe some things rather than others?

We all form beliefs and opinions about issues that confront us in our daily lives. We often have **reasons**, sometimes seemingly convincing reasons, to support our points of view. But it is also true that sometimes we don't. Sometimes we believe what we want to believe **despite evidence to the contrary**. We still want to think we are right – that the evidence is not real or not convincing. This is an example of **a cognitive bias.**

To be an effective critical thinker, we need to be aware of our own **cognitive biases** and try to overcome them.

What is cognitive bias?

A cognitive bias is a type of error in thinking that occurs when people are processing and interpreting information from the world around them. It makes us biased towards accepting a particular answer or point of view rather than another. This is not always bad. Psychologists believe that many of these biases serve an adaptive purpose – for example, we jump to conclusions quickly based on limited information or past experience. This could save our life or protect us from potential harm. In our modern diverse societies, however, cognitive biases are generally harmful.

Most cognitive biases are a barrier to good critical thinking. They reduce our capacity to reach fair and objective conclusions, even when we think we are being fair and objective. **They can make us believe things that are not true.**

Cognitive biases can be caused by a number of different things – personal motivations, time pressures, social norms, emotions, prior beliefs and attitudes, cultural or social traditions, as well as the psychological limits on the mind's ability to process information objectively. Here we look at the two most dangerous cognitive biases, which are the hardest to overcome and the most common – **confirmation bias** and **belief preservation.**

Confirmation bias

Confirmation bias is considered to be one of the most potent biases and one of the most destructive. It is considered responsible for many of the disputes and misunderstandings that occur among individuals, groups and even nations. As an example, the US withdrawal from the Climate Change Paris Accord in 2017 was already decided in 2016 and was justified by selecting only those economic reports that showed potential job losses from a move away from coal. There were alternative reports that indicated beneficial long-term gains from renewables that were ignored.

Confirmation bias literally means we are **biased towards having a belief confirmed**, rather than refuted. The result is we are more likely to notice and favourably evaluate evidence that confirms a belief we already hold, or that supports a belief we are biased towards holding. We remember the information or event that agreed with a belief and ignore, discount or even forget the information that argued against it. We only look for confirming evidence and fail to critique that evidence appropriately, often accepting it at face value.

*** Important point ***

Just because you focussed only on positive or confirming evidence doesn't entail your belief or conclusion is *necessarily* false. It may be true, and there may be good grounds to believe it to be true. **BUT** if you ignored strong evidence to the contrary, evidence that indicated your belief may be false, then this shows a bias. Social and moral issues are complex and context matters. There may be another perspective that is worth acknowledging. Make sure you deal with all evidence as fairly and objectively as you can. We all like to think we are right! But sometimes there is no simple right or wrong answer.

Belief preservation

A more extreme version of confirmation bias is **belief preservation or perseverance**. Humans have a negative tendency to interpret evidence that favours our existing beliefs and to actively ignore or discount evidence that contradicts those beliefs. This is most apparent when the belief is very personal or emotional, such as with moral, religious or political beliefs. We can interpret or twist evidence to support our point of view and even hold the belief more strongly if it is challenged. When confronted by evidence that contradicts the belief, we discount it or claim it is fake. **Conspiracy theories** are an extreme form of confirmation bias and belief preservation. Any evidence that contradicts the held belief is seen as part of a conspiracy to deceive.

We like to be told what we already believe to be true. We seek out friends who think like us and join groups that support our ideology. If our beliefs feed into our self-image and are part of our identity, it is hard to change them without changing our self-concept. So **we tend to avoid situations and people that threaten those beliefs.**

Exercise 2

Current false beliefs

These claims or beliefs are currently held to be true by certain groups of people, despite strong evidence that they are false (note claims (2) and (5)!). Why do you think people believe these statements to be true when they can be shown to be false?

1. The holocaust was fabricated and millions of Jews did not die (David Irving).
2. The Earth is stationary and shaped like a pancake (Flat Earth Society).
3. Vaccinations cause autism (Andrew Wakefield).
4. Barak Obama was born in Kenya (Donald Trump).
5. Anglo-Saxons are more intelligent than Africans (James Watson).

Why preserve or perpetuate a false belief?

The prevalence of false beliefs despite contrary evidence demonstrates why we need well-developed critical thinking skills. Often the false claim/belief serves a purpose, such as supporting an existing and strongly held prejudice. A prejudice is **a negative belief bias** towards something or someone. Claims (1), (4) and (5) could be said to fall into this category. Should the claim turn out to be false (i.e. Black Americans are no different to White Americans; the Holocaust did happen and was as bad as claimed), then the more general prejudice (in this case, racial/ethnic bias) loses some of its underlying justification. If the claim is part of a wider web of related beliefs, then to not accept this belief may mean that other related beliefs will be brought into question as well. The COVID denial campaign and QAnon are current examples of sets of beliefs based on misinformation.

EXAMPLE 1

Example of confirmation bias

A teenager in Ohio went against his mother's wishes when he turned 18 so he could get vaccinated. He said he had shown his mother scientific studies to show it was safe but that she turned to other less reliable sources of online information that supported her belief that vaccinations were dangerous. He believed his mother was a caring person who had his interests at heart but that she was biased.

In the above example, the boy's mother consciously sought out information that supported her already formed belief that vaccinations were dangerous. She was not open to an alternative position and was unwilling to allow contrary information to change her mind. This is evidence of bias.

Research findings

In California, they found that the autism rate increased by 373% between 1980 and 1994 but the immunisation rate was fairly constant during that period, increasing by only 14%. If there were a link, the pattern of change in the autism rate should reflect the pattern of change in the immunisation rate. Similarly, in 2005, researchers reported on the incidence of autism (ASD) in an area of Japan where the MMR (measles, mumps and rubella) vaccination was withdrawn in 1993. They found that the incidence of autism had continued to increase, even after the withdrawal. If there were a link, one would expect it to have dropped. A recent 20-year Danish study tracked 657,461 children born between 1999 and 2010 from 12 months of age until August 2013, including 31,619 who had not received the MMR vaccine. It found that autism occurred equally in both sets of children.

A lot of people/parents who are against vaccinations (**anti-vaxxers**) hold a range of interrelated beliefs around health and healing and what causes and cures illness. The related websites indicate a lack of trust in Western science and in the motivation of the scientists or researchers. According to some websites, there is concern about the profit motive and vested interests of research institutes working on vaccines. There is also a separate concern about multiple or over-vaccination and the potential consequences of that to the health of their children. Both of these issues are legitimate concerns. They are, however, separate from the issue of whether particular vaccines are harmful in and of themselves. To strengthen their case, anti-vaxxers would need to demonstrate that the following are true.

- Vaccinations are unnecessary (the instance of the disease is rare; the immune system will fight off any disease).
- Vaccinations do not work or are ineffective against the disease they target (i.e. polio, yellow fever, cholera, typhoid, small pox, diphtheria).
- Even if effective, the vaccine causes negative side effects (such as those from drugs like thalidomide).
- The side effects are serious and widespread enough to counteract the benefits of the vaccine (more people suffer death or disability from the vaccine than from the disease itself).

There is currently strong evidence that many of the established vaccines do work in most cases and side effects are rare or low risk. We should, however, not be complacent; we need to pay attention to the effects of any new vaccines to ensure they too are both necessary and safe (COVID19 is a case in point as there are some people who do not believe the threat is real or that a vaccination is necessary). As critical thinkers, we need to ensure the science is rigorous and that we respond to new or counter evidence.

How do we know if we are biased?

We all have some form of confirmation bias. It is a human frailty. We can all hold a belief so passionately we do not want it to be proven wrong. That is why we are prone to discount any evidence that contradicts that belief, especially if that evidence comes from someone or some media who is ideologically opposed to us. This is, nevertheless, a clear indication of bias.

If there is no evidence that would ***ever*** make you change your mind about something, then your belief has become **dogma.** Your bias is overriding your reason.

You may have heard someone say 'I will never change my mind, no matter what you say'. They are saying they will not change their belief, **even if you present good strong evidence to the contrary**. They are content to hold a possibly false belief. In other words, what they believe is not based on reason but emotion. Donald Trump supporters, for example, believe him when he says he is the best president ever, despite any evidence that suggests this may not be the case. There have been 45 presidents in the United States so he has a lot of competition. It is history that determines how great a president is, not their own opinion.

Tribal epistemology

The truth or falsehood of a statement depends on *who* says it

If one of us – true; – If one of them – false

Statements made in Trump's tweets are considered 'fact' because he said them. His suggestion that taking bleach may be a treatment for COVID19 led to at least 30 Americans ingesting bleach the next day, and his endorsement of hydroxychloroquine led to mass stockpiling and a shortage of the drug's availability.

Just because someone is powerful or in a position of authority, doesn't mean what they say is always right or that they have expertise in all areas. Even experts in their respective field should be asked to justify their claims. Accepting someone's claims at face value because of *who they are* is akin to following a guru. Don't accept or believe something just because someone you admire says it is true. Find out *why* they believe it to be true.

It is, however, a human trait to listen to those we agree with and to not listen to those we do not. But being aware of our potential for this kind of bias can help to reduce it. Learn to think for yourself. Be critical and demand solid reasons that can be checked.

Remember, all claims can be challenged and any claim should be falsifiable in theory, if not in practice. If a claim is not theoretically falsifiable, be wary. Ask under what conditions it could be shown to be false. What evidence would you accept that would disprove the claim? Religion is a special case, as belief in its tenets are based on faith rather than evidence. I can continue to believe in a God despite any evidence you put forward as you cannot show me categorically there is no God because God by definition is unknowable, invisible, non-physical. All you can say is that it is unlikely, but you cannot prove it is so. God may have hidden the evidence to test my faith. The nature of the belief makes it unfalsifiable. Astrology falls into a similar category.

As critical thinkers we need to treat all facts, evidence or reasons as **objectively** as we can.

Exercise 3

Critiquing a conspiracy theory

Read the passage below carefully. The claims made in it are very different to the claims you would have heard or read at school. Do you find the claim plausible? If not, is that because you believe in a round Earth, or is it because you think their reasons are not convincing? Are you the victim of a round-Earth conspiracy or are Flat Earthers deluded? Their website encourages everyone to be a critical thinker so let's start with an open mind. To check for yourself, go to https://www.tfes.org/

Case for a flat Earth

Flat Earthers believe that the Earth is shaped like a disc, surrounded by a wall of ice. It is not orbiting around the Sun or spinning on its axis but sits at the centre of the surrounding planets which orbit around it. The Earth is constantly accelerating upwards, creating gravity. The moon landing, space travel and space stations were all faked by NASA (along with China and Russia) to maintain military supremacy during the space race. They claim the Earth is depicted as a sphere in the faked satellite images because, like all of us, that is what NASA staff have been taught to believe. Flat Earthers claim all evidence for a spherical Earth can be debunked or given alternative flat Earth explanations.

Cambridge Analytica and Facebook

The world was shocked in 2017 to find out Facebook had allowed a right-wing funded organisation, ***Cambridge Analytica,*** access to users' personal data for political gains. They wanted access to this data so that they could profile users and influence the way they think and vote. The aim was to influence voting patterns that favoured pre-designated outcomes, such as the election of Donald Trump and Brexit. Through ***Facebook***, people were sent carefully selected images and stories that were not true, or which were deliberately misleading, giving a false picture of events and people. The 'facts' appeared to be 'confirmed' because they came from multiple sources and were verified by people's social networks who were sent the same things. Sometimes they just sent subtle messages or ads that worked on the emotions, deliberately promoting fear or anxiety. Cambridge Analytica (and Facebook by allowing access) has since been found complicit in feeding our political biases. Cambridge Analytica no longer exists under that name. Facebook was fined $5 billion dollars for breaching privacy regulations.

A cautionary tale!

In 2016, Mr Nix boasted to *Sky News*: 'Today in the United States we have somewhere close to four or five thousand data points on every individual... So we model the personality of every adult across the United States, some 230 million people.'

Cambridge Analytica gathered thousands of pieces of data to categorise voters into one or several of 150 possible psychological profiles, which then allowed selected political parties and candidates to tailor their campaigns accordingly (machine learning can be used to identify deep-rooted fears among pre-profiled user groups, which social media bots can subsequently exploit to foment anger and intolerance).

All of this information was collected mostly without the users' permission or knowledge

According to the European Data Protection Supervisor (EDPS) – 'If there is anything we should learn from the Cambridge Analytica revelations, it is that unless things change, we can expect the spread of disinformation and the systemic manipulation of voters to happen all over again, not only in U.S. national elections but throughout the world.'

Campaigns like the above work by playing on our insecurities and fears. The perpetrators know our vulnerabilities and that we are prone to confirmation and other biases. Being aware of what influences our thinking is the first step to guarding against those influences. We do not want to be manipulated unwittingly. We want to carefully choose the beliefs we hold.

We are living in a post-truth era!!

The Oxford Dictionaries Word of the Year 2016 – **post-truth** – defined as 'relating to or denoting circumstances in which objective facts are less influential in shaping public opinion than appeals to emotion and personal belief' (The Oxford Dictionaries 2016, https://global.oup.com/academic/content/word-of-theyear/?/cc=au$lang=en&).

People will always disagree about something. We have different interests and values; we live in different circumstances. What is important to one person is of little consequence to another. There are, however, some better and worse ideas, and some true and false beliefs. A critical thinking framework can provide tools to help sort out the good ideas from the not so good, the better ideas from the bad, the true from the false. But we need to put the effort in. It is not easy.

If someone has good grounds for a belief or position, they do not need to rely on emotion or subterfuge to demonstrate that this is something we should believe in. They can present the idea openly and convincingly. We can then choose to agree or not agree.

There is not just one way to think, nor is there just one solution to a problem. However, that **doesn't mean that all or any answer is equally legitimate** or acceptable. Some will be just plain wrong or nonsensical, while some answers and solutions will be much better than others.

Relevance to academic study and life

At university, we are often confronted by new ideas or controversial information. We are faced with ideas that contradict our current beliefs or the traditions we grew up with (e.g. feminism, euthanasia, abortion, socialism). We often need to decide between competing positions (global warming, fossil fuels, GM foods, freedom of speech, political correctness). How do we deal with difference when we confront it? How do we cope when our own position is challenged? How do we stop getting angry and defensive?

The best defence of your belief is to make sure you are justified by having reliable grounds for the belief. Remember what counts as justification – **evidence must be reliable, relevant and sufficient**. Our beliefs should be based on sound reasons and reliable knowledge as much as possible. People are still free to disagree with you. This may be because they have their own cognitive bias. But it may also be because they see things from a different perspective (we discuss this in the next chapter).

For all of us to become better critical thinkers, we need to recognise and overcome our biases as much as we can. There are things that we can do to help overcome our biases, especially confirmation bias. However, none of the techniques are easy as we all have a natural resistance to information that may make us change our mind. Even those of us who are used to exploring and analysing arguments will critique those arguments that are against our views more thoroughly than we do those that support our views. It is easy to come up with counter examples. When all else fails, we say things like 'you can't trust the internet' or 'scientists can still be mistaken'. It is, nevertheless, worth putting the effort into checking our thinking processes to try to improve them (Halpern, 1997; Govier, 2010).

How to overcome confirmation and other cognitive biases

Having a disposition towards seeking the truth is an advantage, as well as having an inquiring mind. Most of us don't want to hold false beliefs and would prefer our beliefs to rest on fact. Here are some techniques we can engage in:

1. Be aware of our biases – just knowing that we can all suffer from confirmation bias or belief preservation can help us reduce its effects. Try to be more cautious in your conclusions and be aware that you may not be treating an objection seriously.
2. Access more information – more information can prevent us from forming false or irrational beliefs. It could also provide us with alternative points of view. Unfortunately with Google, we can find a lot more information that *confirms* our beliefs, making us think they must be right or logical. Because we have to be selective, we tend to select information that accords with our views. Make sure you don't just look for confirming information or articles.
3. Seek out alternative views – scientists have long realised that confirmation does not prove truth, whereas disconfirmation shows there is a problem. Try to find information that would disprove or change your view. What would falsify your theory or idea? What evidence would you accept as very strong counter evidence? If there is nothing you would accept, then you are saying your belief is not changing regardless of any evidence to the contrary. This is called dogma!
4. Test your beliefs against empirical data – sometimes we hang on to a belief against the evidence (no one found weapons of mass destruction in Iraq). Make sure that the empirical data supports your belief and does not argue against it. If you believe *x*, cite your evidence for it. If there is none but there is evidence to the contrary, maybe it is best to put that belief on hold.
5. Question its plausibility – sometimes our beliefs are implausible but we still believe in them, especially when with a group of like-minded people. How plausible is it that the US Government has managed to hide all evidence of aliens visiting Earth? Why haven't aliens visited other countries? Make sure your beliefs pass the plausibility test.
6. Is there an alternative explanation? It may be the case that there is an alternative theory or explanation that fits the facts and is much simpler than the theory or explanation you are expounding. If there is, find out what it is and see if it is feasible. Think about why you prefer your explanation. Would those reasons stand up to scrutiny?
7. Pay attention to emotional influences – sometimes emotion will influence our support for a position we would not have taken previously. Fear of terrorism makes it easy to be harsh towards refugees. Remember we can be manipulated by selective reporting of events. Examine the role that emotion is playing in your support of a position. Be honest.
8. Engage in open debate – put your views to the test in an objective and rational manner. If they are well-grounded, you will be able to defend them and counter any alternative views.

Chapter summary

- We want to be sure, as much as we can, that what we think is the case really is the case.
- To be an effective critical thinker, we need to be aware of our own cognitive biases and try to overcome them.
- Most cognitive biases are a barrier to good critical thinking. They reduce our capacity to reach fair and objective conclusions
- If there is no evidence that would ever make you change your mind about something, then your belief has become dogma. Your bias is overriding your reason.
- There is not just one way to think, nor is there just one solution to a problem. However, that doesn't mean that all or any answer is equally legitimate or acceptable.
- As critical thinkers we need to treat all facts, evidence or reasons as objectively as we can.

Answers to Exercises 1–3

Exercise 1

Reasons for beliefs

1. This claim was based on observation and the experience of our senses. The Earth feels stationary and the sun appears to rise in the east and set in the west. So strong is this visual effect that we still talk about sunrise and sunset, even though we know this is not the case. Imagine being told that the Earth is really a spinning ball that orbits around the sun? It would seem to go against common sense. This is a good example of the appearance/reality distinction. How something looks is not necessarily the way it is.
2. This claim was based on the false belief that all matter was made of four elements – earth, water, fire and air – and that (theoretically) one could change one type of matter into another. It was also driven by greed and wishful thinking. While alchemy was based largely on superstition and mysticism, it was an early form of science and led to the discipline of chemistry.
3. This claim was based on ignorance, fear and religious superstition. At the time, there was limited understanding of natural events, cause and effect, or infections. When crops failed, babies died or disease spread, people blamed 'witches', often the local midwife or herbalist who they had consulted. This belief was promulgated by the Church who claimed witches consorted with the Devil, giving them supernatural powers like flying or turning themselves into animals. Witches were handy scapegoats for any problem. This false belief led to the violent deaths of many innocent women.
4. This claim was initially a consequence of Darwinism and his argument that humans had evolved from ape-like ancestors. It allowed a justification for colonisation and slavery as Africans were judged to be physically closer to apes and so less evolved. A controversial book in 1994 by Herrnstein and Murray claimed there was a measurable difference in IQ between White and Black populations in the United States, suggesting a genetic or racial link to IQ. This has since been debunked.

5. This claim was first put forward by Descartes, who argued that the body and mind were distinct substances. Using dreaming as his analogy, he argued that one could doubt the existence of the body but not one's mind. Thus the body was seen as a purely physical mechanism controlled by the non-physical mind or soul. As animals did not have souls or minds, they were seen as mechanistic like clocks and wind-up toys.
6. This claim was based on wishful thinking and the opinion of an historian who authenticated the diaries after they were found. The historian compared single pages of the diary with other material supposedly written by Hitler and concluded they had been written by the same person (they were forged by the same person). No forensic tests were conducted. Nazi sympathisers desperately wanted the diaries to be real, so were easily fooled.

Exercise 2

Discussion of false beliefs/claims

These claims or beliefs are all examples of **confirmation bias and/or belief preservation.** Each claim represents a case where the proponents want to believe the claim, **despite evidence to the contrary**.

- They cannot count as *fact or knowledge* because there is little or no justification to support them. What evidence there was to support them has been refuted as false, unreliable or misinterpreted. On the other hand, there is strong counter evidence to show an opposite or counter claim is true (i.e. Obama was born in the United States; the Earth is a sphere). Despite this, the statements are believed to be true regardless of any evidence that shows they may be false. This demonstrates a bias.
- While it could be the case that more convincing evidence to support (3) or (5) could emerge in the future, it is not likely given the weight of current evidence that disproves the truth of both claims. Not only was Wakefield's original research discredited, recent research trying to establish a causal link between autism and the MMR vaccination failed. Likewise with (5); the initial research by Hernstein and Murray has been shown to be flawed. The intellectual achievements of Black Americans in all spheres are also clear counter evidence.
- Claims (1) and (4) are historical occurrences that happened in the recent past. At the moment, we still have living witnesses and relevant physical evidence available to demonstrate the falsity of both claims. Obama has a US birth certificate; he could not become president if he were not born in America. Gas chambers, human remains, testimonials and documents all attest to the reality of the Holocaust. Both these claims represent malicious wishful thinking. Proponents either want them to be true or knowingly spread a false claim to achieve a particular outcome.
- Claim (2) is interesting as there have been round Earth sceptics since 500BCE. Yet today there is an abundance of physical evidence to argue for a round Earth orbiting in a solar system. The shape of the Earth can be proved in numerous ways, not least by observations such as flights at high altitude. The movement of the stars and planets, the

seasons and the transition from day to night are best explained by the movement and rotation of the Earth. Evidence from satellites and the Hubble telescope attest to the spherical shape and orbital motion of not just the Earth but other planets. There is no advantage to be gained by governments or scientists from pushing a false round Earth theory. The flat Earth theory represents a conspiracy theory. Their scepticism is directed towards all scientists and mathematicians throughout history, governments and agencies of all nations, and the efficacy of technology from the telescope to space travel.

Exercise 3

The flat Earth

Think about how you would prove the claim to be either true or false.

- What evidence would you need on each side to justify the claim for or against?
- What evidence do we have now that is reliable that supports the round Earth theory (many would argue it is no longer a theory as it has been shown to be true by observation)?
- Do we have similar evidence to support the alternative theory that the Earth is flat?
- Which theory best explains the physical phenomena and can also be used to make accurate predictions about possible future events?
- Can we accept the evidence presented by science and technology such as satellite or telescopic images, or are there grounds to be sceptical of it?
- How likely is the conspiracy theory that there has been no space exploration or successful space flights, that satellites do not orbit the Earth and the satellite pictures of the Earth are fake?
- How likely is it that all the mathematicians and scientists throughout history have been mistaken in their calculations that indicate we are spinning on our axis and orbiting the sun?
- How plausible is the claim that the round Earth theory is a conspiracy?

Space travel is once again the focus of technological advances as is new satellite technology. There are space research centres being created and moves to develop commercial space flights. There have been recent manned orbits that have included space walks creating more footage of a spherical Earth. The evidence is not on the side of a flat Earth.

CHAPTER

3

Overcoming Barriers – Problems with Perception

Epistemology and perception

It is a common position for most of us to assume that the world really exists and that it exists as we perceive it to be. We discover the world or find out what it is really like through our experiences of living in the world and the information we gather through our senses. This position is known as **empiricism** (it represents **a realist view** of the world). Empiricists believe all knowledge is derived from **our experience** (i.e. *a posteriori*) of a world that exists independently of us. An alternative view argues that we can gain knowledge of the world through reasoning (i.e. *a priori*). In fact, this view (**rationalism**) holds that we need to use our minds, our logic and rationality, to uncover the truth about how the world really is because our senses can only tell us what *appears to be the case*. Scholars have known since Plato's time (500 BCE) that what appears to be the case is not always the case, and that there is an appearance/reality distinction. The sun appears to rise and set; the Earth appears to be stationary, but we know this is not the case.

The terms **'a priori' and 'a posteriori'** are used primarily to denote the foundations upon which a proposition is known. A given proposition is knowable *a priori* if it can be known independent of any experience other than the experience of learning the language in which the proposition is expressed, whereas a proposition that is knowable *a posteriori* is known on the basis of experience. For example, the proposition that <u>all bachelors are unmarried</u> is *a priori*, and the proposition <u>that it is raining outside now</u> is *a posteriori*.

http://www.iep.utm.edu/apriori

Scepticism about knowledge

The appearance/reality distinction creates a problem for all knowledge claims. Even if the world exists independently of us, we can never know what it is really like because we can only ever experience it through our limited senses. What we perceive may not reflect reality at all. But how would we know? How can we trust our senses when we know they can be wrong or easily deceived? How can we make claims about anything with any certainty? Most of our knowledge comes through our experience of the world. And we know past scientific claims have been proven wrong despite the evidence. If we have been wrong in the past, we can be wrong in the present. It may be the case that what we think we see and hear doesn't exist at all.

Pyrrhonian scepticism – founder Pyrrho of Elis (c. 360 to c. 270 BCE)

'Neither our sensations nor our opinions tell us truths or falsehoods. Therefore, for this reason we should not put our trust in them one bit, but we should be unopinionated, uncommitted and unwavering, saying concerning each individual thing that it no more is than is not, or it both is and is not, or it neither is nor is not.'

(https://www.iep.utm.edu/skepanci/#H1)

This kind of thinking has led to some extreme sceptical positions, many of which you will encounter at university and in social media, and some of which you may even endorse. Are we really just brains suspended in a vat, being fed information? Is our external reality a constructed fantasy as portrayed in sci-fi movies? Are we just a computer-generated Avatar? Is the world created by our minds? Is all knowledge relative or even subjective?

Our job as critical thinkers is to find out what we can believe with certainty and what remains open to debate. This requires us to understand and overcome our cognitive limitations and the barriers to clear thinking.

To avoid extreme scepticism we need to ensure our claims are as reliable as they can be. We need to be **aware of the barriers to knowledge** and seek ways to compensate for them.

Problems with perception – observation

For many of us, observation is the main source of information that shapes our initial beliefs/ideas about the world. Although we use all our senses, we rely mostly on our sight to give us a true picture of the world around us. People who are visually impaired perceive a very different world to those with sight. For them, the world may be richer in other sensory ways.

However, observation is not always reliable. Our eyes can be tricked. What do you see in the pictures below? Do the dots flicker and change from white to black? Are the circles spinning in different directions? If so, these are illusions, as both images are static. It is not always clear what creates the illusion of movement but it relates to how the eye receives visual stimuli and the brain processes and interprets it. It is likely that the mechanisms that have evolved to recognise real moving objects in the world can be tricked to perceive movement when there is none.

Herman grid illusion

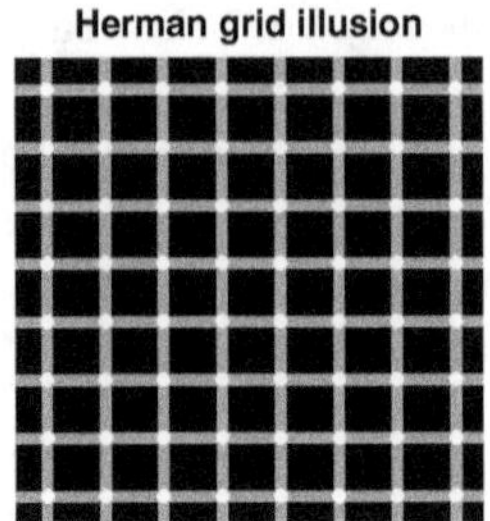

Notice how the white dots in your peripheral vision change to black, then back to white as you shift your focus.

Enigma

The rotary motion appears to alternate between a clockwise and a counter-clockwise direction.

The bent stick

Another common visual illusion is caused by the way light refracts in water. A pencil in a glass of water looks bent but we know it is not. Even though we know this is an illusion, we cannot override it. We cannot make ourselves see the stick as straight. So while there is a belief that we can alter reality by just changing our perspective, there are limits to this capacity. What we see and how we see it will be largely determined by the interaction of our bodies' perceptual apparatus with the physical world.

The Necker Cube – inside/outside

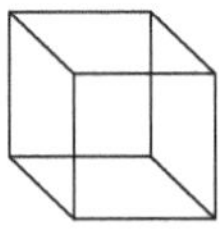

This next visual illusion has to do with the way we perceive dimensions in the real world and how we interpret representations of three-dimensional objects in a two-dimensional medium, such as a picture. The Necker Cube illusion represents a three-dimensional (3D) cube which we can view from different perspectives. The darker square can either be the front of the box facing towards the right or the bottom of the box angled upwards and towards the left. We should be able to easily alternate between each perspective.

The Mueller-Lyer illusion is another perspectival illusion. Again, it is related to how we represent 3D objects in two dimensions but it is also related to how we interpret visual information to ascertain height and depth. This perceptual capacity is a useful ability to have but means we can misjudge the length/height of a line when it is taken out of context or the background is neutralised. The two lines in the image are identical in length even though one appears longer than the other depending on the angles of the attached lines. Again, knowing that this is an illusion cannot change how we perceive the lines. Similarly, although A and B look different sizes they are identical.

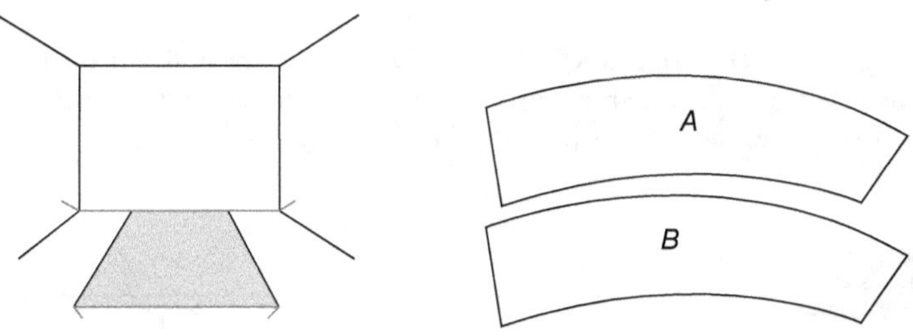

Appearances can be deceptive. We need to be aware that our perceptions can be tricked and that what appears to be the case may not be the case.

Perspective matters: how perceptions influence our beliefs

You may have seen photos on Facebook that show seemingly impossible scenes – a tourist holding the Eiffel Tower between their fingers, a young boy riding his bike over a cliff, a domestic cat bigger than a car. These all represent an unusual or distorted perspective which fools our eyes into seeing something which is not real. Changing the perspective changes how each object appears in relation to each other object. Because a different perspective will provide a different view, we can be tricked into coming to a false conclusion or belief about something. But while we know that it is impossible for the lady to really be holding the Eiffel Tower, other illusions are not as obvious and so may be believed. The person we saw running away from the shop may not be the robber but just an innocent jogger.

It is important to remember that what we see is *always* from a particular perspective or point of view. Our observations are limited by our visual range (how far we can see) and our visual acuity (how well we can see), our human physiology (forward facing eyes), and our physical position in space. More importantly, our observations are always from **one single perspective**, from where we look at the world.

Perspective is not just about visual or other sensory information. As we have mentioned in earlier chapters, what we experience through our senses shapes our beliefs about the world. Because what we experience is unique to our environment and lifestyle, we will see things in a certain way. This means we are likely to form beliefs that may differ from those of other people. Not only will you have had different experiences from other people, but each of you will see things from a different perspective because of those experiences and the subsequent beliefs that have been formed. We need to be aware that we all have unique cultural, ethnic and social experiences that may not be shared by others. We literally 'see' things from our own singular point of view (this is discussed later in Chapters 10 and 11). This will have an impact on how we interpret and weight the information we encounter and what we deem relevant or reliable. When we conduct research, we need to be aware of how we rate or value some information or facts above others and why. We need to pay attention to our thinking processes.

Becoming a critical thinker requires us to acknowledge that we have our own **singular point of view**. We may not see the whole picture and we may get things wrong. There may be another way of seeing something.

Exercise 1

Different perspectives on objects

Think how differently people view these items depending on their social, ethnic or cultural background. Can you think of different ways these items could be viewed? Can you think of other items that may be viewed differently depending on one's background (e.g. education, wealth and status can influence our perception of items and events)?

- Music – entertaining...
- Food – nourishment...
- Water – thirst-quenching...
- Trees – firewood...
- Insects – pests...
- Tattoos – gangs...
- Dogs – pets...

As critical thinkers, we can broaden our singular perspective by understanding what shapes our perspective and why this may differ for other people. Like us, others also have narrow views, so it is important to encourage sharing of information to find out what the other person sees and why they see it that way. Where do the differences lie? What might be the particular information you have access to that they don't? What might they have access to that you don't? Could this extra information change your perspective? Remember we like to preserve our beliefs when we can, so this openness is not easy but it is something we should try to foster.

Be open-minded. We cannot see from another perspective unless we deliberately shift our perspective to see that of the other. This can help our understanding of differences.

Beliefs matter: how our beliefs can influence our perceptions

Just as our perceptions shape our beliefs, our beliefs can influence the way we perceive. As any good magician knows, sometimes we do see what we expect to see, not what is really there. Because our beliefs shape our perception, we may interpret what we see rather than just report what we see. Similarly, if we expect someone to behave aggressively, we will interpret their behaviour as aggressive. It is often the case that innocent people are blamed for crimes they didn't commit because they looked a certain way and they were in the vicinity. In America, there are frequent cases of Black Americans/people of colour being accused of crimes they didn't commit because they were the victims of racial stereotyping. In England, a young Colombian student was shot dead at a Tube station because he fit a terrorist stereotype: he looked Middle Eastern and carried a backpack. False beliefs and misperceptions can cost lives.

We need to be aware that **our beliefs can influence our perceptions** which, in turn, reinforce our beliefs, which are confirmed by that misinformation. Be cautious and seek confirmation from other sources. Ask yourself, 'Could I be wrong?'

EXAMPLE 1

Mind over matter – ***How to get drunk cheaply…***

We know from magicians that our beliefs and expectations can lead us to being tricked into seeing things that are not there. In an experiment to see how powerful mind over matter can be, subjects were given a drink that they thought contained alcohol, but which in fact did not. They experienced reduced social anxiety just as if they had been drinking. However, other subjects who were told they were being given non-alcoholic beverages when they were, in fact, given alcohol did not experience any reduced anxiety in social situations. This experiment shows how our expectations can dramatically alter our perceptions.

Adapted from David R. Aronson, *Evidence-Based Technical Analysis*. Wiley, 2007

Making observation more reliable

Police and psychologists have known for some time that eyewitness accounts can be unreliable. People will often only see one part of an accident or will misremember a sequence of events. Observation is not a simple matter of just looking at something. You need to know what you should be looking at or for. A trained observer will see and notice things that we do not. Doctors can look at an x-ray, for example, and see evidence of disease where we see only shadows. A geologist will notice changes in rock formations that an untrained eye will not see. A piano tuner hears notes that we cannot detect unless trained to recognise them. A wine-taster can detect elements in a wine that we cannot taste. Forensic scientists detect clues at crime scenes that are invisible to others.

Not all research relies on observational or experimental evidence (i.e. philosophy, literature, languages) but those that do must overcome observational and perspectival shortcomings. Scientists and social researchers have to make sure their observations of events are as accurate as they can be; they are carefully measured, recorded and **verified** by others. Experiments have to be repeatable and the results replicated. They follow a method that helps minimise mistakes and allows and encourages any mistakes to be identified. The method is rigorous. They observe a phenomenon, develop an hypothesis, then devise a test to prove/disprove the hypothesis. They isolate the variables, conduct controlled tests, compare results with control groups, and test again. Critiquing is built into the method (different research methods are discussed in more detail in Chapter 8).

As critical thinkers, we should know and understand **the scientific method** and why it is used.

How do we know that we know?

In epistemology, it is generally accepted that the majority of our knowledge claims can never be 100% certain. It is argued that we cannot rely on observation and experience to give us an accurate picture of the world because it is too easy to be mistaken. Our perception is limited and prone to error. Our conclusions will be constrained by our current knowledge base and there will always be things we don't yet know. We know that our prior beliefs dispose us to seeing certain things and ignoring others. It is also true that we make mistakes; we are fallible reasoners. We don't always draw the best inferences from the text or data and, even when we do, it may be coincidental rather than because of our reasoning (this is discussed in more detail in Chapters 4 and 5).

In addition, most of the more important knowledge claims we make are about objects we can't directly observe, called **unobservables**. In science these are things like atoms, genes, gravity and radiation. In the social sciences, they tend to be things like health, economies, communities, minds and emotions. In the humanities, they may be literary theories, genres and traditions. How do we know that these things exist or that the claims we make about them are true? More importantly, how do we know that what we think we see or sense can be relied upon? The answer, according to epistemologists, is that we don't, and we can't. At best, all we can claim is that our statements are likely to be true (or a fact about the world), given what we currently know. Some will turn out to be neither true nor false.

Because reliable knowledge of the world (both social and physical) is not readily available for us to see and act on, we can easily be led to draw false conclusions, which is why we need to develop our critical thinking skills. One important way that we can limit or minimise such potential mistakes is to carefully examine our reasons for believing something.

We should ask ourselves ('*p*' stands for proposition)

- Why do we think '*p*' is true?
- What evidence do we have that supports '*p*'?
- Why should we rely on that evidence?
- What relationship does it have to '*p*'?
- Could that evidence support something other than '*p*', such as '*q*'?
- Do we have any evidence that doesn't support '*p*', which might even show '*p*' to be false?
- Is the evidence we have for 'p' enough for 'p' to be counted as true?

What we are doing here is asking ourselves, **'what justifies our belief in '*p*'?'** Do we have good strong reasons to believe '*p*' to be true? Epistemology is about exploring how we know what we know and whether or not we are right in believing that we know it. There are ways we can break down our reasons for accepting something to see if what we think is true really is true (or likely to be true).

Ultimately, what makes a claim acceptable or not is how well it can be **justified.**

Exercise 2

Look at these statements. How might we justify each claim?

Example:* It is windy** – ***can be justified by evidence from observation (the trees are swaying; my hair is blowing)

1. That car is an Alfa Romeo
2. There are more cyclists on the roads than 10 years ago.
3. If you need a degree to be a doctor then my doctor has a degree.
4. Cycling is a popular alternative to driving to work.
5. Adding nitrates to plants helps them grow.
6. The Conservatives are more likely to win the next election.
7. An atom is a fundamental particle of matter consisting of other subatomic particles called electrons, protons and neutrons.

Our limitations can be addressed

We need to be aware of our limitations so we know what we can rely on and what may not be so certain. As biological creatures we have evolved certain useful perceptual capacities in order to survive. But we know there are limitations to our perceptions. We do not see as well as eagles; we do not hear as well as dogs; we do not navigate as well as terns. As stated earlier, we are susceptible to illusions. We know that the way things appear are not always the way they are. Even though the Earth looks flat, we know it is a sphere. Even though we still talk of the sun setting and rising, we know this is not the case. It is just the way it *appears.* We don't *feel* the Earth spinning; it doesn't *seem* to be moving.

Despite our limitations, the physical world does have its own constraints in terms of what we can experience, which is why most people see the same or similar things when they look at the physical world. Our perceptual apparatus has evolved to enable us to survive and thrive in this particular physical environment. We can be sceptical about the details of objects or the meaning of a physical event but most of us will see a tree when there is a tree or hear a bird when there is a bird. We can live together because **we share a common world** and share our knowledge of that world. We can end up more or less agreeing about many things (it is raining; fish need water; rice is edible). We can, and have, gained reliable knowledge about our world.

Is climate change a real threat?

'What if we are wrong about climate change and we create a better world for nothing?'

Adapted from Daniel Kurtzman

The reliability of empirical evidence and the different types of cognitive reasoning are discussed in more detail in the ensuing chapters. Remember – our own experiences are particular to us, are limited and may be anomalous. They may be unique to you. Be aware of your limitations but know these can be overcome with care and rigour. Be cautious, be sceptical and be critical. Be convinced by reason, not emotion. Become a critical thinker.

Chapter summary

- To avoid scepticism we need to ensure our claims are as reliable as they can be. We need to be aware of the barriers to knowledge and seek ways to compensate for them.
- Appearances can be deceptive. We need to be aware that our perceptions can be tricked and that what appears to be true may not be the case.
- Becoming a critical thinker requires us to acknowledge that we have our own singular point of view. We may not see the whole picture and we may get things wrong.
- Be open-minded. We cannot see from another perspective unless we deliberately shift our perspective to see that of the other. This can help our understanding of differences.
- We need to be aware that our beliefs can influence our perceptions, which, in turn, reinforce our beliefs, which are confirmed by that misinformation. Ask yourself, 'Could I be wrong?'
- As critical thinkers, we should know and understand the scientific method and why it is used. Ultimately, what makes a claim acceptable or not is how well it can be justified.
- Be aware of your limitations but know that these can be overcome with care and rigour.

Answers to Exercises 1–2

Exercise 1

Examples of perspective (this list is not finite)

- Music – entertaining, religious, blasphemous, sexual, pagan, primitive, highbrow, working class, defiant, political, meditative, therapeutic, cultural, tradition, identity.
- Food – nourishing, cultural, hospitality, friendship, social, healthy, necessary, poison, fattening, social status/wealth, allergies, addiction, sensual.
- Water – thirst-quenching, dangerous, fun, life-saving, essential, drought-breaking, cleansing, soothing, food, sport, transport, therapeutic.
- Trees – firewood, building material, lungs of the Earth, woody weeds, habitat, shade, obstacles, employment, craft, mystic.
- Insects – pests, disease carriers, pollinators, food, nutritious, part of life cycle, ecosystem.
- Tattoos – gangs, art, tribal, initiation, manhood, fashion, identity, disfigurement, self-expression, protest, tradition, culture, enhancement, beauty.
- Dogs – pets, companions, helpers, workers, food, therapeutic, rat catchers, killers, diseased, warmth, hunters, guards, protectors.

Exercise 2

1. That car is an Alfa Romeo – *This can be proven by observation, checking the car to see what name is on it. But you could be dreaming or delusional. It could be a trick. To ensure you are not mistaken, seek confirmation. In most cases, we trust simple observation but it is not foolproof.*
2. There are more cyclists on the roads than 10 years ago – *Use statistics of bicycle users over the last 10 years to compare numbers. This requires relying on a method of data collection and knowledge of basic statistics and maths.*
3. If you need a degree to be a doctor then my doctor has a degree – *A priori – this is a logical deduction drawn just from the statement itself. You have to also understand the language and the implication of the grammatical structure of the sentence.*
4. Cycling is a popular alternative to driving to work – *Drawing an inductive inference using statistics from an appropriate survey. What is popular? How was the survey conducted?*
5. Adding nitrates to plants helps them grow – *Experimental evidence measuring growth of plants, hypothesis testing. Requires accurate measurements, a control and verification.*
6. The Conservatives are more likely to win the next election – *Probability inference usually based on statistical sampling of a population. Polls are problematic as they depend on representative sampling, political context and how questions are phrased.*
7. An atom is a fundamental particle of matter consisting of other subatomic particles called electrons, protons and neutrons – *Observation using an electron microscope and interpretation of the data. Requires skilled analysis of the observational data and an understanding of physics.*

CHAPTER

4

Knowledge Claims – Recognising and Writing an Argument

Knowledge claims and justification

In the last few chapters, we have been discussing how important it is to have reliable evidence or justification to support the claims we make and what we need to be careful about when making judgements. When we make claims about the world we live in, we want to make sure they are true, are likely to be true, or they are the best account or explanation of events we can make in line with the evidence and what we know. Critical thinking is all about examining what we and others say or write, in light of the physiological, psychological and epistemological barriers that can influence our judgements and our capacity to reason objectively.

Being aware of our cognitive limitations will help us minimise the effect those limitations have on our judgement, making us **better critical thinkers**.

One of the most important ways we can check claims for credibility is by examining the grounds or reasons put forward to support them. We are bombarded by written information of all kinds, especially at university or when reading media or accessing the internet. A lot of that writing is descriptive. It is telling us about something. It is usually informative. Textbooks are like this. We are not expected to critique the content in a textbook but to accept it, learn from it and, in some cases, apply it. Although the knowledge claims or facts were once new and contentious, they have now become the basic lore of our respective disciplines. It is, however, important for us to understand *how* they became knowledge and *why* they have become accepted. There will be good reasons for believing the claims to be true, given what we currently know. The claims will have been successfully **argued for**.

As critical thinkers, it is vital that we can recognise **an argument** and distinguish arguments from non-arguments. Then we are in a position to evaluate the quality of the argument to see if the claim it makes is acceptable. Much of our critical thinking skills will be directed towards the claims that others make (critiquing is discussed in the ensuing chapters). At the same time, we need to think about our own claims. We need to know when to argue and how to argue. We need to know what an argument is.

Why and when to use argument

When we want someone/everyone to accept a new idea, a new practice or a new piece of information as a fact, we need to persuade them that the new idea is better than (or as good as) a previous one, or that the new piece of information is likely to be true. We do this by presenting convincing reasons to support the new claim. We *argue* for the claim by presenting convincing evidence that the claim should be accepted, given what we know.

An argument is an attempt to persuade someone to accept a claim or point of view by using reason.

The term '**argument**' is generally used to describe a dispute or disagreement between two or more people. Within academic writing, published position papers or reports, however, an argument does not always indicate a disagreement. The argument form is used when we want to convince someone (the reader or listener) of something, such as to:

- Support something we think has merit – a position, a point of view, a program, an object, an action.
- Persuade someone that something would be beneficial to do (or not to do) – a particular course of action.
- Convince someone that something is true, likely to be true or probable – supporting an hypothesis, establishing a fact or a likely outcome.
- Show someone the problems or difficulties with something – a theory, an approach, a course of action.
- Reason with someone to get them to change their mind, their belief or their practice.

You **do not need** an argument if you are describing a process or event, listing certain items, explaining how to do something, how something works or identifying key points or factors.

You **do need** an argument when the point you are making is not well known or may not be well accepted (it is not obviously true) or where you know there is some disagreement, controversy or alternative perspective. If this is so, you have to give **reasons** to support your position.

What is an argument?

An argument must be *for or against* something. It must present a case. In order for something to be an argument, it must contain some justification for the claim it is supporting . For example, the statement '*we should support the Black Lives Matter movement*' is *for* something, but it is not an argument. But if we were to add a reason why, then it would become an argument – '*We should support the Black Lives Matter movement to show that we are against the unequal treatment of people based on their ethnicity or skin colour.*'

As well as giving a reason, the language used by the author should indicate what the relationship is between the claim and the evidence or justification. It is the strength (or weakness) of that relationship (the relevance), as indicated by the words chosen to express that relationship, that will persuade us to accept or reject the truth of the claim. This is what we call **the logic** or reasoning element of the argument. In the Black Lives Matter example, the words 'to show that' really mean '*because this* shows that...'. The assumption is we would want to show we are against racism.

Examples of logical connectives

There are certain words we use to demonstrate the logical relationship between statements.

And; Or; If....then; Either/or; Not; also All, None, Some.

There are some words we use to describe causal or inferential relationships

Because; in the first (second, etc.) place; follows from; for; since; as; the reason is that; may be inferred from; this is why; given that.

There are other words we use to describe inferences and consequences

Therefore; consequently; implies that; hence; so; proves that; it follows that; which means that; infers that.

An argument presents a claim or conclusion which is supported by at least one reason or piece of evidence (the claim is justified)

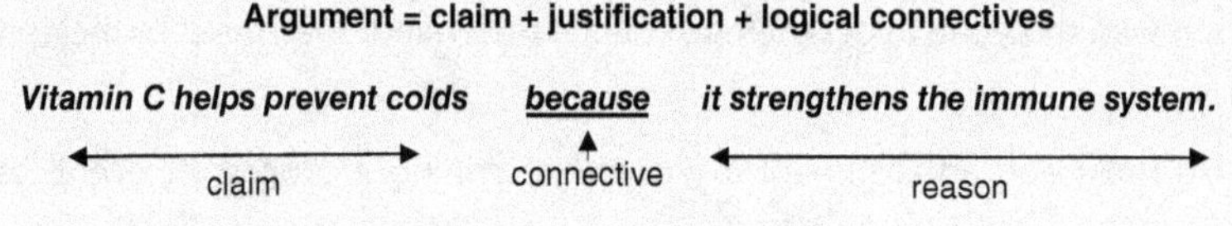

EXAMPLE 1

Recognising what is or is not an argument is not always easy. Look at these examples

- People with dementia tend to have problems with communication skills, concentration, abstract thinking, recognising objects and remembering. They may not function well in employment and social settings – *This is descriptive only, there is no claim supported by evidence, it is not arguing for anything.*
- George always found it hard starting a new school. His awkward gait attracted bullies and his stutter made him shy and prevented him talking freely to the other children. He was always the weirdo – *This is part of a story or narrative setting a scene, there is no claim supported by evidence, it is not arguing for anything.*

- *The Body Sense* by Fogel is fundamentally a book about maintaining health and well-being. Fogel sets out to demonstrate 'how everyday life, as well as serious stress and trauma, can cause us to lose contact with our sensations and emotions', along with the way our body moves and feels. This, he claims, can lead to illness – *'This is called an exposition or excerpt which summarises a text, it may be discussing an argument but there is no claim being argued for.*
- When taking a blood sample be sure to perform hand hygiene first then put on surgical gloves. Choose the site for needle entry carefully to ensure vein is adequate, then disinfect area. Next push prepared needle carefully into vein... – *This is a description of a process (instruction), there is no argument but it is providing information.*
- The people who drop rubbish on the ground have no respect for the environment, otherwise they wouldn't do it – *This is called an explanation, which sets out why an action is/was performed (but not that it has occurred), it can sometimes look like an argument because it contains reasons.*
- The reason vinegar turned the litmus paper red is because vinegar is a weak acid – *This is a causal explanation but is not arguing for anything; it explains how or why things work. It is most like an argument because it contains reasons.*
- If the world were flat, we would be able to reach its edges – *This is called a conditional or hypothetical statement, often used as part of an argument. It is making a claim but is not arguing for something. It is raising a possibility.*
- Solar power is a more sustainable source of power than coal. It is unlimited, does not create the same levels of air pollution and has less physical impact on the environment – *This is an argument as it presents a claim (first sentence) which is supported by reasons given to accept the claim.*

Persuasive writing and identifying an argument

There are many different types of writing, from poems, to stories, to newspaper articles, to websites, to text books. More often than not, the texts we access are intended to persuade us of something. Someone has a point of view about something and they want to encourage other people (the reader) to have the same point of view. The writer wants you to agree with them or believe what they say. They want to be convincing or persuasive.

Even though a poem or a fictional story may be written to entertain you, or to capture a mood, it may also intend to convey a message. The author may want you to adopt a certain attitude or feeling towards something that they feel strongly about. A novel might want to encourage you to change your thinking or behaviour (to stop bullying or to plant trees). A political pamphlet or an advertisement might try to get your support by appealing to your emotion or your vanity (don't be a loser). Although each of these texts may want to influence your thinking, they are not necessarily presenting you with reasons or evidence. They are more likely using persuasive or emotive language or evocative scenarios that convey a feeling. As such, they are not presenting an argument.

EXAMPLE 2

Examine this passage. Is it trying to persuade you? What of? How?

(Extracted from an opinion piece targeting teachers who allowed or encouraged their students to take time out from school to demonstrate about climate change.)

We should all be **outraged** by the mobilisation of children to serve the **wacky** climate change agenda. Activist teachers are **bullies, misusing** their position to push their **crazy Leftie** politics – anti-capitalism, pro **illegal** immigration, and **unscientific** global warming **alarmism** – on our **innocent** children. It's **disgraceful** that they can spread their socialist **lies**, while being paid from public money, **our** taxes.

Examine the language choice

It is clear that this passage is intended to persuade. Look at the choice of words. The language is designed to make you think a certain (negative) way about a particular belief or group of people. 'Outrage' denotes a moral stance, as does 'should'. Note how the terms 'left' and 'socialist' are used as insults. But does it constitute an argument? Is the author making a claim?

The first step in recognising an argument is to **identify the claim** or point of view of the author has taken. What does the author want us to believe or accept?

While it is clear that the author wants to persuade the reader to think a certain way (i.e. view the teachers in a negative light), this is not stated directly. The author's own point of view is assumed to be the opposite of the ones he/she is attacking (i.e. right-wing, pro capitalist, anti-refugee and a global warming denier). The author does say 'we should be outraged by…', which could count as a claim, but there are no reasons given why we should be outraged. Are the children being mobilised? Is the climate change agenda wacky? The author then goes on to describe the things he claims the teachers are doing, but this doesn't constitute evidence for his claim either. If the author said we should be outraged by *our teachers' behaviour* because they are doing all these things, then that would constitute an argument, albeit a bad one.

Target audience

With passages of this kind, opinion pieces in newspapers or vlogs, the authors are not trying to put forward well-reasoned arguments. They want a reaction. Think who the intended audience is, who are the readers that this piece is written for? *It will not be written for people who support climate change and refugees.* The intended audiences are most likely of several types. One, it is likely directed at those members of the public who are sympathetic to the views expressed in the piece; readers who already disagree with climate activism and who will have their beliefs confirmed by this piece. Two, it is likely directed at readers who may feel uncomfortable with one or other of the more radical or 'leftie' beliefs expressed here. The opinion piece will clarify and confirm their reasons for that discomfort. Third, there are readers who are ignorant of the facts or events around a range of public debates, including climate change, who read opinion pieces for information. They will be shocked (and outraged) by the 'revelations' contained in the passage. And that is what this piece is primarily designed to do – evoke moral outrage rather than to inform.

Donald Trump is well-known for using personal insults against his opponents in his tweets. Rather than presenting arguments against their ideas, he deliberately discredits them by calling them names. (Clinton was 'heartless', 'crooked Hillary' and a 'nasty' woman; James Comey was a 'rat', a 'slime-ball', and a 'liar.') These are called 'ad hominem' attacks because they target the person, not their position or what they say (we discuss ad hominems and other fallacies in Chapter 5). It can be an effective technique in debate and may win an argument. If I belittle you or make you seem unworthy, then what you say becomes unworthy as well (why would you listen to an idiot or a liar?). It is, however, a *fallacy* as it deflects attention away from what the problem or real issue is. It doesn't address the issue under discussion. Watch out for this technique when listening to political speeches or when reading articles. As a rule of thumb, if a writer needs to resort to insults or excessive praise to get their point across, it generally indicates they lack sufficient evidence or reasons to counter the opponent's claim or to argue for their own position.

EXAMPLE 3

Fallacious appeal to prejudice to persuade voters

Mr Austin said (Dec. 2019) that 'decent, traditional patriotic Labour voters' should vote for Mr Johnson and the Conservatives rather than let Mr Corbyn take power.
The implication is if you were to vote for Corbyn, you are not decent or patriotic. Often people use phrases like 'as a good Christian/Muslim...' or it is 'not British' / 'un-American' to get you to support or oppose a particular act.

We find some pieces of writing more persuasive than others. It is much easier, for instance, to be persuaded by something that aligns with our own beliefs, rather than something that conflicts with our worldview (refer back to Chapter 2). So we need to be watchful. Persuasive writing is not always the text with the best reasons. Ideally, we want to be persuaded by something because it is the most convincing case: it has the best **argument**.

The second step in recognising an argument is to see if there is any evidence given to support the claim. If there is, you have identified **an argument**. If not, there is no argument.

Exercise 1

Which of these statements is an argument?

Can you work out which of them is an argument and which is not? Try to explain why or why not. [HINT: If it is an argument, there should be a reason given that supports the claim being made]

1. Michael Moore is a film producer who produced the documentary '*Sicko*', which looked at medical insurance in the States. ☐yes ☐no
2. Nobody expects foreign taxi drivers to discourse at length on world affairs, but they should at least understand the address of the passenger's destination and be able to answer questions about the fare. ☐yes ☐no
3. Withholding information is just the same as lying, and lying is wrong in any situation, so withholding information is wrong. ☐yes ☐no
4. An activity need not be financially rewarding to be valuable. However, housework is not valued because it is not paid work. ☐yes ☐no
5. When newcomers (migrants/refugees) arrive too fast, they gather in enclaves and resist learning the national language. ☐yes ☐no
6. You shouldn't eat grapes before bed as they will give you indigestion. ☐yes ☐no

Explanation or argument?

As previously mentioned, some passages look like arguments when they are not because they contain reasons and reasoning words like 'because' or 'so'. This is the case with explanations and causal explanations. An explanation seeks to explain *why* something happens; we usually know that it has occurred. An argument, on the other hand, attempts to argue *that* something will happen or *that* something is the case, by giving reasons to convince someone of its likelihood. An explanation is used for human behaviour whereas a causal explanation is for physical phenomena and is most common in the sciences for explaining how things work or interact, i.e. that tremors occur when the ground is unstable; the bird's eggs didn't hatch because the weather was too cold.

EXAMPLES OF EXPLANATIONS

1. The window had been shut all day so the air was hot and musty.
2. She had difficulty concentrating because of the pain in her leg.
3. The chemicals were considered highly volatile. As a consequence, the students were carefully monitored.
4. Excess nutrients and warm weather can cause blue-green algae to bloom, creating toxic scums. As the bloom decays, it reduces oxygen levels in the water, causing the fish to die.

Exercise 2

Identify the claim/s in this passage. Is there an explanation or an argument? If it contains an argument, you should be able to identify the supporting evidence.

Explanation or argument?

It is easy to see why Realty Home Loans collapsed. When the factory in their town closed, people lost their jobs and they couldn't keep up with their mortgage payments, so they didn't pay back their loans. The company could set up in the neighbouring town but it is likely they will end up in a worse situation. The town has only one industry, and if they lose their contract with Nigeria, which is likely, the industry will close and over 1000 people will be out of work. This would affect the economy of the town and Realty Home Loans would collapse again.

Exercise 3

The statements below are all arguments. Underline the claim or conclusion. Can you identify the supporting evidence?

1. Fear is the main source of superstition and one of the main sources of cruelty to others. To conquer fear is the beginning of wisdom.
2. There is a substance in the human eye that is similar to algae. So human beings are related to algae.
3. Multi-coloured fish are more restricted to particular territories than fish with less dramatic colouration. The bright colours have evolved to warn other fish that they are there and that this is their territory.
4. Elephants have a concept of death because they have been known to cover the corpses of other dead elephants with leaves and branches, whereas they do not cover sleeping elephants.
5. Swimming places no stress on the joints because one's weight is supported by water. It is a safe form of physical exercise for people troubled by joint pain.
6. Charred rhinoceros bones, thought to be about 300,000 years old, have been found in an archaeological site in France. This indicates the rhinoceros species lived in Europe at least 300,000 years ago.

Argument structure and argument mapping

An argument has a structure. A simple argument will have one claim or conclusion with a supporting reason or some supporting evidence, like those in the exercise above. A more complex argument may have several claims, with separate arguments for each one, leading to the main conclusion. Not all arguments will be structured in the same way. The argument may start with the claim and then present one or more reasons to support or justify that claim. Alternatively, it may start with the reasons and end with a conclusion, inferred from those reasons.

EXAMPLE 4

Argument

(a) **Good health requires good nutrition, and good nutrition requires a budget adequate to buy fresh and nutritious food** (reasons). Thus good health requires an adequate budget (conclusion).

(b) Marketing infant formula in the Third World is irresponsible (claim) because **there is limited access to safe water, leading to illness, and it discourages women from breastfeeding** (two reasons).

Often it is easy to see the structure of short arguments without having to carefully analyse the text. However, most texts are more complex. They may include information that is not directly relevant to the argument, such as contextual or background information, the (unsupported) personal views of the author or those of other people, explanations or additional information that is related to the topic but which is not part of the argument.

Academic texts frequently include more than one argument. There may be multiple claims the author is arguing for; they may have a series of sub or supporting arguments and they may include counter arguments. The evidence presented can be equally complex, ranging from a simple statement or quote presented as fact to the presentation of detailed research data (often in tables) drawn from experiments, observations, statistics or questionnaires.

In order to evaluate and critique an argument, we need to understand it, by seeing what is being said (argued for) and why. We need to **analyse it** by breaking it down into its component parts or its elements.

Argument mapping can help in analysing a complex argument (van Gelder, 2005) Mapping our own arguments can also help to identify the logic of our argument, any areas of weakness or where our claims need more support. To do this we need to be able to identify the parts of an argument and how they relate to the main claim. We then demonstrate the relationship between the premises and the claims/conclusion in a diagram.

Premises: A premise is a statement that directly supports the claim/conclusion of an argument. Once you know what the claim is, you need to identify the supporting premises as these contain the evidence or reasons that justify the claim or conclusion. The conclusion is **only** supported by its direct premises, but each premise itself can be supported in a number of ways, using sub-arguments. **Argument example 4a** has two supporting premises. It is an example of a linear argument where one premise leads to the next, which leads to the conclusion, like links in a chain. If you took out premise 2, for example, the conclusion would not follow. This can be seen clearly if we *map* the argument. Mapping makes it easier to see if the argument has assumptions that need elucidating, is logical, or needs more justification. In this instance, we can see that **Argument example 4a** is a valid deductive argument (discussed in more detail in Chapter 5). If we accept the truth of the premises, then the conclusion follows.

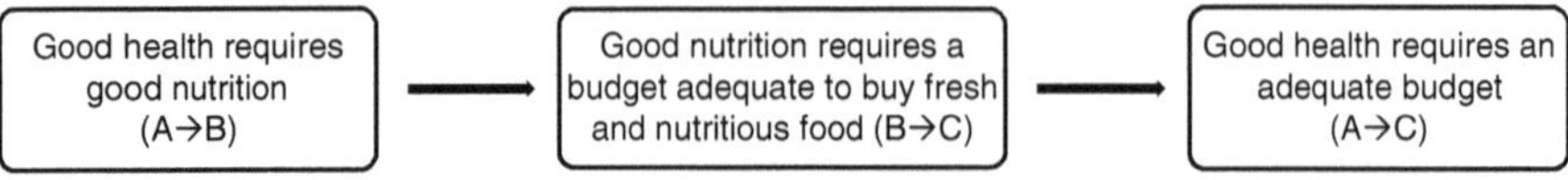

Supporting arguments*:* The main argument can be supported by other arguments, which is often the case in more complex arguments. It may be necessary to *argue for* one of the key supporting premises if you think the premise is not going to be accepted without further evidence or could be questioned. A supporting argument is one which has as its conclusion the same statement as the premise being supported. **Argument example 4b** looks simple but it does have a supporting or sub-argument embedded within it. This can be easily seen if we map the argument. The two supporting premises are – *it leads to illness* and *it discourages women from breastfeeding.* The sub argument is – that *limited access to safe water* leads *to illness.* By mapping you can also see that the reasons given are independent of each other. Arguing against one will not negate the other; it would still hold.

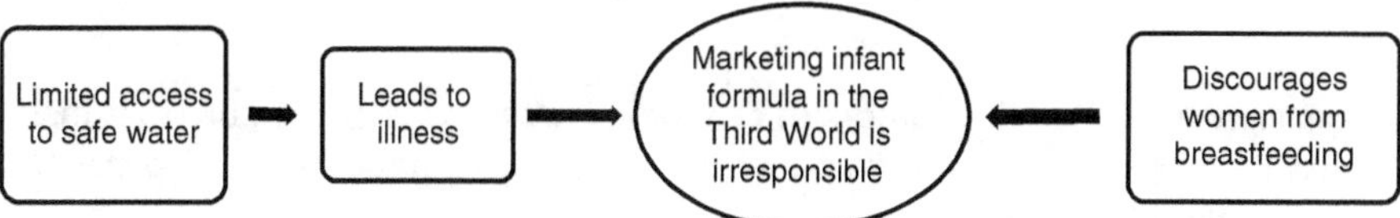

All premises can be supported in this way, but such supporting arguments are often tacit or implied. In the argument above about infant formula, we could add **another supporting argument** that defends the premise '*it is irresponsible to discourage women from breastfeeding'.* This rests on the assumption that '*we don't want to discourage women...'* Justification for this claim would include the positive or negative consequences of (not) breastfeeding taken from, say, a WHO report. This supporting argument would add weight to the main claim that marketing infant formula in Third World countries is irresponsible (see full argument map below).

Counter arguments: An argument can be strengthened by using counter arguments. A counter argument is one which argues against a claim by presenting counter evidence. Counter arguments can be used in two ways: to strengthen an argument by demonstrating that a rival claim is not convincing, or to argue against something by presenting counter arguments to rival claims. Hypotheticals can often be used, such as: *'One could argue that if women in Third World countries do not want to breastfeed, then they should have the right to choose.'* This position is put forward to offer an alternative or counter claim. It would then need to be argued against or *countered* to maintain the original argument. Alternatively, if you were disagreeing with the position expressed above, you could put forward a counter argument. You would then need to argue for this alternate position – '*However, women in Third World countries who do not want to breastfeed should have the right to choose. Providing access to formula means they can choose'* (see argument map on next page).

*When reading text with counter arguments, we need to make sure we don't mistake a counter claim for the author's own claim or position rather than acknowledging that the author is only presenting an alternative point of view or a hypothetical case.

Assumptions: Eventually, all support for premises can be traced back to a set of beliefs which the person making the argument considers to be self-evident, and therefore not in need of further support or analysis. These may be called assumptions, presumptions, suppositions, or, in certain situations (i.e. in the sciences), postulates and axioms. Such assumptions serve as the premises for supporting arguments and, in general, any premise can be called an assumption unless you have argued for it. As we said in the beginning chapters, our discipline-specific knowledge has generally become accepted as fact and is used to help ground new claims. All arguments have to start from basic assumptions. It is important to be aware of our starting assumptions as these are often implicit. Sometimes, we may need to make them explicit.

We should seek to identify the assumptions made in any text we are analysing, just in case they are not self-evident, as this may have an impact on the credibility of the argument. In **Argument example 4b**, claiming that '*there is limited access to safe water, leading to illness*' assumes – (1) that formula needs safe water and (2) that the illness is somehow linked to the use of formula. Claiming that it *discourages women from breastfeeding* assumes – (1) this is a bad thing, (2) breastfeeding is better than formula and (3) all women can and want to breastfeed.

Explicating the *implicit* assumptions can sometimes allow discussion of issues that may be otherwise hidden from public debate. Explicating them may **help clarify** and resolve objections.

Evidence: A supporting premise can be made more acceptable when it is also supported by various kinds of evidence: statistical studies, graphs, tables of data, historical information, physical evidence, observations, experiments, eyewitness accounts or photographs. **Argument example 4b** would be a stronger argument if there were supporting evidence (i.e. from the World Health Organisation [WHO]) of babies adversely affected by formula (see argument map below). The relative strength of the evidence is determined by how reliable a person believes it to be.

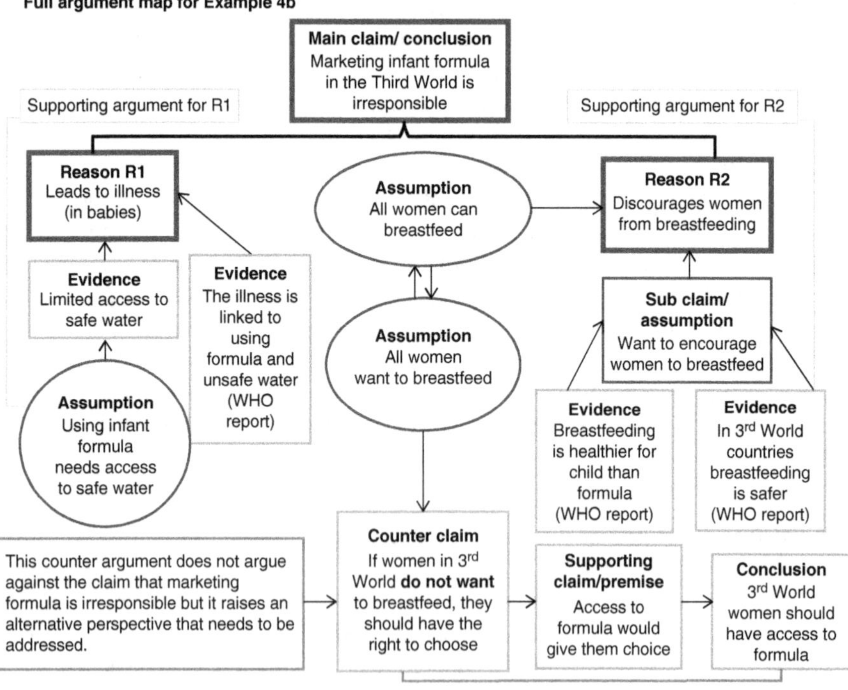

Almost no evidence is totally beyond dispute – we can challenge the research methods of a study, the accuracy of the information, the manner in which physical evidence was collected, the perspective and the eyesight or motivation of an eyewitness. But remember not to turn healthy scepticism into cynicism. Question as much as you can but also recognise when the criteria for acceptance have been reached. We do have to accept some basic assumptions from which to argue.

It is important to note that evidence on its own does not argue for anything – empirical evidence **only supports the premises.** To argue, one has to state what the relationship is between the premises – supported by evidence – and the claim.

***Authoritative opinion**:* Sometimes, we are not in a position to judge supporting evidence for ourselves; there may simply be too much of it, it may be too technical in nature or it may not be directly available to us. In those cases we often rely on the judgements of others, authorities we believe are more likely than we are to come to an accurate evaluation of the evidence. Though we tend to think of such expertise in scientific, medical or other scholarly fields, authority in arguments can also come from religious teachings, traditional or cultural wisdom and accepted folklore – anything or anyone that we accept as able to reach a more accurate evaluation. The relative strength of an authority in an argument depends on how willing a person is to accept the judgement of that source, but even in the strongest of cases, use of an authority merely supports a premise, and does not make an argument by itself.

***Explanations and anecdotes**:* Sometimes, we are more willing to accept a premise if we are given background information or specific examples. Such explanations and accounts are not given the importance of evidence or authority in an argument. Anecdotal evidence, for example, is by definition less reliable than other sorts of evidence, and explanations do not carry the weight of authority. But both anecdotal evidence and explanations may affect our **understanding** of a premise, and therefore influence our judgement. They can both add weight to other more rigorous evidence. The relative strength of an explanation or an anecdote is usually a function of its clarity and applicability to the premise it is supporting. The weight of an expert report on the adverse effects of using unsafe water in infant formula could be increased by adding anecdotal evidence from women whose babies became ill.

***Facts and opinions**:* One can distinguish between three kinds of claims: verifiable, evaluative and advocatory. Generally speaking, factual evidence takes the form of a **verifiable** statement, and authority takes the form of an **evaluative** statement. People tend to think that facts are much more reliable and convincing than opinions, yet statements of fact drawn from statistical surveys, scientific measurements and historical events, are ultimately based on interpretation, albeit expert interpretation. Thus, the difference between verifiable evidence ('the victim's blood was found on the suspect's clothes') and evaluative authority ('according to my analysis, the sample taken from the suspect's clothes matches the victim's blood type'), is not always clear. Unauthoritative opinions do not count here.

Important point

The various sorts of support for a premise – supporting arguments, evidence, authority, explanations and anecdotes – interact in what can be called a **hierarchy of support or evidence**, in which one sort is given priority over another. In a murder trial, for example, the prosecution's case is based on the assumption that the jury's hierarchy of evidence will be weighted according to reliability and strength. It is usually ranked in the following order of importance:

1. physical evidence (fingerprints, blood samples, glass fragments), especially as explained by technical authorities (forensic pathologists, ballistics experts)
2. eyewitness accounts
3. other sorts of authorities (psychologists, sociologists, other experts)
4. explanations and anecdotes (character witnesses, personal histories, testimonies).

If the prosecution is right, any strong physical evidence and eyewitness accounts will outweigh the defendant's character witnesses because of their relative placement in the jury's hierarchy of evidence. In some research, however, anecdotal evidence can be weighted above scientific findings. In nursing, for example, the qualitative reports from patients about the positive/negative effects of a treatment may outweigh test results that fail to show any difference in effect.

EXAMPLE 5

Argument analysis REAL SECURITY

The idea that shutting out refugees will bolster Europe's security is a dangerous illusion. Closing the door to those fleeing violence will increase antagonism, alienation and anti-Western sentiment. Abandoning refugees to sit idly in Middle Eastern camps will allow resentment to fester and increase the risk they fall prey to extremist recruiters. Ensuring their integration into European society, by providing training and opportunities, will reduce the danger of them becoming radicalised. Many will eventually return home with an understanding and respect for European values and help build new societies there. **Daesh is trying to smuggle operatives into Europe among refugees** from Syria, so vigilance is needed, but an overreaction will be counter-productive. Almost all Jihadi terror attacks in Europe have been planned and executed by European citizens or residents. In the United States, the number of refugees admitted since 1980 is 3 million; the number implicated in a fatal terrorist attack since then is zero.

REAL SECURITY – To analyse this passage, first decide if it is an argument. There is a claim contained in the first sentence – shutting out refugees will not bolster security (implied) – and the author lists several reasons that relate to that claim so it is an argument. The author also has two sub-arguments, one suggests how to reduce the risk of terrorism, the other is a counter argument that argues terrorist attacks do not come from refugees (not stated but implied), supported by statistical evidence. Not all the content is relevant to the argument so you need to be able to identify what are the relevant parts. The statement about Daesh raises a potential counter claim, which is why the author has countered this with the final argument. Mapping the full argument would show how the different sub-arguments relate (or not) to the main claim. This will make it easier to identify the relative strengths and weaknesses of the argument, how it could be made more convincing or how it could be critiqued.

Exercise 4

Try to identify the elements in this argument. Mark 'c' for claim or conclusion, 'e' for supporting evidence, 'ca' for counter argument.

The smart pill (*adapted from Laurance, 2003*)

Debilitating mental diseases like Alzheimer's and other forms of dementia have a huge social and financial impact. As a consequence, scientists have been trying to find a cure by developing drugs that slow mental deterioration and enhance memory retention (Laurance 2003). According to researchers in the field (MacNally, 1998; Jones, 2001), more than 200 chemical compounds that will boost memory and learning ability are currently being developed by pharmaceutical companies. Contrary to these claims, the Chair of CIBA Foundation (2002) says that of the 140 'smart pills' already being sold in California, none were effective and some were actually hazardous. One cognitive enhancer, Tacrine, has produced only modest effects – slowing mental deterioration by just six months – but its side effects, such as liver damage, have been very severe. The idea of a smart pill is popular with students and high achievers. There is, however, little evidence that such a pill exists, especially one without risk. While cognitive enhancers may be worth the risk for dementia patients, students would be better off eating nutritiously and studying regularly rather than risking the effects of a smart pill.

The next chapter (Chapter 5) explores how to critique arguments by examining potential flaws in the logic. Chapter 9 looks in more detail at how we can develop and write strong arguments to make them more persuasive and convincing.

Chapter summary

- Being aware of our cognitive limitations will help us minimise the effect those limitations have on our judgement, making us better critical thinkers.
- An argument is an attempt to persuade someone to accept a claim or point of view by using reason.
- The first step in thinking critically about what we read is to identify the author's claim or point of view. What does the author want us to believe or accept?
- The second step in analysing a claim in a text is to recognise whether or not there is any evidence to support the claim. If there is, you have identified an argument.
- You need an argument when the point you are making is not well known or may not be well accepted (it is not obviously true) or where you know there is some

disagreement, controversy or an alternative perspective. If this is so, you have to give reasons to support your position.

- It is important to note that evidence on its own does not argue for anything – empirical evidence only supports the premises. To argue, one has to state what the relationship is between the premises, supported by the evidence and the claim.

Answers to Exercises 1–4

Exercise 1

Which of these is an argument?

1. *Michael Moore is a film producer who produced the documentary 'Sicko,' which looked at medical insurance in the States.* ☐no

This is not an argument but a statement (of fact) with an illustrative example. It would be an argument if the word 'who' was changed to 'because he' as this would constitute a reason for him being a film producer. As it is, it just describes who Moore is.

2. *Nobody expects foreign taxi drivers to discourse at length on world affairs but they should at least understand the address of the passenger's destination and be able to answer questions about the fare.* ☐no

This is not an argument but a statement containing a prescription (should) about the desirable skills of foreign taxi drivers. It does imply that these are lacking. It is a generalisation.

3. *Withholding information is just the same as lying and lying is wrong in any situation, so withholding information is wrong.* ☐yes

This is a (valid deductive) argument where the conclusion is the end of the sentence (so = therefore). The conclusion is a logical consequence of accepting the first two premises.

4. *An activity need not be financially rewarding to be valuable. However, housework is not valued because it is not paid work.* ☐no

While this looks like an argument, it is an explanation. The word 'because' in the second sentence introduces the reason *why* housework is not valued. It is not arguing *that* housework isn't valued (i.e. because we only value paid work). For it to be an argument, we would need to add that premise. In fact, the first sentence states that we *do not just* value paid work.

5. *When newcomers (migrants/refugees) arrive too fast, they gather in enclaves and resist learning the national language.* ☐no

This is a description of what happens when newcomers arrive too fast. It doesn't give reasons and just states that this is so. This is not an argument.

6. *You shouldn't eat grapes before bed as they will give you indigestion.* ☐yes

This is an argument as it is giving you a reason not to do something you might do. The claim or conclusion is do not eat grapes before bed. The reason is they will give you indigestion.

Exercise 2

This passage contains **both an explanation and an argument** (in fact, it contains more than one argument). The first two sentences offer an explanation of *why* Realty Home Loans collapsed. We know it has collapsed so do not need persuading of that fact. What the passage offers are reasons *why* it collapsed. The next few sentences contain both an argument and a sub-argument. It is an argument because it is offering reasons why going to another town will be just as bad for the company. This has not happened but could. It is putting forward an argument, offering reasons to justify the claim that they will end up in a worse situation. The sub-argument, which sets out what would happen if the one industry lost its client, Nigeria, supports the premises that the industry will close and (negatively) affect the economy. The supposition that the industry will close is a hypothetical deductive argument (if x then y).

Sub-argument structure

If the industry lost its client, it will close.
It is likely it will lose its client.
Therefore, it is likely it will close.

Main argument structure

If the industry closes, 1000 people will be out of work.
This will affect the economy of the town.
Therefore, Realty Home Loans will collapse again and be in a worse situation.

Exercise 3

1. Fear is the main source of superstition and one of the main sources of cruelty to others. To conquer fear is the beginning of wisdom. – This passage argues that conquering fear is the beginning of wisdom *because* of what fear causes – superstition and cruelty. This argument is convincing only if we accept the truth of the first premise and the background assumption that cruelty and superstition are the antithesis of wisdom.
2. There is a substance in the human eye that is similar to algae. So human beings are related to algae. – This passage argues that human beings are related to algae because they share an algae-like substance. For this analogy to hold there would need to be more similarities between the two things (human and algae). As it stands, it is a weak analogy, hence not a strong argument.
3. Multi-coloured fish are more restricted to particular territories than fish with less dramatic colouration. The bright colours have evolved to warn other fish that they are there and that this is their territory. – This is an argument using evolutionary adaptation to claim multi-coloured fish are limited to the particular areas they have evolved in. It may or may not be true. The evidence given of the effectiveness of bright colours does not directly support the claim about restriction of territory. It needs additional support.

4. Elephants have a concept of death because they have been known to cover the corpses of other dead elephants with leaves and branches, whereas they do not cover sleeping elephants. – This passage uses the behaviour of elephants towards the dead to argue that they must have a concept of death. The counter-evidence of their behaviour towards sleeping elephants seems to indicate that they do discern a difference between the two, adding weight to the claim.
5. Swimming places no stress on the joints because one's weight is supported by water. It is a safe form of physical exercise for people troubled by joint pain. – This passage argues for the safety of swimming for patients with joint pain. The reason given offers good support for the claim, making it a convincing argument.
6. Charred rhinoceros bones, thought to be about 300,000 years old, have been found in an archaeological site in France. This means the rhinoceros species lived in Europe at least 300,000 years ago. – This passage argues that rhinoceros lived in Europe a long time ago based on the discovery of 300,000-year-old bones of rhinoceros. This would seem a safe conclusion to draw from the evidence.

Exercise 4

The Smart Pill (adapted from Laurance, 2003)

Debilitating mental diseases like Alzheimer's and other forms of dementia have a huge social and financial impact. As a consequence, scientists have been trying to find a cure by developing drugs that slow mental deterioration and enhance memory retention (Laurance, 2003) (**E**). According to researchers in the field (MacNally, 1998; Jones, 2001), more than 200 chemical compounds that will boost memory and learning ability are currently being developed by pharmaceutical companies (**E**). Contrary to these claims, the Chair of CIBA Foundation (2002) says that of the 140 'smart pills' already being sold in California, none were effective and some were actually hazardous (**CA**). One cognitive enhancer, Tacrine, has produced only modest effects – slowing mental deterioration by just six months – but its side effects, such as liver damage, have been very severe (**CA**). The idea of a smart pill is popular with students and high achievers. There is, however, little evidence that such a pill exists, especially one without risk (**C**).While cognitive enhancers may be worth the risk for dementia patients, students would be better off eating nutritiously and studying regularly, rather than risking the effects of a smart pill. (**C**)

- ← Statement/starting assumption (i.e. that this is common knowledge)
- ← Context, rationale/ evidence (E)
- ← Evidence to support claims about smart pill (E)
- ← Counter-evidence to show claims may not be true (CA)
- ← Summary of article; sub-claim/counter argument (CA)
- ← Main claim or conclusion (C)
- ← Conclusion/implication (C)

CHAPTER

5

Critiquing the Logic of the Argument – Logical Thinking and Common Fallacies

Knowledge, justification and logic

We now know there are a great many potential barriers to arriving at reliable or defensible conclusions about the world around us, including the claims we make about our social and political world, which is why we need to become thoughtful critical thinkers. Examining the background beliefs and experiences that influence our own thinking processes is a first step in that process. The next step is understanding how claims are justified through the use of argument. The stronger we can make the argument, the more convincing the claim will be. What makes an argument strong (or weak) is how well the claim is justified. Having reliable, relevant and sufficient evidence to support a claim should make it justifiable and, therefore, convincing.

> Critiquing a statement starts with asking for its justification; critiquing an argument starts with **questioning the justification** for the claim.

A common barrier to reaching reliable conclusions or in justifying our claims with appropriate evidence is **flawed logical thinking**. It is easy to make mistakes in our reasoning. We may draw conclusions from unrelated evidence or reason from the evidence to a false conclusion. In this chapter, we are going to examine reasoning or logical arguments and the fallacies we can fall into. Understanding how reasoning can be flawed will help us to both critique the claims that others make and better justify the claims we want to make. It will help us improve our reasoning to become better critical thinkers.

> Cucumbers are green; Some frogs are green;
> Therefore some cucumbers are frogs

Assessing arguments

When assessing the strength of an argument, we are looking to see how well its premises support its conclusion. Is the support strong enough that we are willing to accept the truth or reliability of the conclusion? Our acceptance of the conclusion should depend on several things:

- The strength and reliability of the evidence
- The relation of the evidence to the claim/conclusion
- The reliability of the conclusion in relation to the evidence
- The logical structure of the argument
- Underlying assumptions that influence the acceptance of the evidence

Remember! We want to avoid accepting a conclusion *just because* we agree with it.

Critiquing the argument requires us to **identify the author's reasoning** so we can decide if it is logical and actually supports the claim.

Types of justification for arguments

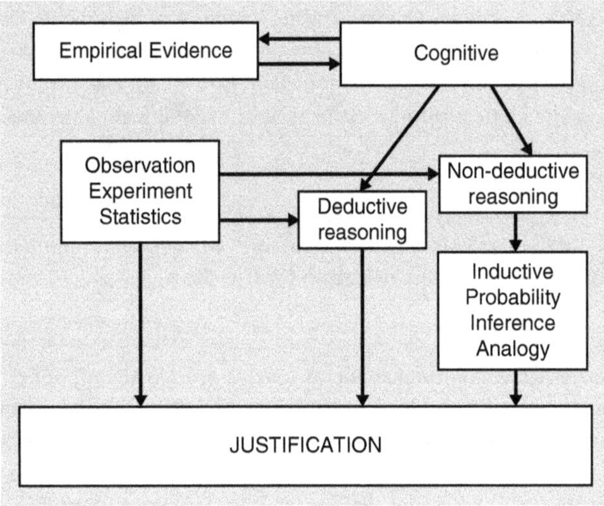

This diagram illustrates the different ways we can justify the claims we make – using what is called empirical evidence (information or facts), and using what is called cognitive evidence (reasoning or logic). Having the right kind and amount of empirical evidence is essential to support most of our claims (evaluating evidence is discussed in more detail in Chapter 8). It is, however, not enough on its own. It is the reasoning that connects the evidence to the claim, and shows us how it is relevant to that claim. This is what makes an argument and this is what makes it convincing or not. But this is also where we make mistakes.

Simple example of an inductive and deductive argument

Inductive argument
All the crows anyone has ever seen have been black, so all crows are black.
Deductive argument (Aristotle's 3-step syllogism)
All crows are black; this is a crow; therefore this crow is black.

All logical argument forms are either a type of **inductive or deductive** reasoning. Inductive reasoning includes use of analogy, probability and inductive inference. Deductive reasoning uses a set of known logical forms that can be valid or invalid. Sherlock Holmes is considered the archetypal deductive reasoner who solved criminal cases by using logic. What type of logical form we use will depend on what kind of evidence we have. Each form has its own strengths and weaknesses. We will look at each of these separately.

Inductive reasoning

Inductive reasoning is our most common form of reasoning. It draws from experience and examples, using past events as evidence and the future for predictions (all crows are black example). It enables us to form generalisations or make predictions about what we think is the case, or what is the most likely cause or the most likely outcome. It allows us to generalise from specific instances to making claims about categories of similar things. The strength of the generalisation will be proportional to the strength of the evidence supporting it and the strength of the relationship between that evidence and the claim.

Other than *a priori* truths, which are by definition deductive, all our assumptions, initial claims or starting premises are derived using **inductive reasoning**.

Example of the process of induction

Claim/conclusion	**Creatures with wings tend to fly**

This statement is an example of an **inductive inference** because it is drawn from our experience of particular instances of creatures with wings flying. We observe individual instances of flying creatures and note that they tend to have wings. We then infer a conclusion that appears to follow from the observed instances and explain them. We form a **generalisation**. The reasoning (argument) is spelt out below:

Inductive argument 1:

Birds have wings and fly;

Bees have wings and fly;

Bats have wings and fly;

∴ **Creatures with wings tend to fly.**

Note that the inference applies to all creatures with wings, not just those we observed. It has become a broad general statement that applies to creatures we can't see, both past and present. We also assume it will apply in the future too. This is why it is called a **generalisation.**

Examples of generalisations or predictions (inductive inferences)

- Atomic bombs cause mass destruction.
- Artificial intelligence (AI) is the next stage of evolution.
- Health is more important than money.
- Alcohol makes you aggressive.
- Labour will win the next election.
- Our perception is limited and prone to error.

A **generalisation** claims more than we can possibly know just from the supporting premises. Despite this, we sometimes feel confident enough that the information in the premises is sufficient to warrant such a leap. If we are right, then we have been able to make legitimate claims about things we can't know or see directly. We have added to our knowledge base.

Strong inductive arguments infer things that **add** to our knowledge of the world.

Strength and limitations of inductive arguments

In an ordinary inductive argument, we draw an inference or make a claim based on the available evidence. What we hope for is that it is the best, most reasonable conclusion to come to or the best inference to draw, based on what we currently know and what we want to achieve. This is sometimes called the **inference to the best explanation.**

Examples of inductive generalisations in a text (notice how most of the statements here could count as inductive generalisations; they are general claims). Note also that the reliability of the inferences drawn depend on the reliability of the research used to generate the data.

Evidence indicates that about a third of students drop out of university because they made few social connections in their first year and had little personal contact with academic staff. As an additional risk, mature-age students and those from lower socioeconomic status backgrounds are more likely to live off-campus, study part-time and/or have work and family responsibilities. This has become a pattern for all students. Over 70% of students do some form of paid work and an increasing percentage (up to 30%) are working full-time. These conditions make it more difficult for students to participate in co-curricular and extra-curricular activities that allow the building of robust social networks, thereby making it easier for them to feel disengaged. A lack of engagement can reduce the sense of belonging, which, in turn, reduces the likelihood of students seeking help if faced with difficulties. It is generally believed that if students can engage with university life by understanding the culture, making friends or developing a sense of belonging, they are more likely to persevere and to report a positive experience.

While inductive reasoning is the most common and useful way we draw inferences, it is also the most fraught with difficulties. It is easy to make mistakes. There may be exceptions and there could always be another explanation. At one time it was believed that 'All swans are white'. For thousands of years every swan ever seen was white, so this seemed a safe **inductive inference or generalisation.** Then settlers arrived in Australia and discovered *black swans*. This raised the problem of how many examples do we need before we form a generalisation.

Inductive arguments can be **strong or weak** but not valid. All inductive arguments are actually invalid deductive arguments.

Problems with inductive reasoning

- We do not know how many instances of something are enough to warrant a claim that 'x is so'. (the destruction of Hiroshima alone was enough to show that 'atomic bombs cause mass extinction' but millions of white swans were not enough to prove 'all swans are white').
- We assume because things happened a certain way in the past that they will happen the same way in the future, but this is not the case (polls are based on past practice and how people say they would vote; COVID 19 showed that the future is not predicated on the past).
- Just because one thing precedes another does not mean it caused that thing to happen (the economy may have improved regardless of who won the election).
- Correlation between two events is not always causation (the two events could be consequences of something else or coincidence).
- What counts as evidence for some one thing rather than for something else? (we interpret and infer things from specific events that could be interpreted differently).
- Our knowledge of things is incomplete or unknown (there may be relevant facts we do not know).

- There can always be an exception or anomaly (albino crows, flightless birds).
- There can always be another inference or alternative explanation (think of Newton and Einstein, conspiracy theories, religious belief).

Exercise 1

Have a look at these inductive arguments. Decide whether or not they are strong or weak. Explain why you think this.

1. In winter we usually experience a severe storm every week. We haven't had one for two weeks so I expect there will be a storm tomorrow or the day after.
2. Recent statistics indicate that car accidents cause 11% of deaths while cancer is responsible for 76% of deaths. This means we are 7 times more likely to die of cancer than to die in a car accident.
3. There is a 4% chance this product contains peanuts so my son is likely to have an allergic reaction because he is allergic to peanuts.
4. Pig-farming leads to poor quality of life. One woman who lived next to a pig farm said she couldn't hang out her washing because the smell was so bad.

Argument by analogy

An analogy is a particular form of argument model often used in South East Asian writings. We are using **analogy** when we compare one thing (*x*) with something else (*y*) to suggest that what is true (or false) for *x* is also true (or false) for *y*. We can legitimately use analogical reasoning to make a point or to argue a case. It acts as a type of proof or justification. As an argument tool, it pushes us to act or think consistently – if we think *x* is right or wrong in that situation, then we should think *x* is right or wrong in a similar situation.

Example of analogical reasoning

If you gave $150 to Rashad for babysitting, then to be fair you should give me $150 for looking after your fish while you were away!

Some examples of where analogy is used as argument:

- Legal precedents – one case is similar enough to another to be treated the same
- Fingerprinting/DNA – looking for enough similarities between samples
- Evolutionary theory – parallel between natural selection and breeding practices to get certain traits
- Archaeology – similarities between cultural artefacts to infer similar practices
- Animal rights – similarities between animals and humans to claim similar rights
- Medicine – similarities between human bodies and machines or brains and computers

For an analogy to work, however, there must be sufficient similarities between the two things we are comparing. To be effective as evidence in an argument:

- the analogy should be understandable
- at least one of the objects being compared should be known or familiar
- there should be enough similarities between the objects to draw an analogy
- the similarities between the objects will be relevant to the claim
- the differences between the objects are minimal or irrelevant to the claim, and
- all this is made clear and explicit in the text. The parallels are explained.

EXAMPLE 1A

Animal rights analogy

Animal rights advocates often use the **similarities** between animals and humans to argue by analogy that if animals are the same as humans in certain respects (able to suffer, feel joy or pain, fight to survive, care for their young), then they should be treated the same as humans (i.e. not exploited or made to suffer). If humans have rights, then animals should have rights similar to human rights.

EXAMPLE 1B

Animal rights counter analogy

The argument by analogy for animal rights assumes that the **differences** between animals and humans don't matter. However, it can be argued that the **cognitive and linguistic** differences between animals and humans do matter when it comes to rights. Humans can be aware of their rights, exercise their rights and respect the rights of others in ways animals can't. There are many rights we can't give animals because of the differences. So the analogy may only hold in a limited way; i.e. in terms of preventing cruelty or unnecessary suffering.

Exercise 2

Are these good or bad analogies? Why or why not?

1. To say that dreams are wish fulfilment because Freud said so is no better than saying animals don't feel pain because Descartes said so. Nobody would accept the second argument, so why would you accept the first?
2. In scientific reasoning, evidence from experience is a fundamental part of empiricism. Religious mystics fast and meditate and then have sensory experiences. If we think experiences provide evidence for matters of fact about our world, then to be consistent, we should accept the evidence from mystics about the spirit world.

3. If the tiger had its tooth removed without anaesthetic, I would infer that this caused it great pain. We have a reasonably similar nervous system and I know how painful having a filling is without anaesthetic, so I can imagine how painful it would be to have a tooth removed without pain medicine.
4. There was nothing wrong or offensive about Marilyn Manson's concert. Young people are exposed to worse violence on TV and Netflix every day than they saw at his concert.

Argument from probability

We often qualify the claims we make by saying the conclusion is likely or possible or even *probable*, given the evidence. Saying some event is probable is often taken to mean it will happen at some point. This is a fallacy. Probability in this context only means that it could happen (*James will probably pass his exam; Labour will probably lose the next election*).

There is another kind of **probability,** which refers to numerical or statistical probability. Statistical data is a special kind of evidence used to support our claims. It turns information into numbers that can be represented in graphs or tables that can be described or interpreted. When we say an outcome is probable in this context, the statement is usually saying that an outcome is **statistically probable** based on the (statistical) data. Often this refers to the relative frequency of a property in a given population – i.e. the instances of breast cancer or smoking in a population. Based on the relative frequency, one can infer the statistical probability of something occurring (a homicide) or being likely (owning a home). Statistics are used whenever large amounts of data are collected to ascertain trends, likelihoods, or patterns of behaviour. In newspapers, probability is commonly referred to in percentages (alcohol increases the risk of breast cancer by 20%; pancreatic cancer risk is 29% higher in men with a high red meat intake) or as a predictive trend (women are 4 times more likely than men to experience sexual assault at work). In academic papers or official documents, statistics will often appear in a table or graph, followed by an explanation of any (statistically) significant findings. We frequently use probability statements to add weight to our arguments.

EXAMPLE 2

Good use of probability

In a cold-case murder trial it was found that a DNA sample taken from a local man exactly matched the DNA profile of the blood trace found on the victim's coat. It was estimated that the probability that the DNA profile of a random male matches the DNA profile of that blood trace was about 1 in 1500 billion billion, or $0.66 \cdot 10^{-21}$. This meant that the probability of the sample not belonging to the local man was 0. He was arrested and confessed to the crime.

Examples of areas where statistical probability is used:

- Medical matters such as cancer rates or increased probability of a disease
- Effectiveness of drugs or other agents
- Car accidents and fatalities
- Election or other opinion polling
- Predictions of spending patterns
- Education results or achievement levels
- Income and expenditure of a population
- Likelihood of certain behaviours appearing in a population

EXAMPLE 3

Misleading statistics found in a magazine

US researchers claim you can reduce your risk of heart attack or stroke by 31% if you own a dog. Better still, owning a dog can reduce your overall risk of death by 24%!

As with analogies, there can be problems using statistics or probability as support in our arguments. It is easy to misrepresent statistical evidence, to be mistaken about what it means or to distort it to suit our own ends. It is also easy to be swayed by numbers and not think critically about what the data are demonstrating, if anything. As in Example 3, while it sounds convincing, you cannot reduce your risk of death. It remains at 100%! You can only reduce your risk of dying sooner or dying from something specific. Often statistical findings are abstracted from a larger report. The meaning or significance can change when taken out of context (this is discussed in more detail in Chapter 8).

Exercise 3

What claims would these statistics support? Are they persuasive?

Below is a series of statistical 'facts' collected from research findings by authoritative bodies. Have a look at what they say. If we accept their findings at face value, what kinds of inferences could we draw from the data? How reliable do you think those inferences might be, given the evidence? Can you think how someone might argue against the implications of the data?

1. According to Cancer Research UK, the risk of breast cancer increases for postmenopausal women using any type of HRT but is greatest for those using combined HRT, up by 20%. The risk for womb cancer increases to 80% when using oestrogen alone. The risk is also higher for those women who use HRT for more than 5 years.

2. Survey – Adelaide residents feel the least safe in their neighbourhoods, according to research. A survey by insurer AAMI found 14% of Adelaideans said they would feel safer in another suburb, compared to 7% nationally. It also found 92% of Adelaide people knew their neighbour by name. AAMI state manager said there was a link between people feeling safer if they knew their neighbour.
3. The VET in Schools (VETiS) program has a high success rate of putting students in jobs, a new study has found. Conducted by the National Centre for Vocational Education Research (NCVER), the study found that five years after participating in a VETiS program, 78% of students were in a job, while 29% were also studying.
4. Speeding remains the leading behavioural factor in death and injuries on our roads, contributing to about 40% of road fatalities. The RAA found the risk of involvement in a casualty doubles with each 5 km/h increase in free travelling speed above 60 km/h, while a 5 km/h reduction in speed can lead to at least a 15% decrease in crashes.

Deductive reasoning

Most forms of argument use either **inductive or deductive** arguments. These two types of reasoning are often seen as the reverse of each other because induction argues from specific instances to a more generally applicable claim or prediction, whereas deduction starts from a general statement and deduces a specific point or conclusion. Both forms can be visually depicted as a triangle.

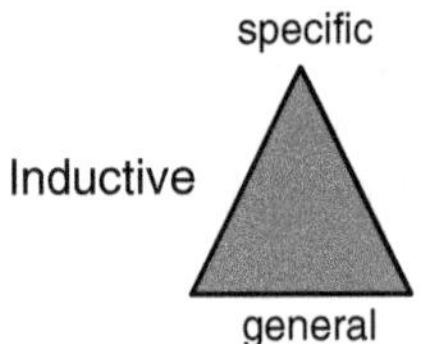

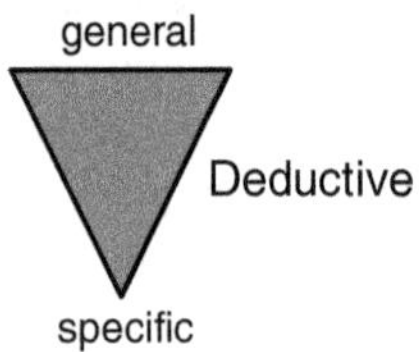

Example of a deductive inference and argument

Deductive argument:	Creatures with wings fly	All As are B
	This beetle has wings	C is an A
	Therefore, this beetle will fly	∴ C is B

The deductive argument starts with **an inductive generalisation** – (all) creatures with wings fly. You can see from the logical structure of the three statements that the conclusion is deduced from the first two. If you accept the truth of the first statement, and you can see that the second is true from observation, then you would also accept the truth of the conclusion as it **follows deductively**. If all creatures with wings fly, then the beetle will fly if it has wings.

Because of this feature, deductive arguments are what are called **truth preserving.** If they are **sound** (valid syntactic form plus true premises), then the truth of the conclusion cannot be denied. This was the case with Aristotle's syllogism. The connection of the conclusion to the premises is a function of the logical implication of the form. The simplest valid deductive form is the three-step syllogism. Any argument that takes the same form is valid, regardless of the content of the premises. This means we can substitute symbols (letters) to replace the content of the premises in order to check the logical structure (propositional logic). There are several types of valid deductive argument that can be represented symbolically. Here are some common examples.

Valid deductive forms

$A \rightarrow B$	$A \rightarrow B$	$A \vee B$	$A \vee B$	$A \rightarrow B$	$A = B$
A	$-B$	A	$-B$	$B \rightarrow C$	$B = C$
$\therefore B$	$\therefore -A$	$\therefore -B$	$\therefore A$	$\therefore A \rightarrow C$	$\therefore A = C$

We can tell that these forms are valid because the conclusion follows logically from the premises: Either we have A <u>or</u> we have B; if we have A, we can't have B too. It is irrelevant what A or B is. If all As are Bs and all Bs are Cs, then it follows that all As are Cs. The form of the argument dictates the validity (or not) of the conclusion. You can test this by substituting premises for letters where you know if the conclusion is true or false.

EXAMPLE 4

Valid

- Either we went to the pictures or we stayed home ($A \vee B$).
- We went to the pictures (A).
- Therefore, we didn't stay home ($-B$).

Because validity takes a very specific logical form, it is easy to tell if something is invalid or not. An **invalid** argument means that the conclusion is not guaranteed to be true through the logical structure of the argument (even though the conclusion may be coincidentally true).

EXAMPLE 5

Valid or invalid?

- If the government passes this bill, we will pay more fees (If $A \rightarrow B$).
- We will pay more fees (B).
- Therefore, the government passed the bill ($\therefore A$).

If you look at the examples of validity above, Example 4 takes an *invalid* form. We can test this by substituting premises that mimic the same form but where we know the conditions of the consequent (B).

EXAMPLE 6

Testing validity

- If the sun is shining, there will be no rain (If A→ B).
- There is no rain (B).
- Therefore, the sun is shining (∴ A).

We can tell this is an invalid argument because we know from experience that the sky could be cloudy (no sunshine) and yet there is no rain. So this can't be a valid form (see above valid forms). It is invalid because the conditional (hypothetical) statement only refers one way (antecedent → consequent). It *does not say* the only reason it's not raining is because the sun is shining; it only says *if* the sun is shining there will be no rain. It does not say if we pay more fees it is only because the government passed the bill. We could be paying more fees (the consequent) for a lot of reasons but not necessarily because the government passed the bill, which we don't know has happened. The conclusion might turn out to be *coincidentally* true, but is not true because of the argument. Deductive arguments can be strong contributing threads in any bigger argument but only if they are sound.

A deductive argument has to be both **valid and sound** – have a valid structure and true premises – before we accept the truth of the conclusion.

Strength and limitations of deductive arguments

The beauty of deductive reasoning or arguments is that we can guarantee the truth of some of our conclusions if our arguments are sound. Rather like mathematical proofs, we can use deductive reasoning to provide strong foundations for our knowledge base. However, there are limitations.

1. Deductive arguments only add knowledge about specific instances. We can know that 'x' is true because it is an instance of 'y'. But we already know 'y' is true, so we are only deducing what logically follows from the premises, given the right logical connectives (if, then; or, and, not) and form. So deductive arguments don't add any *new* knowledge about the world, even though they can reveal a logical (or illogical) consequence of an argument. We generate the initial premises of our arguments through the use of good inductive reasoning.

EXAMPLE 7

Using both inductive and deductive inference

Numerous studies indicate that the emotional quality of the physician/patient interaction has an impact on treatment outcomes (evidence). Health outcomes are improved across domains when there are more understanding relationships between doctors and patients (inductive generalisation). This implies that any empathetic doctor will have patients who get better quicker (deductive inference).

The inductive generalisation is the claim about improved health outcomes, drawn from the findings of individual studies (Numerous studies…). The deductive inference is a logical consequence of the generalisation; if it is true for all empathetic doctors, then it will be true for any one (empathetic) doctor.

2. Deductive arguments rely on being both valid and sound. But it is easy to make logical mistakes. We can argue against or critique a deductive argument if its form is invalid (as in Examples 4–6 above). This means the conclusion does not follow automatically from the premises. The conclusion may or may not turn out to be true but it is not true because of the validity of the argument. Another way we can critique deductive arguments, is if one of the premises can be shown to be false or can be questioned. The argument may be valid (i.e. have a valid form) but have false/questionable premises. This makes it **unsound** or not cogent.

EXAMPLE 8

Valid but unsound argument

- Legalising homosexuality is an attack on religious freedom (A → B).
- Attacks on religious freedom are attacks on human rights (B → C).
- Therefore, legalising homosexuality is an attack on human rights (∴ A → C).

Example 8 has a perfectly valid form according to the formulas above. But we may be reluctant to accept the truth of the conclusion. It seems to be contradictory, as the act of legalising homosexuality is to support human rights. We can argue *not* to accept the conclusion if we can show that one of the premises is not true or acceptable. In this example, the conclusion may not be *necessarily* true if one (or more) of the premises can be questioned (i.e. A→ B or B→C). We cannot argue against the conclusion itself as it follows logically from the previous premises. However, we could reject the initial premise and state that legalising homosexuality is not an attack on religious freedom. The onus would then be on the religion in question (i.e. Christianity or Islam) to say how it impedes religious freedom.

One argument might be that homosexuality is evil in the eyes of God and should be punished. Legalising it means they (the religion) cannot punish those who practice it. They lose that freedom. A counter claim might be that religious freedom consists in allowing the free practice of religion by those who believe in it, assuming its practices do not break civil laws. Those within the religion are not forced to accept or practice homosexuality, so there should be no loss of freedom. On the other hand, those outside of the religion should not be constrained in their practices by religious laws or practices they do not accept.

What about B→C? Are attacks on religious freedom attacks on human rights? Many argue that religious rights are a fundamental human right and that these rights should be protected. So there does seem to be a link between the two. Again, the issue appears to be whether or not legalising homosexuality is an infringement of religious rights. It is not an infringement in a general sense as there are many religions that don't oppose homosexuality; it only applies to Islam and some sects of the Christian church. One can also accept B→C but still not accept the legitimacy of A→B. Ultimately, it depends how religious freedom is interpreted – if it is interpreted to mean the freedom to enact practices that go against the (civil) law, then the statement is correct. If it is interpreted to mean the freedom to practice any religion within the (civil) law, then there is no conflict.

Exercise 4

Write these arguments using the correct logically deductive form. Decide if they are valid or invalid? Are they sound?

1. If there were a Tasmanian tiger, someone would have spotted one by now. No-one has ever seen one, so there are no Tasmanian tigers.
2. Snow only ever falls when it is below 5°C and it is snowing, so it must be below 5°C.
3. Torture is never justified because people lie to stop the torture. This means it never provides reliable information.
4. If you don't vote for Brexit (to get out of the EU) then you want Britain to lose its sovereignty because if we stay, we will be under Brussels and have no sovereignty.

Understanding and **identifying logical fallacies** enables us to detect reasoning errors in the writing of others and to avoid them in our own.

Exercise 5

Identify the argument. Pick out the claim and identify the type of reasoning used (analogy, probability, induction, deduction)

1. You should provide a rich and stimulating environment for your children if you want them to achieve their full potential as adults. Just as plants produce magnificent fruit

when they receive the right nutrients, so too do children. But the opposite is also true; they will wither and die if starved of the right food.

2. The biggest health threat facing the Western world today is obesity. In 2016, nearly two-thirds of adults were classified as overweight or obese, compared to 19% 10 years ago, and the rates are increasing. In some low income areas the rates are as high as 80%. Obesity is linked to many chronic ailments, including some cancers.
3. Many children and youth spend an inordinate amount of time consuming violent media. Research points overwhelmingly 'to a causal connection between media violence and aggressive behaviour in some children'. This means exposure to depictions of violence leads to actual acts of violence.
4. If all men were inherently violent, then there would be no male pacifists, monks or others who are placid by nature or who eschew violent acts. This is clearly not the case as there are many men who live non-violent lives. Therefore, it is not true that all men are inherently violent.
5. 'Before entering a mosque, visitors are asked to take off their shoes – this is a sign of respect', Peter Costello told the Sydney Institute in a speech. 'If you have a strong objection to walking in your socks, don't enter the mosque. Before becoming an Australian, you will be asked to subscribe to certain values – if you have strong objections to those values, don't come to Australia', he said.

Logical fallacies

As we have stated, our thinking processes are fallible. We make mistakes. Some of the frequent mistakes we make are using fallacious reasons to support a claim or drawing incorrect inferences from the available evidence. See below for some common logical fallacies.

Common fallacies

- Appeal to authority – do not accept something as true just because an authority figure said it
- Appeal to common or popular belief – just because it is a popular belief, doesn't make it true
- Appeal to common practice (tradition) – just because it is common or cultural practice, doesn't make it right
- Appeal to fairness – assumes both sides have equal merit, should be treated equally. This is not always the case
- Appeal to indirect consequences – slippery slope fallacy, claims one (bad) thing leads to another and consequences are inevitable
- Appeal to loyalty – peer pressure, nationalism, patriotism; 'it's not American'
- Appeal to prejudice – using stereotypes like 'we all know politicians lie…' 'a real man wouldn't do that…'

- Appeal to vanity – ego, flattery; 'you should know better...', 'as an intelligent person...'
- Hasty or over-generalisation – poor inductive argument
- Ad hominem attacks – attack the person, rather than the ideas
- Post-hoc reasoning – attribute false causal relationship after the event
- Burden of proof – avoid answering question, 'prove me wrong' mentality
- Loaded question – pre-empting answer
- Straw man – superficial characterisation
- Circular reasoning – begging the question
- False dilemma – claiming only two options are possible, 'stay at school or be a loser'.

Most of these common fallacies are found in advertising, popular magazines, personal websites or blogs, political rhetoric or newspapers. However, there are some that are relatively common in academic or scholarly writing.

Check the texts you read to see if they have committed one or more of these logical fallacies. Don't forget to check your own arguments as well.

- **Over generalisation** – it is always a fallacy to generalise across a class of objects as if they were all identical (over generalisation). The most common over generalisation is a stereotype and stereotypes are always wrong; there will always be exceptions (Used-car salesmen can't be trusted; Bikies are criminals; men are better drivers than women).
- **Hasty generalisation** – this is one of the most common fallacies, as we tend to jump to conclusions too quickly (hastily) based on limited information or one or two examples. A hasty generalisation could turn out to be true but it is not justified when based on very limited evidence (Old people shouldn't drive; my uncle is over 70 and nearly ran me over; based on my experience, the NHS is in crisis).
- **Straw man** – sometimes we critique a position by portraying only its worst features or by giving a superficial and selective description of it. This then makes it easy to ridicule or find fault. It is always a good tactic to present your opponent's position in the best light you can and then show why it doesn't work. This makes your argument look better (Labour's policies are all about spending).
- **Shifting the burden of proof** – this is a way of arguing for an unusual claim that has yet to be disproved. However, the burden of proof lies with the proponent of the claim, not with the opposition. I can suggest all sorts of weird theories and say 'prove me wrong' but no-one has to. I should be giving reasons why someone should accept my claim. Lack of a falsifier doesn't make me right (Homeopathy works because no-one has shown it doesn't).
- **Appeal to indirect consequences (slippery slope)** – This appeal is used as a legitimate argumentation tool in all sorts of places but it is a fallacy. It assumes a list of inevitable (and dire) consequences that will follow from taking one action – the first in a series from bad to worst. None of them are directly caused, none of them have just a singular consequence and none are inevitable. Each step on the slope would need to be justified (See arguments against euthanasia or legalising marijuana).

Exercise 6

Identify the fallacy. Do you know why it is wrong?

1. According to a survey in *Variety*, the top-grossing film of all time was *Star Wars*.
2. Chinese medicine clearly has health benefits, otherwise people wouldn't use it. There is also no evidence to show that it doesn't work.
3. Americans are so excessively patriotic that they believe the reason foreigners hate them is because they are jealous! This is not true. We hate them because they are gun-loving evangelists who believe wealth is a virtue.
4. You can't believe CNN news reports. They have done so much dishonest reporting and fake news stories that they should be called fiction writers rather than journalists.
5. Elder's essay was better, because he presented both sides of the issue. Oppenheimer's was more one-sided, so it wasn't as persuasive.
6. If we let the sick refugees on Manus and Nauru come to Australia, we will be opening our borders to people smugglers again. Before long, there will be a flood of refugees arriving by boat.
7. Decriminalising sex workers will open the door to more crime. It will lead to an increase in brothels, more girls being exploited and victimised, more drug trafficking and increased violence towards women. This is a retrogressive step.
8. The last time Labour was in power, inflation increased so this is likely to happen again.
9. The government should make cannabis oil readily available to the public for medicinal use. It has been very effective in reducing chronic seizures in some cases of epilepsy.

Chapter summary

- Critiquing a statement or argument means questioning the justification used to defend the claim.
- Critiquing the argument requires us to identify the author's reasoning so we can decide how well it supports the claim.
- Common argument methods use either deductive or inductive reasoning, or both. Inductive reasoning includes use of analogy, probability and inductive inference.
- Other than a priori truths, which are by definition deductive, all our assumptions, initial claims or starting premises are derived using inductive reasoning.
- Strong inductive arguments infer things that add to our knowledge of the world. However, it is easy to make mistakes.
- Inductive arguments are strong or weak but not valid. All inductive arguments are actually invalid deductive arguments.
- A deductive argument has to be both valid and sound – have a valid structure and true premises – before we accept the truth of the conclusion.
- Understanding and identifying logical fallacies enables us to detect reasoning errors in the writing of others and to avoid them in our own.

Answers to Exercises 1–6

Exercise 1

Are these good or bad analogies? Why or why not?

1. The analogy is that because we no longer accept a claim made by one expert, we should no longer accept a claim made by the other. It is true we should not accept claims by experts just because they are experts. However, we reject their claims because they have been shown to be false or are superseded. Just because one claim has been shown to be false, doesn't mean the other is. The analogy does not hold.
2. The analogy suggests that mystic experience should be treated as reliably in establishing facts about the spirit world as all experience is for the Earthly world. There are marked differences between the two cases, not least the method used for obtaining knowledge and the scope for verification. The latter can be tested and confirmed or disconfirmed. The analogy does not hold.
3. This is a reasonable analogy because we know that animal nervous systems are similar to ours, so it is likely the tiger feels pain without anaesthetic just as we would.
4. This analogy uses the argument that two wrongs make a right. Comparing the concert to other more violent material doesn't mean the concert was not violent.

Exercise 2

What claims would these statistics support? Are they persuasive?

1. These statistics seem scary and would discourage women from using HRT. However, we would need to know the base rate risk to ascertain how much of an increase 20% or 80% were. The overall risk may still be quite small (i.e. 80% of 0.002%), especially when compared to benefits.
2. On the surface, it seems Adelaideans feel less safe (14%) compared to 7% nationally. But the high (92%) of Adelaide people knowing their neighbour by name seems to contradict this finding, so we would need to find out more. We don't know what the sampling process was and which areas were selected for polling. Was it AAMI members?
3. While 78% sounds positive and may encourage getting a VET qualification, we do not know if the ex-students are working as a result of their VET qualification, what the rate of unemployment was before their qualification or whether they went on and got an additional qualification.
4. Speeding is obviously a contributing factor in injuries from accidents (40%). However, this is not the same as 'the risk of involvement in a casualty'. While the risk 'doubles with each 5 km/h increase in free travelling speed above 60 km/h', we don't know what that base risk is. It is not 40%. And a 5 km/h reduction in speeds under 60 km/h may have little impact. Speeding is anything over a set speed limit.

Exercise 3

Have a look at these inductive arguments. Decide whether or not they are strong or weak. Explain why.

1. *In winter we usually experience a severe storm every week. We haven't had one for two weeks so I expect there will be a storm either tomorrow or the day after.* – This argument assumes past events can predict future events but there is no guarantee this is so. Weather patterns are erratic and are not predicated on what happened in the past. **This is a weak inference.**
2. *Recent statistics indicate that car accidents cause 11% of deaths while cancer is responsible for 76% of deaths. This means we are 7 times more likely to die of cancer than to die in a car accident.* – Our risk of one or the other will depend on individual risk factors, which may increase or decrease either ratio (i.e. age, genetics, lifestyle). As a young male, I may have a higher than 11% chance of dying in a car accident and a much lower than 76% chance of dying from cancer. 'We' is too broad. **This is weak.**
3. *There is a 4% chance this product contains peanuts so my son is likely to have an allergic reaction because he is allergic to peanuts.* – You may decide not to take the risk but it is not 'likely' he will react as 4% is not high. The inference **is weak.**
4. *Pig-farming leads to poor quality of life. One woman who lived next to a pig farm said she couldn't hang out her washing because the smell was so bad.* – This claim is based on the anecdotal evidence of one woman and in relation to one feature (smell), a hasty generalisation; so **the argument is weak even if true.**

Exercise 4

Write these arguments using the correct logically deductive form. Decide if they are valid or invalid.

1. If there were a Tasmanian tiger, someone would have spotted one by now. No-one has ever seen one, so there are no Tasmanian tigers. *(If A → B; –B; therefore –A)* ***valid***
2. Snow only ever falls when it is below 5°C and it is snowing, so it must be below 5°C. *(A → B; A; therefore B)* ***valid***
3. Torture is never justified because people lie to stop the torture. This means it never provides reliable information. (there is a missing first premise – *torture is justified if it provides reliable information*- rephrased as *if torture provides reliable information then it is justified – if A → B; –B; therefore –A)* ***valid***
4. If you don't vote for Brexit (to get out of the EU) then you want Britain to lose its sovereignty because if we stay, we will be under Brussels and have no sovereignty. (Can be written as an either/or argument: *either A or –B; –A; therefore –B*) ***valid***

Exercise 5

Identify the argument. Pick out the claim and identify the type of reasoning used (analogy, probability, induction, deduction)

1. You should provide a rich and stimulating environment for your children if you want them to achieve their full potential as adults. Just as plants produce magnificent fruit when they receive the right nutrients, so too do children. But the opposite is also true; they will wither and die if starved of the right food. ***Analogical reasoning***
2. The biggest health threat facing the Western world today is obesity. In 2016, nearly two-thirds of adults were classified as overweight or obese, compared to 19% 10 years ago, and the rates are increasing. In some low income areas the rates are as high as 80%. Obesity is linked to many chronic ailments, including some cancers. ***Statistical probability***
3. Many children and youth spend an inordinate amount of time consuming violent media. Research points overwhelmingly 'to a causal connection between media violence and aggressive behaviour in some children'. This means exposure to depictions of violence leads to actual acts of violence. ***Inductive inference***
4. If all men were inherently violent, then there would be no male pacifists, monks or others who are placid by nature or who eschew violent acts. This is clearly not the case as there are many men who live non-violent lives. Therefore, it is not true that all men are inherently violent. ***Deductive reasoning***
5. 'Before entering a mosque, visitors are asked to take off their shoes – this is a sign of respect', Peter Costello told the Sydney Institute in a speech. 'If you have a strong objection to walking in your socks, don't enter the mosque. Before becoming an Australian, you will be asked to subscribe to certain values – if you have strong objections to those values, don't come to Australia'. ***Analogical reasoning***

Exercise 6

Identify the fallacy. Do you know why it is wrong?

1. *According to a survey in Variety, the top-grossing film of all time was Star Wars.* Appeal to popularity – top-grossing films are determined by how much money they bring in, not by asking the public.
2. *Chinese medicine clearly has health benefits otherwise people wouldn't use it. There is also no evidence to show that it doesn't work.* Appeal to popular belief/burden of proof – just because a lot of people use it, doesn't mean it is good; the burden of proof lies with the advocate, lack of evidence that it doesn't work doesn't mean it does.
3. *Americans are so excessively patriotic that they believe the reason foreigners hate them is because they are jealous! This is not true. We hate them because they are gun-loving evangelists who believe wealth is a virtue.* Over-generalisation; typical of stereotypical characterisations – assumes all Americans are the same and all non-Americans feel the same towards Americans and for the same reasons.

4. *You can't believe CNN news reports. They have done so much dishonest reporting and fake news stories that they should be called fiction writers rather than journalists.* Ad hominem attack – insults the person (CNN) not what they say. Could also be circular reasoning as the reason is the same as the claim.
5. *Elder's essay was better, because he presented both sides of the issue. Oppenheimer's was more one-sided, so it wasn't as persuasive.* Appeal to fairness/equity – assumes both sides deserve equal treatment.
6. *If we let the sick refugees on Manus and Nauru come to Australia, we will be opening our borders to people smugglers again. Before long, there will be a flood of refugees arriving by boat.* Appeal to indirect consequences/slippery slope – assumes first act will lead to inevitable and negative consequences that are not inevitable.
7. *Decriminalising sex workers will open the door to more crime. It will lead to an increase in brothels, more girls being exploited and victimised, more drug trafficking and increased violence towards women. This is a retrogressive step.* Appeal to indirect consequences/slippery slope – assumes first act will lead to inevitable and negative consequences that are not inevitable.
8. *The last time Labour was in power, inflation increased so this is likely to happen again.* Post hoc reasoning – just because one event precedes another, doesn't mean it was causal in that event.
9. *The government should make cannabis oil readily available to the public for medicinal use. It has been very effective in reducing chronic seizures in some cases of epilepsy.* Hasty generalisation – making a general recommendation based on just one instance of limited effectiveness.

CHAPTER

6

Critical Thinking and Digital Literacy: Evaluating the Information Source

The need for digital (information) and critical literacy

In today's world, we are exposed to a wide range of information from an equally large number of diverse sources, all of which contribute to our ideas and beliefs. The Internet and social media have caused an information explosion that is unprecedented. We can access huge amounts of information and data on just about anything. All of this information shapes our ideas and practices, influences our actions and impacts on our emotions and attitudes towards others.

Such availability comes at a price. A lot of the information we access is untrustworthy. There is a lot of fake news out there and some very dodgy claims. We now know that unscrupulous interest groups in conjunction with Google and Facebook can manipulate public information, control what we have access to and 'change audience behaviour' (see Chapter 2, Cambridge Analytica).

This information overload means we need the skills to discriminate truth from falsehoods, rational claims from populist beliefs; we need to distinguish the quality of information from the quantity of it. We need to be digitally and critically literate. Not easy in the ever-changing world of social media. However, if we want our beliefs to be reliable, we need to ensure as much as we can that they are based on genuine, relevant knowledge. We referred to what counts as knowledge in Chapter 1.

EXAMPLE 1

Bots and their cousins – botnets, bot armies, sockpuppets, fake accounts, sybils, automated trolls, influence networks – are a dominant new force in influencing public discourse (https://motherboard.vice.com/en_us/article/mb37k4/twitter-facebook-google-bots-misinformation-changing-politics).

How reliable is the information we have access to? What can we trust?

The Internet and associated media are not our only sources of information. We are, and have been, influenced by a range of sources. Below is a list of information sources that influence (and have influenced) the very way we see the world and the kinds of things we believe about that world, our ontology.

Exercise 1

Rank the following sources of information in order of how strongly you think they influence/have influenced your ideas and beliefs. You can rank some items the same if you believe they carry equal weight (i.e. equal no. 2).

Sources of Information

1. What we hear/learn from family and friends ☐
2. What we observe and experience of our physical environment ☐
3. What we observe and experience in our social environment ☐
4. What we observe about other people and how they live ☐
5. What we hear/learn from school, high school or university ☐
6. What we see and hear on television, film or radio ☐
7. What we access through social media (Google, Instagram, Facebook, Twitter) ☐
8. What we access through the Internet, www, search engines ☐
9. What we access through books, magazines and newspapers ☐
10. What we access through text books, databases, academic books and journals ☐

What did you rank as the most influential? Was it number 1 or number 10? It can be difficult to judge where our ideas come from and what our strongest influences are.

A Jesuit adage states, '*give me the child until he is seven and I will give you the man (sic)*'. Our experiences in the first of our seven-year life cycles, when our brain is still developing, play a major role in shaping our views. This means *item 1* is often the most influential.

Be critically self-reflective. Think about the ideas you have and the beliefs you hold. Where did they come from? Do you know your reasons for believing them?

Becoming a more effective critical thinker (and writer)

While a lot of our beliefs are well-grounded (such as the belief that touching something red-hot will burn), others are just habit or reinforced by selecting confirmatory information (refer back to Chapter 2). Unfortunately, a few of those beliefs will be just plain wrong because the information we had access to was not reliable or was not complete. In addition, we have to guard against those interest groups who set out to deliberately misinform us.

If we want to become more effective critical thinkers (and writers) and ensure that our beliefs are as well grounded as they can be, given what experts currently know, we need appropriate techniques for sorting through the information we have access to every day. Carefully checking the sources of our information is a first step to finding out if the information is likely to be reliable.

Check how **credible** your sources of information are and whether or not you should accept the content.

How do you check for credibility?

In all topics within academia, there is an accumulated body of facts or knowledge that we currently accept as true, even though there has been a long history of research behind the development of that body of knowledge. We accept these well-established facts as reliable and use them as evidence to support our arguments. We assume the sources of that information are credible (see **Credible sources** later in this chapter).

However, we have access to (and use) a lot of other information sources and not all of them are equally credible. Common sources of everyday information are television, radio, newspapers, magazines, books, the Internet, Facebook/Twitter/social media, homepages, blogs, YouTube. Some sources are more reliable than others, so you will need some criteria to discriminate between different sources to help ensure the information you have access to is as reliable as you can make it. Start by asking yourself a few preliminary questions.

- **Who or what is the source of the information?** A person, a newspaper, a website...
  - Be aware that the source of a piece of information you come into contact with is unlikely to be the original source of that information. If the issue matters to you, try to find out where their information originally came from. This change of source may make a difference as to how you view or judge the content (academic texts and reliable websites will always cite the source).
- **Do I trust the source?** – Is it from your uncle who is into conspiracy theories? Was it a story on Facebook/Twitter or in the local newspaper? Is it from a topic textbook?
  - Some sources are more trustworthy than others. Think about your criteria for trusting a source. What do you consider to be reliable sources? Why? As above, try to find the original source if you can. You may trust your friend who sent the information, but you may not trust the website or person it originally came from. Remember how easy it is for us to be manipulated by being fed certain types of information. Don't just accept something at face value just because it fits with your ideology or lifestyle choices.

- **Why should/shouldn't I trust this source?**
  - If we trust a source, we are more likely to accept the truth of the claims from that source. Think what makes a source reliable to you. Do you have good grounds to trust that source? Is it because you share a similar ideology? Are they always reliable (or only 50% of the time)? Even if you trust the source, it doesn't mean the information itself is trustworthy, although it makes that possibility more likely. A trustworthy source can also be wrong and could be fed false information. And just because you *don't* trust the source doesn't mean the information will always be false, although you are right to be more sceptical of a source you don't trust.
- **Does the information sound plausible?**
  - Sometimes the level of trust depends on the nature of the information. This in itself won't tell you whether you should trust it or not but it can separate out bizarre claims from more rational ones. Bizarre claims generally need more verification or supporting evidence than reasonable claims. However, we are more likely to accept claims that *fit with our belief system* than those that don't. So we need to be vigilant, and willing to question. While it may sound reasonable to us, it may not to someone else. And sounding reasonable or believable doesn't make it true.
- **Does the person/website/organisation have a vested interest?** How partisan might they be? Do you think they are neutral?
  - Some sources have a vested interest in the subject matter being presented. While this does not automatically mean the information is false, it should raise doubts about its objectivity. If there is an interest, you need to see if the same information is supported or verified by an independent source as well. It may be that only one part or side of an issue is being presented, or even misrepresented, to give a more positive slant that suits the sender's purpose.

Exercise 2

Look at the information sources below. Use the criteria set out above to assess the credibility of the source and the likely reliability of their information. For each item, rank the credibility of the source and the reliability of the information separately. Rank each on a scale from 1 (poor) to 5 (high).

1. A Facebook or Twitter post from a respected political commentator describing Trump's foreign policies
   Credible 1 2 3 4 5 Reliable 1 2 3 4 5
2. The World Health Organisation website discussing the spread of HIV/AIDS (http://www.who.int/)
   Credible 1 2 3 4 5 Reliable 1 2 3 4 5
3. *The Sun* newspaper (part of Rupert Murdoch's news empire), talking about immigration and terrorism
   Credible 1 2 3 4 5 Reliable 1 2 3 4 5
4. The BBC program *Panorama* talking about immigration and terrorism
   Credible 1 2 3 4 5 Reliable 1 2 3 4 5
5. Yogafusion website (https://yogafusion.com.au/) advertising the benefits of hot yoga
   Credible 1 2 3 4 5 Reliable 1 2 3 4 5

The sources above cover a range of different sources of varying credibility. However, we may rank the information as more reliable if we think it fits with the author's expertise. WHO conducts health research and should know about the spread of AIDS. A Yoga website should know about the benefits of yoga (but note they do have a vested interest!). A newspaper is not renowned for its expertise in any one area, neither is a TV show per se. However, we would expect reporting on *Panorama* to be more informed and objective about issues relating to immigration and security than *The Sun*. A political commentator would be expected to know about Trump's policies, given the role of the United States in world affairs.

The source of your information does matter. A political correspondent is more reliable than a popular broadsheet like *The Sun*. An official website is more reliable than someone's homepage. Business sites (even a yoga site) have vested interests. We need to be cautious.

Exercise 3

Sometimes we judge the truth of a claim based on how plausible or implausible it sounds. Look at the statements below and rank them for plausibility (1 = low; 5 = high). Decide how much the source influenced your rating (circle Y [yes], N [no] or S [some]).

- The CIA used polio vaccinations in Pakistan to access Muslim DNA to find terrorists (Source: *National Geographic*, 2/2015)
  Plausible 1 2 3 4 5 Y/N/S
- Teachers at UK primary schools have 'banned' best friends. Hugging and holding hands are not allowed (Source: *The Sun*)
  Plausible 1 2 3 4 5 Y/N/S
- Russia did not interfere in the 2016 American elections (Source: Donald Trump)
  Plausible 1 2 3 4 5 Y/N/S
- MMR vaccinations cause autism (Source: Wakefield AJ. 1999, *The Lancet* 354, 949–50)
  Plausible 1 2 3 4 5 Y/N/S

Does it matter if it is wrong?

Some misinformation doesn't matter that much; it may have limited or trivial consequences. However, some misinformation can have serious consequences, such as changing the way we vote or how we live, increasing our fear of others, confirming our biases or causing suffering or even death to others. If the consequences matter, don't accept a piece of information at face value. Check it out first.

Use the questions below as a guide to help decide which statements are worth checking (adapted from https://www.politifact.com/truth-o-meter/article/2011/feb/21/principles-truth-o-meter/):

- Is the statement rooted in a fact that is verifiable? (An opinion is not verifiable but the fact it is based on is, if it is stated. We can't check an opinion.)

- Is the statement leaving a certain impression that may be misleading or even false?
- Is the statement significant? Does it matter? Does it have consequences?
- Is the statement likely to be passed on and repeated by others?
- Would a typical person hear or read the statement and wonder if it were true?

If you answered 'yes' to these questions, then it is worth checking your facts.

Seek out other sources of information to check that what you ***believe*** **to be true** ***is***, in fact, true. Can it be verified?

Seek out other sources of information to check that what you **have** ***heard or read*** **as true** ***is***, in fact, true as claimed. Can the claim be verified?

What does verification mean?

When checking whether our own belief or idea (or someone else's) is based on reliable information, it is good practice to search for other sources of information on the same topic. We can check a claim or statement of fact by seeing if it can be verified. First, look for confirming evidence. Find out what is out there on the topic and where that information is coming from. Who else says this is true? Where is that information located? How reliable is the source?

However, confirmation is pointless if the information is not independently verifiable. Cross-reference whenever possible. Do different web pages or articles all quote the same single source or piece of research? Do they just refer to each other? If so, this is not independent verification. What kind of publications are they? Are any of them peer-reviewed, research-based articles? If not, ask why no one has conducted research in this field. Do a search to see if there has been appropriate research conducted by a reliable source. Did their findings agree or disagree with the information you have?

EXAMPLE 2

How would you verify this claim? What is the truth?

Alex Jones, the host of Infowars, claimed that the US Sandy Hook massacre of 20 young school children and six teachers in 2012 was a hoax faked by the Obama Administration to try to restrict access to guns. The 'dead' children and others were supposedly actors paid by Russian millionaire George Soros. https://www.youtube.com/watch?v=mkWAjaVlhHc
[the post has since been removed because of its contentious content]

1. Check the source for credibility. *Alex Jones is a member of the far right, is pro-gun and is known for his support of conspiracy theories. He claims to be anti-establishment and*

claims he is being targeted by big corporations for uncovering the truth about fake claims. Look critically at the types of facts he claims are false.

2. Check the website for credibility. *Infowars is a website that suggests it is uncovering 'fake' news stories and global conspiracies. But it focuses only on traditional far-right targets – e.g. Democrats, CNN, Obama and anti-gun campaigners, raising concerns of partiality. Many of its stories have turned out to be fake themselves or a sensationalised misrepresentation of a true story.*
3. Check the claim for plausibility. *Is it feasible? Parents of the dead children have successfully sued Jones for defamation. He now denies he claimed their deaths were fake. A report by the Connecticut State Attorney in 2013 concluded the shootings were conducted by Adam Lanza who had just killed his mother. Lanza was a former pupil of the school. He used an automatic weapon.*
4. Check other sources of information. *There are many comments online supporting Jones and the idea that the shooting was fake. In 2017, a reporter claimed he had proof one of the parents was lying about holding his dead child. Others claim there is no pictorial evidence that the shooting happened. They claim the school had been unused for four years. However, these comments are by readers of Infowars. They frequently contradict themselves. The changing of stories amongst the deniers suggest the claims are not supported by or based on real evidence.*
5. Check Wikipedia and other official sources. *Wikipedia lists links to official reports and media coverage of the events in 2012. These can be cross-referenced. There are also articles undermining the conspiracy theorists' claims. Those latter claims have since been shown to be false.*

While one can always deny any evidence and say it was faked, this puts you in a position of scepticism about any claim and its proof. If evidence A is claimed to be fake, why isn't the counter evidence B fake too? What is the criterion used to judge one fact as true and the other fact as false? Make the person declare what their criteria are for accepting certain evidence as reliable and other evidence as not reliable. With conspiracy theorists, the criteria will shift to suit a particular conclusion. In the Sandy Hook examples, independent police and coroners' reports confirmed that the Sandy Hook massacre did happen and that the perpetrator, Lanza, died. There is also no evidence that the parents were actors feigning grief.

There is another important question to ask – why would someone fake an elaborate conspiracy? In this case, why would someone go to such trouble to fake a mass shooting like Sandy Hook? The conspiracy theory argument is that the 'massacre' was set up to encourage Congress to reduce citizens' access to firearms in a push to overturn the Second Amendment. Unfortunately, since Sandy Hook, there have been many more mass shootings in the United States, often involving school children. There seems little need to fake a massacre.

Accredited fact checkers

There are sites you can access to check facts you may have concerns about. The **International Fact-Checking Network** (https://ifcncodeofprinciples.poynter.org/) at Poynter, says fact checkers have a process for each claim they deal with. This group issues certificates to organisations that 'regularly publish nonpartisan reports on the accuracy of statements by public figures, major institutions, and other widely circulated claims of interest to society' if those organisations abide by an agreed code of fact-checking principles.

Seek disconfirmation

While confirmation seems like a good idea, and is what we do most of the time, there are some problems with it, as pointed out in Chapter 2 (see confirmation bias). The algorithms of Google search engines are designed to find Google searches all those documents that support the idea you are looking for, so it becomes self-fulfilling. And your feeds on social media will keep adding other related material that contains similar information and points of view to ones you have searched for, seemingly confirming your position.

This is why it is essential that you also seek out information that might disconfirm your belief/idea/fact or even falsify it. One of the easiest ways to check if our ideas and the claims of others are true (or plausible) is to look at what might show them to be wrong. Are there alternative views and opinions? How well grounded are they in terms of plausibility and evidence? Is yours (or the other's view) considered a minority view? What is the mainstream position? On which side does the evidence stack up? You may find that what seemed plausible is actually not supported by reliable evidence, even if the view is held by a lot of people. Just because a lot of people believe the same thing (there really is a flat Earth society), doesn't make it true. Apply the critical thinking skills you have learnt so far.

Seek the **opposite points of view**, or counter claims, to see how they compare. What evidence would make this idea/claim false?

Digital information literacy: critiquing web sources for credibility

There are so many documents available online that it is difficult to know which ones to read. It is even harder to assess them for quality, to know which ones are *worth* reading. The sheer quantity is daunting. More importantly, the academic quality that university students have come to expect is not always present in Web sources.

Be aware that anyone can set up a web page and write about anything they like. No one can stop them. This doesn't make them an expert or someone worth reading. Unlike papers in academic journals, no one has assessed their work and agreed that the content makes a contribution to the field of knowledge. No one has said the information is trustworthy or that the ideas are objective, well supported and likely to be true.

To evaluate websites, you need a few techniques or rules to make sure you are accessing the best quality documents you can. Asking the questions (above) is a good first step. Below are some tips to help. Applying these techniques will help you become digitally literate.

1. **Check out the credentials of the website author.**
   - Who are they? Who are they affiliated with? This matters if we want to know how partisan someone is. If you want balanced information on the holocaust, you would not use a neo-Nazi site. If you want reliable information about Viagra, you don't just go to the drug company's website.
   - Is this site their personal web page or is it part of a bigger organisation or network? If you want reliable information or a reliable point of view, it is best to avoid articles that are from someone's homepage, blog, Twitter, Facebook or popular magazine. Even if the article is written by a well-known expert in the field, it is best not to rely on it. The author would have published (or will publish) the paper, if they thought it could satisfy the scrutiny of their academic peers. This may be just an opinion piece or express ideas that are not well researched or well supported.
2. **If there is no author, check out who the sponsor or owner of the website is.**
   - The organisation can usually be found at the top of the web page or at the bottom of the page. Check out both, as sometimes these affiliations may give you insight into the views of the website and other associated affiliations.
   - See who or what the web page has links to. What other organisations or websites can be accessed from the page? What kinds of sites are they? This will give you some idea of how credible the web page you have accessed is. Organisations have to grant permission for you to link them from your website.
3. **Look at the way the article is written.**
   - You can tell a lot about an article by the tone or language the writer has used. If it is very colloquial, uses a lot of emotive words, or uses phrases that appeal to our vanity, patriotism, humanity, intelligence or some other device to get us on their side, then the article is unlikely to have much objective evidence to support its claims.
   - Watch out for the use of rhetorical devices like 'we all know', 'everyone agrees', 'they say that…', 'no-one would believe'. These are all designed to stop you thinking and accept what the authors say.

Remember, if there is no verifiable evidence then it is just someone's opinion

Assessing credibility

- Who is the author?
- What are their qualifications in this field?
- What are their affiliations?
- Do they have a respected reputation?
- Have they previously published in this field?
- Is this their homepage? Who do they link to?
- Is this article/page part of a larger report or part of a larger organisation's website?
- Do they link to official websites on related matters?
- Is the article referenced?
- Do the references exist? If so, are they also reliable sources for this information (as above)?
- What is the tone or language being used? Is it emotional, friendly, angry, colloquial, technical, academic, opinionated, balanced?
- Is the article well written and is it easy to follow the author's reasoning?
- Have they justified the claims they are making? Have they included evidence or sources of evidence you can check?
- Do you think the information in this article is reliable? Why?
- Could you use this article as a reference in an academic paper?

Can I use Wikipedia? Is it reliable?

Wikipedia is an evolving resource which is self-regulating. Most contributors are experts in their field so it is useful for accessing detailed information on specific topics. Some entries are very thorough and provide a good introductory basis for understanding terminology, definitions or the history or development of an issue or idea. It will often have links from reputable sources that can provide additional information. Many of these links will be academic in nature and can be used in scholarly essays.

It does, however, elicit mixed responses and most academics won't accept it as a reliable enough source for referencing. Use Wikipedia to develop your own understanding and as a source for finding other reliable texts in the field.

Don't rely on dubious sources for your information. Get confirmation/disconfirmation from other sources you can trust that **are credible.**

Do not refer to Wikipedia in assignments.

Exercise 4

Rank how credible you think these sources are.

Rank from 1 to 5 with 1=not credible and 5=very credible

1. The Future of Killing: Ethical and Legal Implications of Fully Autonomous Weapon Systems, Martin Lark, *Salus Journal*. 2017;5(1):62–73

   Rank 1 2 3 4 5
2. This is our truth…, Anthony Temple, http://astraeasweb.net/plural/ourtruth.html, accessed May 2018.

   Rank 1 2 3 4 5
3. Top 5 Anti-Aging Creams - Our Top Pick Will Surprise You, thedoctors.healthfindings.website http://aus.skin.healthfindings.website/InstantYouth.html? Accessed January 2018.

   Rank 1 2 3 4 5
4. The "Depressive" Attributional Style Is Not That Depressive for Buddhists Michelle T. Liu, Fei Wang, Kaiping Peng, *Frontiers in Psychology*. 2017;8 DOI 10.3389/fpsyg.2017.01003

   Rank 1 2 3 4 5
5. Monarch butterflies spectacular migration is at risk... theconversation.com/monarch-butterflies-spectacular-migration-is-at-risk-an-ambitious-new-plan-aims-to-help-save-it-136479..., D Andre Green II, 2020.

   Rank 1 2 3 4 5
6. Heinrichs R. Walter. *In Search of Madness: Schizophrenia and Neuroscience* Oxford University Press, New York, 2001.

   Rank 1 2 3 4 5

Evaluating information sources for academic purposes

As mentioned in Chapter 1, the role of a university scholar is not just to reiterate what we have heard, read or learnt. We also need to think about that information, evaluate it to see how it stacks up as *credible* information, and then use what we judge to be reliable information to inform and develop our ideas and practices.

This is the way that knowledge progresses over time. We learn from past mistakes and build on past successes. But, as we also discussed in Chapters 1–5, it is easy to make mistakes. As humans, we are designed to jump to conclusions and judge by appearances. Unfortunately, our hasty conclusions may turn out to be wrong. And what appears to be the case may be false or misleading. So we need to be wary and pay attention. This is why we put more credence into the claims made in academic papers, government reports and official sources of information. They are public documents that play a major role in informing practice and solving problems. As such, they need to be reliable and defensible.

There are different kinds of texts, ranging from reports to research articles, from history books to experimental procedures, or from poems or novels to reviews. They each have their own format. A novel is not expected to be a source of reliable information, although it may contain accurate facts and figures. A report, on the other hand, is supposed to be accurate and objective. We evaluate each type of text against its own criteria to see how well it achieves its goals.

Each text is written for a purpose and for a particular audience. When you are reading, you have to work out what and who the audience is. Most importantly, you have to work out what is being said, why it is being said and how it is being said. This will take you below the surface of the text to its actual construction. Once you have found some credible sources of information (such as scholarly articles in an online journal, a WHO annual report, or an academic book), it is important to then examine or critique the content.

Never use or rely on articles that are not referenced. If referenced, make sure the sources are academic or professional or from an official source.

Credible sources – accessing reliable academic sources

To check you have access to reliable information, it is best to focus on articles or reports that come from reliable sources that have been peer refereed. Focus on sites such as:

- Academic databases
- Hard copy or online journals and other refereed publications
- Government websites and reports
- Official NGO websites and reports

If you are not sure whether a source is academically credible, check with your tutor.

Finally, how do we check that what they are claiming or arguing for is likely to be true?

Ask questions of the text

- What is the topic?
- Who is writing? Who is the audience?
- What is the purpose of the text? (information, entertainment...)
- What kind of language does the author use? (informal, technical...)
- Where is the author's voice?
- What is/are the point/s the author is making?
- What or whose perspective/point of view is it written from?

- Is the author trying to persuade you of something? Why?
- What evidence do they provide to support their claim?
- How successful/persuasive is it?
- Why do you think it was successful/partly successful/not successful?

Chapter summary

- Check how credible your sources of information are and whether or not you should accept the content.
- Seek out other sources of information to check that what you believe to be true is, in fact, true. Can your belief be verified?
- Seek out other sources of information to check that what you have heard or read as true is, in fact, true as claimed. Can the claim be verified?
- Seek the opposite points of view, or counter claims, to see how they compare. What evidence would make this idea/claim false?
- Don't rely on dubious sources for your information. Get confirmation/disconfirmation from other sources you can trust that are credible
- Never use or rely on articles that are not referenced. If referenced, make sure the sources are academic or professional or from an official source.
- Evaluate the claim in light of the context and the evidence used to support it. Assess how well the evidence supports the claim.

Answers to Exercises 3–4

Exercise 3

Analysis of Exercise 3

1. This claim seems a little far-fetched or implausible. You don't collect blood by giving a vaccination (polio is an oral vaccine) and you can't pick a terrorist by their DNA. On the other hand, the *National Geographic* is a reputable publication and this could influence your rating. It turns out that the CIA did use a Pakistani doctor to extract blood samples from patients in a compound believed to contain relatives of Osama bin Laden under the pretext of giving polio vaccines. However, such an implausible claim should be thoroughly investigated to ensure there is some truth in it as it does seem like a conspiracy theory. All conspiracy theories are unfalsifiable, so flawed. The consequences of the CIA operation resulted in the death of Osama bin Laden but have caused a backlash against polio vaccines, the killing of nurses promoting the vaccines, and a rise in polio cases in Pakistan. (Rank: 2/3)
2. *The Sun* is one of Rupert Murdoch's papers and is known for creating populist, sensational headlines by misrepresenting facts, often to make a particular group look

bad. It is not considered a credible source of information. Is the claim plausible? Superficially, it sounds extreme but with a grain of truth perhaps? This is the case. It is exaggerated but with some truth. While children are not banned from making friends, they are being discouraged from touching each other (hugging) in an attempt to foster inclusion and reduce bullying. (Rank: 1)

3. The claim seems implausible, given what the CIA found. Is Trump a reliable source of information? Unfortunately, he has been caught out in quite a few lies and is well known for making exaggerated claims about his own qualities and those of his supporters, as well as negative claims about his antagonists or political opponents. (Rank: 1)
4. This claim was viewed as so plausible it has spawned an influential anti-vaxxer movement. As a source, *The Lancet* is a reputable medical journal. However, it turned out that Whitehead's research was faked and there was no establishable link between the MMR vaccine and instances of autism. Despite evidence to the contrary, the claims are still believed and have spread to include other vaccines and other ailments. (Rank: 1–5)

Exercise 4

Answers Exercise 4

1. This is a journal article so should be credible. The article should have been peer reviewed. You need to check the quality of the journal as well to see if it is legitimate and ranked. Check the qualifications of the authors in relation to relevant expertise.
2. This is a personal blog, so while it may represent the author's perspective, it should be treated with caution as reliable evidence for multiple personality disorder (MPD/DSD).
3. Although this website claims to have conducted research into these products, it is a commercial site, so its claims should be treated with caution.
4. As a journal article, it has more credibility. What do commentators say? You need to check the quality of the journal as well to see if it is legitimate and ranked. Check the qualifications of the authors in relation to relevant expertise.
5. *The Conversation* is a site that interviews people on various topics. While the author will have academic credentials, this is a conversation piece. Check the sources and refer to the author's peer reviewed publications on this topic, not this site.
6. Oxford University Press is a well-respected publisher, so this book has credibility. It still pays to check out the author and their expertise in the field.

CHAPTER

7

Critiquing the Literature – How Do You Know That Is So?

Academic texts and critical thinking

We learn about the topics we study through accessing textbooks, journal articles, websites and other material that inform us about the topic. This constitutes the **literature** in the field. However, most of the texts we access will be doing more than just providing information for us to learn. They will be presenting data and interpreting that data; they will be drawing inferences from that data and other research findings; they will be evaluating that data and coming to conclusions. In fact, they will be putting forward hypotheses and arguing for (or against) them, or they will be defending their theses or main claims, based on their research.

A big part of **critical thinking** at university and elsewhere involves evaluating the ideas the various authors put forward as a consequence of that research. It involves assessing how well they have conducted their research and how convincing their subsequent arguments are. What we are doing when we engage in this kind of evaluation is a form of interrogation. We are interrogating the authors by asking questions of the literature.

The two broad **epistemological** questions we are asking the authors are:

1. **How do you know that is so? (what is the evidence?)**
2. **Why should I believe you? (Is the evidence reliable?)**

As we have seen in earlier chapters, asking appropriate questions is a key characteristic of a critical thinking approach. Given that ideas are mostly communicated through publishing via a written text, we use that as our starting point. So we start with what the researchers or authors actually write (not what we think they mean).

Critiquing the literature involves examining the written text – what is actually written and how it is written – as it is.

When we **critique the literature**, we are critiquing what has been written – the text (the blog, the article, the book). We analyse and evaluate the content of the text to decide if the claims are believable or convincing. We do this by examining *how people say* they have conducted their research (where the information or evidence has come from) and by assessing *what they claim* the research results indicate (what they have inferred).

Critiquing involves applying rigorous academic standards to a piece of work and judging that work against those standards.

We critique the text by evaluating the claims that are made *in that text* and by judging how well those claims have been supported, defended, or **argued for**. This means that at the heart of critiquing is an understanding of what constitutes a good argument. We are engaging in a process of argument analysis and evaluation of the argument as it is presented in the literature, the piece of written text.

Critiquing the text is **critiquing the argument** – how have the authors argued for this? Is it a strong or convincing argument?

Critiquing is not the same as criticising

Critiquing is being critical; but it is not just about finding fault or criticising. We are assessing a text and critiquing its arguments against a given set of criteria to see how it measures up, given what we know constitutes best research practice, a strong argument and knowledge. The text may well turn out to be an excellent piece of research that is clearly written and well argued. It may make a significant contribution to the field and add to what we currently know.

Don't think you must always find fault or shortcomings. **A good critique** will identify strengths as well as, or not just, weaknesses.

Reading academic articles

As students, you will spend a lot of time researching for your essays; you will spend large amounts of time searching for, selecting, reading, understanding and then referring to selected academic articles. You will select and read articles that you judge to be relevant to your topic. In addition, each article or book chapter will have contributed something to your understanding of the topic. During this process of researching and selecting, you will also find articles that are not relevant, that do not suit your purpose or which do not contribute to your knowledge of the topic. They won't be what you wanted or what you were looking for.

What you are doing is engaging in **a process of evaluation**. You have an idea of what you want – a set of criteria that you are judging the article against. Based on those criteria, you either reject an article or retain it for future use and closer reading.

We engage in a similar kind of evaluation process when we **critique a text**. Our standards, however, may differ depending on the context. Evaluating an article to see if it is of use to us in answering an essay question will require a different set of criteria to critiquing an article to see if its conclusion is (1) justified and (2) significant. This means we can judge the same material differently depending on what we are looking for and what our aim is. So we need to be clear why we are evaluating something and what our critique will contribute.

We cannot critique or judge something if we do not have **a standard** to critique or judge it against. We need to be clear what that standard is.

Critical reading

Although most of the texts we read at university will be articles published in academic journals or books, some will not be. Other texts may be from websites, magazines or newspapers or some other form of media. Unless the article is written purely to entertain, rather than inform or persuade, we should still apply a critical mindset to reading and understanding the text. The same epistemological questions still hold (how do you know and why should I believe you?) as do the same criteria for judging the evidence offered in support.

Critical thinking entails **critical reading and writing**. You can't think critically if you don't read critically and vice versa. You can't write critically if you don't think and read critically.

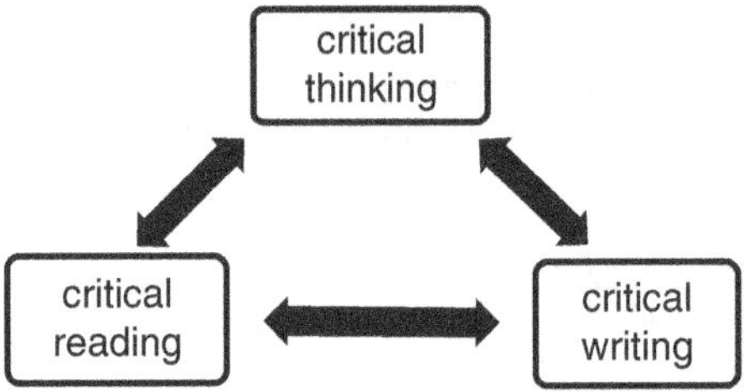

To read critically, you must always interrogate the text you are reading. Ask yourself questions. If you can answer the questions easily then you have understood the text. Understanding the text is the first step to thinking critically about it. Initial questions are useful to elucidate our understanding (Bean, 2011; Horning, 2007). We would follow these questions with more critical ones (see review criteria below).

- What is this text about?
- Why do you think the author is writing about this topic?
- What is the point the author is trying to make?
- How does the author get across his/her point? What linguistic devices do they use?
- Is the author expressing his/her particular view on a topic?
- Has the author presented information or evidence to support the point they are making? Is there an argument?
- Does this information/evidence appear reliable?

- Would a broad spectrum of readers agree with the author's point of view? Why/why not?
- Do you understand why the author has taken the position they have?
- Do you agree with them? Are you sympathetic to their position?
- Do you think your own views influenced your reading of the text? If so, in what way?
- How might you address this?

Critical reading example: EUROPE CAN'T COPE

Europe is full. The European Union (EU) registered 1.2 million first-time asylum seekers in 2015, and a further 954,000 over the first nine months of 2016. It is simply too many. Our social services, housing departments, health systems and schools can't cope with any more. The influx is concentrated in certain places, creating local tensions, and strains within communities. The absence of a workable re-distribution scheme within the EU, and the unwillingness of refugees to relocate, means some countries and regions are unfairly burdened – Germany and Sweden in particular. The arguments over where to locate incoming refugees places undue pressure on European solidarity. With Britain preparing to split and euro-hostile parties on the rise in other countries, the very fabric of the EU is under threat. It would be foolish to add to those strains by importing more refugees.

The first thing to do as a **critical reader** is to read the passage all the way through. This gives us a feel for the text and an idea of what it is about. The first sentence gives a clear indication of what the topic is (refugees) and the author's position – no more refugees. This idea is repeated at the end of the text. From the tone and content, one can tell that the author is writing this piece because they are concerned about the number of refugees and what they fear is/will be the impact on EU social and political life.

A **second reading** is necessary to encourage a more critical approach (if a text is difficult, we may read it multiple times). Notice the use of short sentences. This is a powerful linguistic device for emotional effect (Europe is full; It is simply too many). This piece is an argument for the claim – *It would be foolish to add to those strains by importing more refugees.* The author provides information or reasons to support their view, so it is not just an opinion piece, which means we can evaluate it. To really critique it, we need to pull it apart to see what claims are being made (our social services, etc. can't cope; unwillingness of refugees to relocate; European Union under threat) and how relevant and reliable the evidence is supporting those claims. Are the threats real or exaggerated? The author's tone is quite passionate. They appear genuinely concerned about the stability of the European Union. We can understand and even empathise with their position as the numbers of refugees have increased dramatically even since 2016. If this passage resonates with our own views, we may find it persuasive. But we should be persuaded by the strength of the argument, not the sentiment. It may seem less persuasive once we critically examine the evidence and its relationship to the claims. What might counter the claims here? Is there evidence for an alternative perspective? At the same time we may feel the author is raising some good points. Critically examining the argument may indicate how we can strengthen the argument and counter any alternative views.

Thinking critically as you read requires a bit more effort but it is worth it. Your appreciation and understanding improve exponentially, no matter what the text. Reading critically will also help you to write a more critical and informed response to the text.

Exercise 1

A Practice Critique – Start by thinking why the author is writing this article. Do you find it persuasive? Identify the argument and the evidence provided. Is the evidence relevant, sufficient, reliable? How might you verify the evidence?

Evolution or Creation? *By Duane T. Gish, PhD. 2016*

The Evolutionist states that all life gradually evolved from a single cell, which had evolved from dead matter. The evidence the Evolutionist needs to establish his claims is fossils showing a gradual step-by-step development of lower animal life into more and more complex forms. And this should be evident by the presence in the fossil record of many transitional forms. But there is absolutely no fossil evidence showing that this took place. For example, not a single fossil with part fins, part feet has ever been found. There are no transitional forms. So evolution did not take place.

Alternatively, Creationists believe that life and our existence came by the acts of a Creator. The evidence needed to support creation is fossils showing complex life appearing suddenly, with no fossil evidence of lower animals developing into new and complex forms of life. If we look at the actual fossil evidence, we find there is a sudden appearance of fossils of a vast array of invertebrates in Cambrian rock strata. And the billions of fossils found there are *all* of highly complex forms of life, with *no evidence* of these complex forms gradually developing from a simple form of life. All higher categories of living things, such as complex invertebrates, fishes, amphibians, reptiles, flying reptiles, birds, bats, primates and man, *appear abruptly*. Therefore life came into being through the acts of a Creator.

The strength of Gish's argument lies in presenting an either/or scenario – either there is evolutionary theory or there is creationism. Gish argues that there is no evidence of evolution, so there must be creationism. However, most either/or scenarios are *false dilemmas*. Even if evolutionary theory is wrong, it doesn't make creationism right, and vice versa. There can be other options.

Critiquing an argument like this requires us to really pull it apart to see how it is constructed. This helps us get to a deeper understanding of the text. It should uncover the strengths and weaknesses in the argument which would either make us dismiss it as unconvincing or imagine ways it could be strengthened, mapping the argument could help with this analysis. (**See full analysis at end of chapter.**)

Reviewing (critiquing) an academic article

When we review something we judge it against a given set of criteria that are relevant for that object. We use that specific set of criteria to see how well our object measures up. Generally, our criteria will include standards of (good) quality that are appropriate for the object. An academic article will be evaluated against a different set of criteria to a novel or a blog.

The purpose of any review is to tell the person reading it whether or not the object under review – the film, the book, the article – is worth spending time (and money) on. What is important to keep in mind is that a review is *always* **evaluative** and never just descriptive. A review passes judgement; it doesn't just describe what something is like. We are, in effect, writing a ***critique*** of the object under review (setting out our criteria), which means we are putting forward an argument explaining why we evaluated it the way we did. The review is our own assessment of the piece of work.

A (critical) review is a special kind of critique. Its purpose is to evaluate the object under review against a set of criteria and to make a judgement or evaluation based on how well it fits the criteria.

At university, we are often asked to **critique the literature** by writing a review of a given article. Academic articles are important because they contain the research that we use, or want to use, to inform our ideas and practice. We want to be sure that the findings, the conclusions drawn from the research and presented in the article, are as reliable as they can be.

An academic article should add something to our understanding or knowledge in a given field. This means the article has to be written a certain way. It should set out what it was trying to find out (hypothesis), how it went about finding out (research methods) and what it found out (thesis). By reviewing the article we learn what makes a good article or a good piece of research. We understand what the criteria are. Our review then passes judgement on that article based on how well it measures up against our criteria.

Two main types of article

There are several different sets of criteria we can use to evaluate an academic article, depending on what we are looking for. As academics, we search for articles on specific topics that are making particular claims. This determines the field or scope of the article. Once we have chosen an article, however, we need to assess it against what makes something a good research article, regardless of what the topic is.

There are two main categories of article – **empirical articles and conceptual articles**. We need to determine which one we are dealing with first because this will have an impact on how the article is evaluated and which criteria we use to critique it against.

Empirical	An empirical article supports its claims by using evidence gathered from *primary* research that the authors have conducted themselves. This will be data collected from observations, experiments, statistical analysis, field studies, questionnaires, focus groups or case studies (*primary data*). The article should outline the methodology and research methods and include a description of how the data were analysed and interpreted, along with any limitations.

Conceptual A conceptual article supports its claims by using evidence gathered from *secondary* research, empirical findings that have been reported by somebody else, drawn from the literature (*secondary data*). The author has not created or collected the data themselves so does not have to report on how the data was collected or analysed, unless this is relevant to their argument.

Either article may also include logic, theoretical or linguistic analysis as evidence.

Sets of criteria for evaluating and critiquing an academic article

- **Criteria A – Article structure**
  There is an expectation that an academic article will follow a determinate structure. Most research-based academic articles will be organised in a similar way. Conceptual articles will have fewer sections than empirical articles and will refer more to the literature.
- **Criteria B – Assessing research quality**
  It is important to understand how the research was conducted, how reliable the evidence cited is, and how strong the conclusions are in relation to the research evidence presented.
- **Criteria C – Critiquing the argument**
  The article is putting forward a particular claim or claims which it argues for by showing how the evidence leads to or supports the conclusions. This should be clear and set out logically and convincingly.

We can now critique the article by assessing how well it satisfies each of the sets of criteria we expect from a good research article. Ultimately, the article should be understandable, be clear about what issue it is addressing and put forward a strong case to support its contribution to solving the problem or clarifying our understanding of the issue under discussion. We weight its value based on that contribution.

Criteria A: Article structure

1. An article should have a title that captures the content of the article and its main contention or claim.
2. It should have an abstract that explains what the issue/problem is and the context in which this occurs; what the paper will be arguing for in relation to solving the problem or addressing the issue; how it went about getting its answer (the evidence); what it concluded.

3. It should open with a summary of what has happened in the past (context/past research/literature review), where things are now and what has yet to be done (the gap/new research).
4. It should set out what it is going to do to fix the problem or fill the gap and explain why the methods they used addressed this and why they were best suited for this purpose.
5. There should be a discussion of how the authors conducted their research, how the data were analysed and what it showed (empirical) **OR** a discussion which uses and refers to other research articles that are cited as evidence to support (or not) the authors' case (conceptual).
6. There should be a discussion of their findings and their interpretation in light of the issue or problem being addressed **OR** pros and cons of various positions and an evaluation of these in relation to the issue being discussed.
7. It should have a conclusion that re-iterates the objectives, summarises key points of evidence and discusses the implications of the conclusion/s to the issue under discussion.
8. There must be a comprehensive reference list of reliable sources and articles referred to or cited in the paper.

Once you have been able to identify the relevant parts of the article, you can now start to evaluate it against those criteria. As we have discussed already, critiquing involves asking appropriate questions. The same is true for writing reviews. Questions are a good way of pulling something apart to better evaluate its effectiveness. Think about what makes a good academic article. Does it have the parts we would expect? Do they contain/explain what we expect them to? **This is a process of analysis.** Note that article reviews in some topics have strict evaluation criteria.

Nursing, health and medical students may be asked to evaluate a research article according to a critical appraisal checklist drawn from evidence-based practice. This sets out a list of criteria or questions designed to find out if the research was a good example of, for example, a randomised clinical trial (RCT) with an intervention, a cohort study or a qualitative study.

Check with your discipline area to find out whether or not there are specific evaluation criteria or questions that must be answered.

The main point of reviewing an article is to evaluate how well it makes its case for its thesis statement or main claim. **Remember the epistemological questions driving our critique – how do you know this is so? (what is the evidence?) and why should someone believe you? (is it reliable?).**

The criteria guiding the answers to these questions are about **evaluating and critiquing the justification.** We need to identify and assess the evidence that is presented as support for the claims being made and how well that evidence relates to and supports the claims. How strong is the argument? The research quality will be assessed according to how well the research process is conducted and how appropriate it is for the problem under investigation, as outlined in *Criteria A* above. (Research methods are discussed in more detail in Chapter 8.) Asking questions helps to focus our thinking on what we want to know.

Criteria B: Assessing research quality

(These questions are a guide. There are more to ask depending on the nature of the research. Refer to criteria A)

- What evidence have the authors cited/presented to support their claim?
- Did they conduct primary or secondary research?
- If primary, was it observational (recording what is observed); experimental (taking measurements, recording results from tests); statistical (collecting and tabulating data, analysing data); verbal/written (what people say or have written)?
- Have they accurately described their research methods and how the data were collected and analysed?
- Did the research method suit the problem or issue under investigation?
- Do they identify any problems or limitations with their method?
- Did you identify any weaknesses in the research method and their findings?
- If secondary, have they covered relevant literature and accommodated alternative findings or counter arguments?

The final set of criteria look at the article as a whole and assess the strength of its argument in relation to the evidence presented and what we may know from other similar research. This set of criteria focuses on **the logic of the argument** and how reliable the inferences drawn from the data are, in light of what is presented.

Criteria C: Critiquing the argument

The easiest way to think critically about what you read, is to ask questions.

- What is the context of the article?
- What is the issue or problem being addressed?
- What is the author claiming?
- What is the argument?
- How is it justified?
- Is the evidence convincing? Is there enough?
- Does the evidence support the claim/s?
- What are the limitations of the evidence?

- Can the conclusion be inferred from the premises?
- Is the argument logical?
- Is it clear and easy to follow?
- Could there be another conclusion or interpretation?
- Do you know other work that supports these findings?
- Do you know other work that contradicts these findings? Have these been acknowledged and addressed?
- What assumptions has the author made? Are they acceptable?
- Was the overall argument persuasive? Why? Why not?

Writing the review

What we write depends on the length of the review. A short review will be a summary plus critique; a longer review will look at all aspects of the work, the quality of the research, the originality of its contribution, its relationship to other similar articles and any alternative reports that might contradict or disagree with its findings or claims.

At a minimum, the **final review** should carefully describe what the article is about, identify what its main argument is (including the evidence) and present some kind of discussion about how effective the article is in making its point. In the process, you will evaluate its significance or contribution to the topic under discussion. See below for the elements a basic article review should include.

Basic article review structure

- Bibliographic information about the article – author, title, journal, volume, page numbers (this appears at the top of the review under the title).
- A brief summary of the essential content (what the article is about), the problem or issue that has triggered the article, the author's main claim/hypothesis/conclusion (what new ideas are being argued for) and a summary of the evidence used to support the claim.
- An evaluation or critique of the work presented, its contribution to the field, its strengths and weaknesses and any limitations or problems identified (supported by selected quotations from the article or elsewhere).

Have a look at the review below. Note how it starts by summarising the content of the book first by outlining the issue as identified by the author and then what the author's main claim is going to be. This is followed by a critique which raises both positive and negative attributes of the text. It is standard form to focus on the positive aspects of a text first before moving to any negative comments or areas for improvement. It is also important to end with a summary of your overall response to the text.

EXAMPLE 1

Basic academic review (edited)

A student review of *Body Sense: the science and practice of embodied self-awareness, by Alan Fogel, 2013, Norton, USA.*

Body Sense is fundamentally a book about maintaining health and well-being. **Fogel** sets out to demonstrate 'how everyday life, as well as serious stress and trauma, can cause us to lose contact with our sensations and emotions', along with the way our body moves and feels (p. 1). Stress, trauma, bad physical habits, or suppressed emotions for example, cause a (natural) repression of the body's sensations or natural reactions. If unaddressed, this suppression or repression can change the way the brain reacts to stimuli, leading to major ailments such as chronic pain, PTSD and arthritis. According to **Fogel**, we have the capacity to heal ourselves by changing the way we experience our bodily selves through changing our brain-body patterns of responses. Pain, he claims, is a state of mind so we don't have to suffer from it.	The review should refer directly to the *author* and what he says about the topic. This first paragraph summarises his main points. Setting out topic/ context, main argument for body awareness Problem/ Consequences
One of the strengths of this book is the use of neurochemical and neurophysiological detail to illustrate the various mechanisms in the brain that make up the body's schema. **Fogel** spends time describing how various parts of the brain interact to respond to stimuli to create the sense of an embodied self. In this way, he establishes the importance of interoception to our overall perception of ourselves and the world we inhabit. The sheer complexity of all these interacting systems, the roles they play in maintaining bodily stasis and how easily they can be affected or disrupted by our life choices is well-argued and supported by research.	Thesis statement – what author argues for Outlines positive aspects of book Describes how the author uses reliable evidence to argue his case; which is evaluated as strong
There are, however, a couple of shortcomings. Because **Fogel's** focus is on the therapeutic practice of embodied self-awareness, he never questions the neurological data he presents nor the psychological or philosophical implications he draws from them. Those of us with some knowledge in the field of neuroscience know that a lot of this research is new, is still developing and is highly contentious in relation to conscious experience. This should be acknowledged and addressed. It is also misleading to say that pain is not real and is something we don't need to feel. As **Fogel** himself acknowledges, pain draws our attention to wrongness, so it plays a necessary role in maintaining health. Similarly, suppression mechanisms serve a healthy purpose, especially in dealing with every day stresses and traumas. Whether or not (and to what extent) we should override them is not going to have an easy answer, but this is also something that Fogel fails to answer. **Fogel** raises some interesting points about the causes of pain and illness and the role body awareness therapy could play in healing, which may be useful for people in chronic pain. However, he does not discriminate between healthy and unhealthy suppression and indicates that both can lead to illness. This implies there is little one can do to avoid the impact of stressors on our health especially as we are unlikely to be aware of when they are being suppressed.	Introduces a weakness (however), Fogel's lack of critique Explains why this is a problem. Could include a ref to this Highlights another problem and a contradiction in the author's argument Raises a related problem re normal functions Summarises author's contribution, with positive evaluation and recommendation. Ends with note of scepticism

Exercise 2

Practice critical review

Imagine you are asked to write a short critical review of this article. Try to answer the questions below.

You are not so smart: a celebration of self-delusion

By David McRaney (edited)

https://youarenotsosmart.com/2010/06/23/confirmation-bias/

Check any Amazon.com wish list, and you will find people rarely seek books which challenge their notions of how things are or should be. During the 2008 U.S. presidential election, Valdis Krebs at orgnet.com analysed purchasing trends on Amazon. People who already supported Obama were the same people buying books which painted him in a positive light. People who already disliked Obama were the ones buying books painting him in a negative light. Just like with pundits, people weren't buying books for the information, they were buying them for the confirmation. Krebs (2008) has researched purchasing trends on Amazon and the clustering habits of people on social networks for years, and his research shows what psychological research into confirmation bias predicts: you want to be right about how you see the world, so you seek out information which confirms your beliefs and avoid contradictory evidence and opinions.

In a 1979 University of Minnesota study by Mark Snyder and Nancy Cantor, people read about a week in the life of an imaginary woman named Jane. Throughout the week, Jane did things which showcased she could be extroverted in some situations and introverted in others. After a few days the subjects were asked to return, and the researchers divided the people into two groups. One group was asked if Jane would be a good librarian; the other group was asked if she would be a good real-estate agent. People then searched their memories for examples that might suggest she was right for that position. In the librarian group, people easily remembered all the moments that made her seem like an introvert, ignoring the moments she seemed more extroverted. The real-estate group did the same thing, searching the same kind of memories but for different information and coming to the opposite conclusion. The study suggests even in your memories you fall prey to confirmation bias, recalling those things which support your beliefs, forgetting those things which debunk them.

An Ohio State study (Knobloch-Westerwick and Meng 2009) showed people spend 36% more time reading an essay if that essay aligns with their opinions. Thanks to Google, we can instantly seek out support for the most bizarre idea imaginable. If our initial search fails to turn up the results we want, we don't give it a second thought, rather we just try out a different query and search again. As Francis Bacon said in 1620, 'the human understanding when it has once adopted an opinion (either as being the received opinion or as being agreeable to itself) draws all things else to support and agree with it'.

Over time, by never seeking the antithetical, you can become so confident in your world-view no one could dissuade you. In science, you move closer to the truth by seeking evidence to the contrary. Perhaps the same method should inform your opinions.

Critical review questions

- What type of article is it? (i.e. academic, blog, opinion piece) Who is his target audience?
- What is the topic? What is the article about?
- What is the author's main claim?
- Is he presenting an argument? Does he present evidence to support his claim?
- What are his sources? How reliable do you think this evidence is?
- Do you think his argument is convincing? Why/why not?
- What do you think the author's objective is?
- Do you think he is successful in getting his point across?
- Is there a shortcoming? How could it be improved?

Chapter summary

- Critiquing the literature involves examining the written text – what is actually written and how it is written – as it is.
- Critiquing involves applying rigorous academic standards to a piece of work and judging that work against those standards.
- Critiquing the text is critiquing the argument – how have the authors argued for this? Is it a strong or convincing argument?
- Don't think you must always find fault or short-comings. A good critique will identify strengths as well as, or not just as, weaknesses.

Answers to Exercises 1–2

Exercise 1

Analysis of Gish

There are two arguments here, one counter argument against evolution and one pro-argument supporting creationism. Gish uses fossil records as evidence to support both arguments. He also uses deductive rather than inductive reasoning (refer back to Chapter 5 for a discussion of inductive/deductive arguments). His argument can be analysed as follows.

- Evolution needs evidence of fossils showing gradual development of lower animal life into more complex forms (such as transitional forms). **If A→B.**
- There is no evidence of fossils showing transitional forms. **–B.**
- Therefore, evolution did not take place. **Therefore, –A.**
- Creationists need evidence of fossils showing complex life appearing suddenly. **If A→B.**
- The fossil evidence shows the sudden appearance of invertebrates with no evidence of simple-to-complex transition. **B.**
- Complex species appear abruptly **B.**
- Therefore, creationism is true. **Therefore A.**

Let's start with the second argument first. This is an **invalid argument** (See Chapters 5 and 8 for examples). We can best see this by substituting different premises to make the invalidity clear. *For it to be true that I made this house, there would need to be tools in my garage; there are tools in my garage, therefore I made this house.* It is easy to see the flaw in the logic in this example. Likewise, having fossils showing complex life does not make creationism true; it is merely one (of many) factors that does not contradict creationism and which may undermine an alternative theory, such as evolution. However, there may well be other theories that could explain life that don't rely on a creator and which the fossil records support.

However, the first argument is a **valid deductive argument**. As the evidence referred to appears *relevant* (fossils *are* used as evidence for evolution), if we accept the truth of the premises, then we are forced to accept the truth of the conclusion. There is nothing wrong with the logic as it stands. In order to critique the argument, we need to demonstrate that the premises are not acceptable; they are false or misleading. We could do this in two ways – (1) demonstrate that the evidence cited is not *reliable or sufficient* enough to support the truth of the premises (it is misrepresented or false), and/or (2) argue that the initial conditional premise of the argument does not hold. Is it the case that evolutionary theory relies solely on the existence of transition fossils for its proof? You may need to research this. The theory of natural selection relies on selection pressures on phenotypes caused by gene variation over time, not fossil records. So it is likely that the fossil evidence is insufficient and possibly misrepresented. However, Gish's overall argument rests on a false dilemma – if evolution is wrong then creationism is right. The former (no evolution) does not logically entail the latter (God/creationism).

Exercise 2

Critical review of McRaney

- This is not an academic article. It is written in a colloquial style for the general public, more like a blog or opinion piece.
- The topic is on confirmation bias and self-delusion. The article discusses how our beliefs influence what we see and how we tend to choose information that fits with our beliefs.
- The author's main claim can be found at the end of the introductory paragraph – you want to be right about how you see the world, so you seek out information which confirms your beliefs and avoid contradictory evidence and opinions.
- He is presenting an argument because he presents evidence to support his claim.
- His sources are Valdis Krebs, Snyder and Cantor from Minnesota University, and Knobloch-Westerwick and Meng. These can be checked for credibility. A search for Knobloch-Westerwick and Meng, for example, yields several scholarly articles on selection bias; similarly Snyder has a large number of scholarly articles in psychology; Krebs is also a researcher of repute in the field of network analysis. McRaney's sources appear to be credible.
- The evidence McRaney presents is reliable and relevant to his claim. It is sufficient for a short piece like this. It does indicate that we do practice confirmation bias and it will affect our objective seeking of alternative perspectives. It is convincing.
- One imagines that the author's objective is to make us aware of our biases in the hope we may seek to overcome them. The last paragraph indicates his belief in the scientific method as a way of moving closer to the truth by seeking counter evidence (disconfirmation).
- Yes, he does get his point across.
- He doesn't provide any evidence that we can overcome this trait so it is all negative. He could also explain the relevance of the scientific method to everyday life in more detail to offer an alternative approach to seeking information (disconfirmation) and ways we can evaluate information more objectively.

CHAPTER

8

Critiquing the Evidence: Quantitative and Qualitative Research Methodologies

Critiquing the evidence

When we critique the literature, especially academic literature, we are assessing whether or not we should accept the claims that have been put forward by the authors. Importantly, we want to make sure that the **justification or evidence** they have presented is sufficient for us to accept the probability of the claim or conclusion. The strength of the argument is proportional to the strength of the supporting evidence. Thus, we need to evaluate the evidence to check whether or not it is relevant, reliable and enough to support the claim. It is always important to keep in mind our knowledge criteria.

Epistemological requirements (knowledge criteria)

How do we know **what** we know? (what makes us believe that x is the case)
How do we know **that** we know? (how do we know we are not mistaken – evidential scepticism)

Some evidence is acceptable *a priori.* This is the case with mathematical statements, logical arguments and claims which are self-evidently true. (Reminder – *a given proposition is knowable a priori if it can be known independent of any experience other than learning the language in which the proposition is expressed, whereas a proposition that is knowable a posteriori is only known on the basis of experience.*)

- If the plant has <u>edible</u> berries, they are not poisonous.
- No object can be round and square at the same time.
- He is not home so he must be out.
- 9 is the square root of 81 ($\sqrt{81}=9$).

All other evidence is derived from experience – *a posteriori*. Some of that evidence informs the basic assumptions we need to start any discussion. These will be statements such as:

- Common sense generalisations
- Well-known facts or common knowledge
- Basic assumptions in a discipline
- Simple observational statements

As noted in Chapter 1, however, most knowledge claims are about things that are not self-evidently true. These claims need additional support or evidence to make them acceptable. That evidence has to be discovered, established or created and be shown to support the claim.

All evidence needs to be relevant, reliable and sufficient for the type of knowledge claim.

In a lot of cases, the research process is designed to find out as much information as we can about some item or event, usually driven by a particular research question. In other instances, the evidence presented to justify a claim will be the result of research conducted purposefully to test the truth or not of that claim or hypothesis. Research is not as simple as just collecting up all the information there is on a topic. It is about finding out things we don't already know the answer to, by identifying the 'gap' in our knowledge. We then need to work out how we fill that gap. We do this by choosing the most suitable **research methodology and research method** for the kind of inquiry we are undertaking.

Research is the systematic exploration of an item (a problem, issue, event, process) that is intended to increase our knowledge and understanding of the item being researched.

Types of evidence

The most common types of data or evidence that are collected as part of a research project, and which you will find in **primary** research empirical texts, tend to be examples of the following:

- Observational – recording what is observed (plant growth, weather patterns, animal or human behaviour, chemical reactions)
- Experimental – taking measurements, recording results from tests (usually controlled, in a laboratory or clinical practice)
- Statistical – collecting and tabulating data, analysing data (questionnaires, census material, surveys, recording numbers or other features, population data and demographics)
- Verbal/written – recording what people say or have written (interviews, questionnaires, newspapers, diaries, films)

Most of the time, we accept the data (experimental results, statistical data, observational records) as it is presented in the article or book, especially when it is in a peer-reviewed academic text or on an official government/non-government website. We then use the findings to justify our own claims or to support our own ideas (or to argue against someone else's claim).

The **reliability** of the inferences drawn from the data are proportional to the reliability of that data or evidence.

All evidence can be questioned and each type of evidence has its own criteria of acceptability (discussed in Chapters 1–5). When thinking critically about the data or the interpretation of the data, we need to know how and why the data was collected and why it was collected in the way it was. To evaluate or critique this, we need to understand what an acceptable research process is for the kind of research conducted. As you progress in your topics, you will learn more about how knowledge in your field is created, what is accepted and why. This will enable you to feel more confident about critiquing relevant texts.

The research process

At university, we commonly conduct research by searching for information on a specific topic of interest. This information is then extracted from the relevant literature on that or related topics. We may start with a research question we want to find an answer to or an essay topic we have been assigned. We then conduct a search of the relevant literature. This is called **secondary research.** We access already existing research that has been conducted by other people, or we source relevant documents that have been compiled by established organisations. Although we could end up using **primary sources** (records, journals, maps, census data), we are not creating the data ourselves. When we (the general public or scholar) research the answer to a question, we generally engage in **secondary** research, often by doing a Google or database search.

A research methodology is the framework used to structure the research. The **research methods** are the processes or methods used to conduct and carry out the research.

First, we need to identify what areas of primary research there are and the kinds of research evidence applicable to each of them. We can't critique the research findings unless we understand how and why the data was collected and interpreted. We need to ensure both processes are as reliable as they can be.

Simplistically, there are three distinct areas of research, depending on what the object of research is (there is some overlap between humanities and social sciences when examining human behaviour and human artefacts).

- Physical or material objects and their Laws – represented by studies in the (natural) sciences, including medical science
- Social, political and cultural objects – represented by studies in the social sciences
- Philosophical, historical, literary objects – represented by studies in the humanities

There are a range of research methodologies and methods for different types of research, each with its specific strengths and weaknesses.

The (natural) sciences

Science deals with the material world rather than the social world. Broadly, science focuses on finding out about the physical world we live in, how it is constituted, what laws govern its operation and how physical objects interact with each other to cause events. Scientific disciplines methodically conduct careful observations and experiments, driven by hypotheses.

Basic elements of the scientific method

- Characterisations (of objects/events under investigation, relevant features)
- Hypotheses (what is proposed as causal explanation)
- Predictions (if true/false, what will happen)
- Experiments (to test predictions)
- Evaluation (to ascertain if hypotheses are confirmed or falsified)
- Verification (repeatability, replication of tests)

A hypothesis should *always be falsifiable* in principle, even if it is not falsified in practice. A hypothesis is falsifiable if there is an observation statement or statements that, if true, would show the hypothesis to be false. This gives it content. It means it is saying something useful about the world (compare to conspiracy theories, Chapter 2).

EXAMPLE 1A

Falsifiable hypotheses

- All planets move in ellipses around the sun.
- Metals expand when heated.
- Acids react with alkalis to form water and salts.

EXAMPLE 2B

Unfalsifiable hypotheses

- All human acts are motivated by self-interest.
- All things evolve.
- Animals are designed to obey their instincts.
- Breaking a mirror will bring you bad luck.

In **Example 1a**, there will be observational evidence that could falsify each claim. We could also test them. Based on appropriate evidence, they will be either confirmed or falsified. In **Example 1b**, there is unlikely to be any evidential statement that would falsify the claims. Any event could be interpreted such that it is taken to confirm the claim. For example, any human act can be interpreted as self-interested, including altruism (she did it to look good/to get praise, etc.). The selfish gene theory is another example of an unfalsifiable hypothesis as all existing genes must be self-seeking to have survived. Evolution itself has become a truism; this statement just says things change. With superstitions like breaking a mirror, there is never a timeframe given or the timeframe is long (seven years) and good and bad things happen all the time anyway. Much like the frequency illusion, we may associate an event (bad) with walking under a ladder or breaking a mirror and claim it was caused by that event but this commits the **post hoc ergo propter hoc fallacy** – arguing that 'A preceded B, therefore A caused B'. This is also called **false cause** reasoning. The same is true for astrological claims. When something happens that was predicted, it confirms that astrology can predict the future.

Exercise 1

How accurate would this prediction be? Can it be falsified? Why or why not?

Astrology – Prediction for Leo

There's something you've set aside that you need to recall this week. As Saturn changes direction, a small action will have a big result. Try to be flexible. As the full moon links with Neptune, it brings an important message.

Science tends to look for **causal explanations** – reasons why or how 'x' occurred, or what does/does not result from 'x' occurring. This is important in all sciences – for example, when trying to examine the effects of a drug on a disease, or what caused the blue-green algae to bloom. To establish a **causal** relationship, there must be a connection between one thing and another such that we can say 'x caused y'. If there is no 'y' present but we have 'x', then it may be that 'x' does not cause 'y'.

If there is no constant conjunction between two things in a controlled experimental situation, then there is **no causal connection** between them.

Establishing causal relationships between variables is done by isolating a single factor that is common or different in known cases – the proposed cause of the effect on an object. Causal explanations predict what might be the case (what would happen) should the hypothesis turn out to be true. There are limitations to this process.

Critiquing the method

- Must know if the similarities or differences are relevant.
- Must be aware of all relevant circumstances.
- What are ALL relevant circumstances?
- Have the circumstances been analysed correctly?
- Can events/objects have only one circumstance in common?
- Is there only one cause?
- Is an observed constant conjunction always a cause? (Do two things always occurring together mean one causes the other?)
- How do we know that the right cause has been identified?

Exercise 2

How would you identify and isolate the possible causal variables in this example? How could they be tested?

Scientists have recently discovered a three generational family living in a remote village whose average age is over 80. Several of the older generation members of the family are over 100 and there are stories of other members living to 120. One of the children claims their good health and longevity were the result of eating yoghurt every day. The grandmother said it was due to hard work.

Critiquing or evaluating causal justification

- Identify the causal explanation and any evidence presented.
- What kind of evidence is it? What and how have the factors/variables been examined?
- Remember the limitations (above). Have these been addressed?

Problems with scientific observation and research methods

As critical thinkers, we need to be aware of the limitations of the scientific method and what we need to critique to make sure the evidence given to support the claims is reliable. It should be noted that all scientific laws or theories are **inductive inferences**, not deductions. This means they can always turn out to be wrong (even if this is unlikely). There could always be another theory that explains the facts better or more succinctly, or that makes more successful predictions. For instance, Einstein's theory of relativity explained more than Newton's theory of gravity because it could be successfully applied in space. See the example below.

EXAMPLE 3

Deductive inference of a theory (invalid)

- If Newton's physics and suitable background assumptions are true, then a comet will appear in Dec. 1758. **(If A → B)**
- A comet did appear in Dec. 1758. **(B)**
- Therefore, Newton's physics is true. **(Therefore A)**

Remember what makes a deductive argument valid or invalid. Confirmation of the consequent does not establish the truth of the antecedent. So the above argument is invalid. Despite this, **it doesn't show that Newton's theory is false**; confirmation is the best we can hope for. If the comet *had not appeared* then it would be a different story and the theory may have been falsified (depending on the background assumptions).

Null hypothesis

In classical science (and psychology), the null hypothesis is the opposite of the hypothesis we want to establish or prove. It is most typically the statement that there is *no effect* of a particular treatment; in observations, it is typically that there is *no difference* between the value of a particular measured variable and that of a prediction.

EXAMPLE 4

Testing the variable (Vitamin C) on cold symptoms (null hypothesis)

Research findings suggest that taking vitamin C has **no** discernible therapeutic **effect** on the symptoms of a cold.

A common mistake students can make is to assume that if the null hypothesis is *not* true, and there *is* a measurable effect or difference, then our hypothesis or theory is true. This is wrong. Similar to **Example 2**, all we can say is that the null hypothesis is likely to be false. Formulations of the null hypothesis (H_0) take the hypothetico-deductive form: If A→B; A; therefore B. Similarly, we cannot say that the null hypothesis is true if there were no effect.

Let's imagine you want to find out if the colour of a light source affects the growth of plants.

The null hypothesis (H_0) will be – *Plant growth is not affected by light colour.* If plant growth is not affected by light colour, then there will be no discernible difference in growth between plants exposed to different coloured light sources. If plants are affected, then there will be a discernible difference. We can represent the possible outcomes as deductive arguments.

EXAMPLE 5

Valid formulation of the null hypothesis argument

- If the null hypothesis is true (no effect), data Y (variations in plant growth) are unlikely to be observed. **(If A → –B)**
- Data Y (variations in plant growth) were observed **(– –B)**
- The null hypothesis is unlikely to be true **(Therefore –A)**

EXAMPLE 5A

Invalid formulation of the null hypothesis argument

- If the null hypothesis is true (no effect), data Y (variations in plant growth) are unlikely to be observed. **(If A → –B)**
- Data Y (variations in plant growth) were not observed **(–B)**
- The null hypothesis is true **(Therefore A)**

EXAMPLE 5B

Belief that the rejection of the null hypothesis establishes the truth of a theory that predicts it to be false (invalid formulation)

- If plant growth is affected by light colour, the null hypothesis (no effect) will prove to be false. **(If A → B)**
- The null hypothesis proved to be false. **(B)**
- Therefore plant growth is affected by light colour. **(Therefore A)**

Using deductive logic, we can see that both Examples 5a and 5b are invalid. The conclusions cannot be proven. Only Example 4 is valid. All we can say is data Y (variations in plant growth) were observed, which may confirm our theory but not prove it. Likewise, claiming the null hypothesis is true is too strong. It may be likely but it cannot be proven.

Theories or hypotheses can only be **confirmed** or falsified but cannot be proven to be true.

Setting up a (scientific) experiment

1. Use your experience – what is the problem, event, effect that you want to solve, explain, prevent? Try to make sense of it.
2. If new, conjecture about possible causes, identify the variables – hypothesise
3. Deduce a prediction; if your hypothesis is correct what would be a consequence?
4. Test – what would make your consequent false? (hypotheses can only be shown to be false, not true)
5. Re-examine and repeat.

Remember, in the sciences you deal with physical objects, processes or effects.

The (natural) sciences deal in testable, measurable effects that can be observed and verified, then recorded, tabulated, graphed and mathematically analysed. The results can be **quantified**, often using statistics and a relevant statistical software program. This removes the results as much as possible from the vagaries of human actions. It is why science considers its research to be **objective**. The process is repeatable and the results can be replicated by anyone else. This is an example of **quantitative** research.

Humanities

Subjects that fall under the humanities vary across institutions but mostly their focus is on human and cultural ideas and artefacts as represented in law, politics, philosophy, literature, language and art. Research in these areas is mostly **conceptual, secondary** research, although frequently using **primary sources** such as human artefacts or other cultural products. If primary research is used, its methods will be similar to those in the social sciences.

Social sciences

The social sciences use the term 'science' because they adopted the principles of the scientific method as the *exemplar par excellence* of knowledge formation. They wanted their knowledge claims to have the same objectivity, rigour and acceptance as claims made in the natural sciences. Much of the research in the social sciences uses a similar method of hypothesis generation, prediction and testing, including use of the null hypothesis. Psychology is the exemplar here.

The major distinction between the (natural) sciences and the (soft) sciences is the object under examination – the former deal with matter or the material world, while the latter examine the social or human world, including human behaviour. This is fraught with difficulties, not least because the objects under investigation are not concrete or stable. They are also very complex and less understood.

Because the object of research in the social sciences is the **human world**, many argue that we cannot use the same research methods as the sciences. Humans are not objects like other material objects. Societies are not objects like other artefacts.

Humans have a **subjective** realm. This means they can be both object and subject of research. Being a subject of research means participating. Unlike inanimate objects, humans can contribute their own perspective to the research. They can talk about the **quality** of their experience.

Additionally, postmodernists and anti-positivists argue that what counts as knowledge is driven by social/political interests and values. They argue that knowledge creation is a relativist or subjective human enterprise; that what counts as knowledge is contextual and dependent on time and place, and it is multivariate. The qualitative methodology acknowledges these differences, as well as the value of the individual in creating meaning.

This means that the human or social sciences (can) use both **quantitative and qualitative research methods**. The (natural) sciences can only ever use quantitative methods, except when engaged in human research (neurology, medicine, physiology, etc.).

Quantitative and qualitative research methodologies

As critical thinkers, it is important to know what the limitations and strengths of the different approaches to knowledge formation are. There are ongoing debates within many social science disciplines about the value of different research methods, of quantitative versus qualitative research methods. Often, the disagreements are driven by differences in ontology and epistemology because these differences inform how we conduct our research.

Ontology → Epistemology → Methodology → Method
(Worldview) → (How we know) → (Research framework)

Our ontology (metaphysics or worldview) will influence how we understand the world and our relationship to it. This will have an impact on our concepts of truth and knowledge. In Chapter 3, we discussed the ontological and epistemological position taken by realists who believe the world exists independently of our knowledge of it. Within that ontological framework, knowledge of the world is something we can discover or uncover, despite our limitations. They believe that we can discover objective facts that can be represented by statements that describe true features of that world. Most scientists would hold this position.

There is, however, an alternative ontological/epistemological position that believes there is no world independent of our minds. This framework assumes that knowledge is not objective and truth is relative to our situation; it is something we construct. It can never be independent of our beliefs and perceptions. As such, they argue that there are various 'knowledges' that describe the world differently but no less accurately. Indigenous knowledges fall within this ambit as do some feminist epistemologies. When critiquing research findings, see if you can identify what ontological/epistemological frameworks are informing the research methodology and methods, as this will affect how it is conducted.

In the social sciences, the conflicting ideas that knowledge is either objectively discoverable or subjectively constructed has led to two different approaches to conducting human research, a *quantitative* approach drawn from the natural sciences or a *qualitative* approach. Prime examples of areas where both methodologies are used are education, sociology and the health sciences, including nursing. The medical sciences tend to mirror the natural sciences, although case studies often include a mixture of both.

Quantitative methodology	Qualitative methodology
• Considered objective and rigorous • Researcher an objective instrument • Emphasises quantification in collection and analysis of data, mathematical/ numerical (aligned to the natural sciences) • Methods employ large-scale surveys, questionnaires, repeatable experiments • Driven by hypotheses • Findings broadly generalisable across a group or population • Seen as positivist, reductionist, analytic • Can generate reliable predictions and probabilities • Assumes regularities in human behaviour governed by laws	• Considered subjective • Researcher an active participant • Emphasises words/qualities, rather than numbers • Methods employ interviews, observation, documentary analysis, case studies, personal anecdotes • Generates hypotheses • Findings narrow and pertaining to individual personal experience, not broadly generalisable • Seen as holistic and non-reductive • Multiple meanings and interpretations; findings may change; context dependent • Assumes human behaviour individual and institutions reflect human culture

Mixed methods

One can, of course, use a combination of both methods. A mixed methods approach tries to utilise the best of each methodology. It can be argued that this is not feasible as each has its own very different ontological and epistemological framework. That difference, though, may not matter depending on the item or object under investigation. Some items are better understood using one or other method. *If we want to know the frequency of breast cancer in a population, then a quantitative methodology will work best. If we want to understand how patients react to having a mastectomy, then a qualitative study will be more suitable.*

As critical thinkers, it is our job to assess **the relevance of the research methods** to the object under investigation, as well as assessing how rigorous the research process was.

Most researchers agree that mixing methods can increase the accuracy of data, provide a more robust picture of the phenomenon, and address the shortcomings of each approach.

Exercise 3

Choose a suitable research methodology for each example (Qt is quantitative; Ql is qualitative and MM is mixed methods)

1. Observing and recording the behaviour of mice after they were given an appetite suppressant. **Qt ☐ Ql ☐ MM ☐**
2. Conducting a postal survey to find out how a community is likely to vote. **Qt ☐ Ql ☐ MM ☐**
3. Giving students a questionnaire asking what they like to study and why. **Qt ☐ Ql ☐ MM ☐**
4. Measuring the growth of fungus on wood in a laboratory over several weeks. **Qt ☐ Ql ☐ MM ☐**
5. Recording the quantity and types of vehicles that use an underpass. **Qt ☐ Ql ☐ MM ☐**
6. Observing the behaviour of children at a playschool before and after eating a sweet dessert. **Qt ☐ Ql ☐ MM ☐**
7. Talking to a focus group of women about their experiences of undergoing chemotherapy. **Qt ☐ Ql ☐ MM ☐**
8. Interviewing three politicians about the impact of the war in Yemen on petrol prices. **Qt ☐ Ql ☐ MM ☐**
9. Comparing the journals of ten migrant women for common themes. **Qt ☐ Ql ☐ MM ☐**
10. Analysing the discourse in newspaper stories about refugees. **Qt ☐ Ql ☐ MM ☐**

Critiquing quantitative (research) data

Collecting demographic data (such as age, gender, postal address, ethnicity, education, health status, weight) is a common form of **quantitative** research that results from individuals filling out personal details in a questionnaire. Data can be collected on a range of items depending on the purpose. We fill out forms every time we register at a new medical clinic, enrol in something, or register for benefits. Data like this can be analysed to discern patterns *(increase in obesity; decrease in smoking)*, correlations (i.e. *postal address and weight/obesity; education and income*), or changes in social behaviour (i.e. *more or less crime in a suburb; ethnic mix).* The census is often used as a source of demographic data.

The data can be easily represented in a graph or table to show what the average (mean) income is or what relationships there might be between the different variables (*gender and income*). The findings drawn from this kind of data are reliable as they describe what is the case for the population in question (descriptive statistics). The reliability of the data collected, however, depends on the accuracy of reporting and the size of the data set collected.

Researchers construct questionnaires or surveys to find out answers to their research questions. In theory, the larger the number of responses the more reliable or representative the findings will be. Quantity can also reduce the incidence of random errors or the effect of anomalies in the data. But it is impractical, time consuming and costly to target everyone, so we generally select a sample group of the population we want to research. If the sample is big enough for the item being investigated, the researchers can generalise their findings to the whole population, make probability statements or infer what might be the case (inferential statistics). This predicts likely outcomes using **inductive probability.**

Sampling

The most crucial factor influencing the reliability of statistical data collected by surveys, questionnaires or polling is the sampling method. Opinion polls are a common example of sampling a population to gauge what they think or to predict how they will vote. However, recent polls have been very wrong. They were wrong about the 2015 Tory win in Britain, the probability of a Trump victory in 2016, and the 2019 Conservative Party win in Australia. This indicates there may be a problem with the polling method. Four critical questions to ask researchers are:

- Who are you asking? How are you selecting your respondents?
- Will this selection process give you a representative sample of the target population?
- What is your means of communication? How are you contacting people?
- Would your sampling method bias your findings to a certain demographic?

Exercise 4

Sampling methods

According to the Brexit data, online polls had a better performance record than phone polls. Online surveys, on average, predicted a 'leave' win with a 1.2% margin, whereas those with a phone methodology had 'remain' win with a 2.6% margin. All in all, 63% of online polls predicted a Leave victory, while 78% of phone polls predicted that Remain would win.

Why do you think the online Brexit polls were more accurate than phone polls?

Exercise 5

How accurate do you think the 2019 poll below would have been and why? What information do you need?

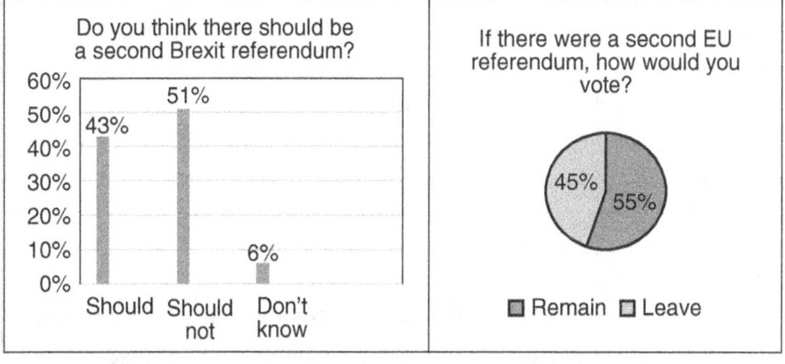

Misrepresentation or vagueness of statistical results

Another problem with using statistical data is how it is represented in the text. This can often be misleading.

EXAMPLE 6

What do these statistics mean? Is the conclusion warranted?

200 women, some of whom had a multiracial or immigrant background, were surveyed about their support for refugees coming into the country. Of those with mixed heritage, 40% supported refugees' right to settlement, while only 7% said they should be sent back. Those with an immigrant background were less supportive at 25%, but more than half felt there should be a clear process for assessing claims. Of those with a non-immigrant single ethnicity, only 15% supported refugees' right to settlement, while 35% said they should be sent back. This shows that people with a multicultural background are less likely to worry about refugees or illegal immigrants and are more sympathetic to their plight than non-immigrant women.

Analysis: How reliable is the inference drawn? Although it may seem convincing (40% compared to 15%), we need to examine the figures carefully. First, we don't know how the women were chosen so there could be a selection bias. We don't know what proportion of the 200 women were multiracial, immigrant or single ethnicity. This means we cannot judge how significant those percentage figures are. Let's assume that of the 200 women, 50 were from a multiracial or immigrant background. Let's further assume that 50% of that 50 were either immigrant or multiracial, making 25 for each. This means that a total of 10 women (40% of 25) from a mixed background supported refugees, compared to 4 immigrant women (15% of 25). Similarly, there were only 35 women from a non-immigrant background who said refugees should be sent back, while 15 supported settlement, more than the immigrant/mixed race category. Even if the ratios are not accurate, none of these numbers are large enough to be representative or to draw any reliable inferences.

Saying '40% increase in x' sounds like a lot but figures can be misleading and are often misused to serve a political purpose. This is especially so with crime statistics, data on immigration, drug use or prisoner recidivism.

Note: Always ask – 40% of what? Compared to what? When the statistics say you have a 20% increased risk of breast cancer if you drink alcohol, ask what is that 20% of? It may be a negligible increase (20% of 0.06).

Exercise 6

Study of gender bias

Look at this example. How might you critique the reliability of the conclusion?

A study of 60 mixed gender undergraduate responses to male and female lecturers presenting identical content showed that both male and female students remembered more information from the male lecturers than from the female. A possible explanation is that males are considered to be more competent or more interesting. Based on these findings, it is likely the public will pay more attention to a male speaker than a female speaker.

Be cautious with statistics; learn what they mean

Different ways of seeing stats

Michael Blastland, 2009; http://news.bbc.co.uk/1/hi/magazine/8153539.stm

A scanner to detect terrorists

Imagine you've invented a machine to detect terrorists. It's good, about 90% accurate. You're in the Houses of Parliament demonstrating the device to MPs when you receive urgent information from MI5 that a potential attacker is in the building. Security teams seal every exit and all 3000 people inside are rounded up to be tested by your new machine.

The first 30 pass. Then, dramatically, a man in a mac fails. Police pounce, guns point. How sure are you that this person is a terrorist?

- 90% ☐
- 10% ☐
- 0.3% ☐

If 3000 people are tested, and the test is 90% accurate, it is also 10% wrong. So it will probably identify 301 terrorists (out of 3000 people) – about 300 by mistake and 1 correctly. You won't know from the test which is the real terrorist. So the chance that our man in the mac is the real thing is 1 in 301 (**0.3%** chance).

Why? Because what you are trying to find is rare, which means there will be a lot of false positives and false negatives.

1. How many people in the selected population will have the characteristic which the test is intended to find? (i.e. T= terrorist; You need to know the **relative frequency** of the characteristic in a given population first)
2. Let's take a population of 300,000 people. Divide them into those with T, and those without T. Let's say 100 will be terrorists (T). This means not terrorists = 299,900 (not T).
3. Calculate how many of those with (T) will be true positives. According to the test, this will be 90%; of 100, this is 90.
4. Calculate how many of those without T will be false positives. This will be the remaining 10%; 10% of 299,900 is 29,990.
5. Think about the balance of true and false positives. You don't need to do any sums to see that 90 is small compared with 29,990.

Response adapted from Jane Hutton, Department of Statistics, University of Warwick, 2009.

Critiquing qualitative research

While there are a lot of potential problems with quantitative research, many people argue that it is much more reliable than *qualitative* research because the findings are more generally applicable and the methods of data collection and analysis are both transparent and rigorous. They can be easily replicated to see if the findings are reliable.

Unlike quantitative research, qualitative research relies on individuals expressing their reactions, feelings, views or attitudes towards something when asked. This can be through a questionnaire using open-ended questions (i.e. why did you come here? What could be improved? How did it make you feel? Explain your reaction, comment on...), a structured or unstructured interview, or a focus group. A case study is another particular method that may follow and document the effectiveness of a new art program at a school or just one person's journey (health, professional). While qualitative research produces a rich amount of data not available through a quantitative approach, it takes a lot of skill and understanding of the methods to do it properly.

Limitations of qualitative research

- It is time-consuming, which limits the scope of the research (smaller numbers of participants; large amounts of data).
- The small number of participants (sometimes only 1) limits the generalisability of the findings and their applicability to other contexts or situations.
- The interviewees or participants are unlikely to be representative, may have unique experiences and may have characteristics that bias the results.
- Widely different, subjective results make comparisons difficult to draw.
- The presence of the interviewer/researcher can influence how and in what way subjects respond.
- The personal biases of the interviewer/researcher can influence how and in what way subjects respond.
- Data can be misinterpreted or misrepresented more easily in the open format.
- The quality and reliability of the data collected depends on the expertise of the researcher.

Rigour and reliability

There are known problems with ensuring the data from qualitative research is reliable. Participants respond based on their lived experience of whatever is being researched. As a consequence, they can respond emotionally on the day, can change their minds, can feel differently over time because circumstances have changed, can disagree with an interpretation and can withdraw consent. They may have faulty memories or feel constrained (embarrassed, nervous) to share their thoughts and feelings. The interviewer or observer can determine what is asked or what is noted. This means the data collected **can be unstable.**

As critical readers and thinkers, we need to understand what the problems are and ensure they have been dealt with appropriately. As with any claim, we need to know that the findings can be trusted. Mechanisms can be put in place to strengthen the reliability and rigour of the data collected and, hence, the inferences drawn from that data. Such mechanisms include:

- Careful recordkeeping of all decisions and decision-making processes
- Explanations for the chosen method and choice of participants
- Documentation of any and all interactions (audio or video recorded and transcribed)
- Multiple researchers able to conduct the interviews/observations to ensure non-partiality and to minimise the effect of the researcher
- Allowing others to check data and conduct analyses
- Comparing results and looking for discrepancies
- Wherever possible, using triangulation (different standpoint) to seek correlation of findings – i.e. observation, interview and questionnaire; different timelines; different places
- If results differ widely, trying to understand why this might be – i.e. cross cultural or subgroup research findings
- Being aware of confirmation bias, halo effect and other cognitive bias.

EXAMPLE 7

A qualitative case study in nursing

Patient X was recently diagnosed with breast cancer and subsequently advised to have a double mastectomy. Her mother had died from breast cancer 10 years earlier. Researcher Y (her sister) was asked if she would document Patient X's journey. Both women were interested in exploring the impact of a mastectomy on a woman's sense of self or identity and the adoption of a new identity as a 'cancer patient/survivor'.

What are some of the issues facing the researcher that may have an impact on the study's rigour and reliability?

The researcher has several issues to consider. Any qualitative study has ethical considerations. The main consideration is doing no harm to the participants. In this study, the researcher will be dealing with very emotional issues, including the real risk of the death of the patient. This is complicated by their familial bond. The sister may feel more comfortable with her sibling conducting the research than with someone unknown, which may produce interesting findings, but it will be fraught. The close bond and emotional investment may be an obstacle to objective reporting and the interpretation of any results. How will Researcher Y guarantee rigour and reliability?

Another issue is the purpose of the research. What is it for? Is it to enrich our understanding of having cancer? What contribution will it make? Researcher Y will need to clarify what the research questions are to be and what she hopes the outcomes will show. It is likely Researcher Y will choose a **phenomenological** framework as the most suitable to explore the lived experience and perspectives of an individual. As this will be a study of one person's experiences, how broadly applicable will any inference drawn from the data be? The researcher will need to pay special attention to how she interprets the data in light of her relationship and feelings towards her sibling. Her own grief (both for her sister and her mother) may also impact on her ability to interpret the data without bias. She may need to invite an outsider to assess her data and any interpretations to provide an alternative perspective.

Exercise 7

How would you critique this research? What questions do you need to ask?

In this article, the author argues that modern women yearn for more traditional marriages with more traditional gender roles. When interviewed, working women expressed higher levels of stress and a desire to be supported by their partner so they could work less. The author claims women are turning their backs on careers so they can spend quality time with their children.

Chapter summary

- All evidence needs to be relevant, reliable and sufficient for the type of knowledge claim.
- Research is the systematic exploration of an item (a problem, issue, event, process) that is intended to increase our knowledge and understanding of the item being researched.
- The reliability of the inferences drawn from the data are proportional to the reliability of that data or evidence.
- A research methodology is the framework used to structure your research. The research methods are the processes or methods you use to conduct and carry out the research.
- There are a range of research methodologies for different types of research, each with its strengths and weaknesses.
- As critical thinkers, it is our job to assess the relevance of the research methods to the object under investigation, as well as assessing how rigorous the research process was.

Answers to Exercises 1–7

Exercise 1

How accurate would this prediction be? Can it be falsified? Why or why not?

Astrology – Prediction for Leo

With any astrological prediction, it is important to bear in mind how many people in the world it is supposed to apply to, in this instance all those born between July 23rd and August 22nd (>10^6). The language of horoscopes are deliberately vague for this reason, and tend to highlight common human concerns or traits that we all have (e.g. 'something set aside you need to recall' or 'a need to be flexible'). Purely by chance, there are bound to be some people who will fit this horoscope because of the large numbers within the star-sign and because it can fit any set of circumstances. If we do get 'an important message', which is likely at some point (importance is a variable assessment), it will confirm its predictive capacity. It is hard to falsify as the way it is worded will fit most people, even those who are not Leos.

Exercise 2

How would you identify and isolate the possible causal variables in this example? How could they be tested?

Testing for what might cause longevity is going to be near impossible. There could be any number of causal variables. It could be genes, a healthy environment or luck. They may even work together. How could any of them be tested? There are also likely to be many people who worked hard or ate yoghurt every day who didn't live long lives. In a person's life, how could you control the environment such that only certain identified measurable factors varied in a controlled way while all others were kept constant? The only way to test for 'longevity' factors would be based on laboratory research and then finding a large cohort of people who had the 'longevity' factors and who consequently lived a long time.

Exercise 3

Try to identify the research methodology in each example

1. Observing and recording the behaviour of mice after they were given an appetite suppressant – **quantitative (laboratory controlled)**
2. Conducting a postal survey to find out how a community is likely to vote – **quantitative (inferential statistics)**
3. Giving students a questionnaire asking what they like to study and why – **qualitative (possibly mixed method as there is likely to be demographic information too)**

4. Measuring the growth of fungus on wood in a laboratory over several weeks – **quantitative (laboratory controlled)**
5. Recording the quantity and types of vehicles that use an underpass – **quantitative (descriptive statistics)**
6. Observing the behaviour of children at a playschool before and after eating a sweet dessert – **qualitative (rigour would be a problem as it would be hard to determine if the behaviour was the result of the dessert)**
7. Talking to a focus group of women about their experiences of undergoing chemotherapy – **qualitative (phenomenological)**
8. Interviewing three politicians about the impact of the war in Yemen on petrol prices – **qualitative**
9. Comparing the journals of ten migrant women for common themes – **qualitative**
10. Analysing the discourse in newspaper stories about refugees – **mixed method (content analysis is considered quantitative, discourse or meaning analysis is qualitative)**

Exercise 4

Sampling methods

Why do you think the online Brexit polls were more accurate than phone polls?

One has to think about the demographics of who voted for or against Brexit. Who were they and where were they from? Data are complex and indicate that those who voted to leave were mixed: a lot were older, white, middle class and conservative, but many were also low social-economic status (SES), disenfranchised and with a lower use of smartphones or internet. So it is confusing. One reason could be that phone polls now target mobile phones. These are not fixed like landlines so are no longer a reliable indicator of a physical location, which means you are not guaranteed representative sampling. One can also access bigger datasets with online sampling of social media like Twitter and Facebook. More data make the findings more reliable. Users tend to be more honest about their intentions in an online forum than they are when face-to-face. So the online responses were more likely reflective of true voting patterns than the phone data.

Exercise 5

Polls prior to 24th of June, 2016 predicted Remain would win (52 to 48%). The result was Leave 51.9% to Remain 48.1%. **How accurate would the 2019 poll have been and why? What more information do you need?** Given the lack of accurate predictions from recent polls on Brexit, there is no reason why we would believe this latest poll. Our confidence levels will be quite low. At a minimum, we would need to know how data were collected and who from, and whether or not this was different to previous polls, and whether or not this was an improvement in sampling methods from the previous polls.

Exercise 6

Study of gender bias

Look at this example. How might you critique the reliability of the conclusion?

The first issue is deciding how reliable the initial finding is. How many lectures were there and how many male:female students? Did they all produce the same results? Did the presentation style differ in relevant ways? How was the retention of information measured? If we are satisfied that the findings did show that the students responded differently to the gender of the lecturer (and we may not be satisfied), our next question is how representative are graduates of the general population? Would the general public respond similarly? Is retention of information an indicator of how much attention we pay?

Exercise 7

How would you critique this research? What questions do you need to ask?

This research uses a lot of generalisations and terms that need unpacking. What is meant by traditional marriage and traditional roles? What counts as more support? Is it purely financial? How many working women expressed higher levels of stress? Compared to who? Does the desire for more support and more time at home equate to wanting a return to traditional roles? To generalise to all women would require a large sample size as well as information about who was selected and what was asked. It would be relevant to see who was behind this research and if there were any vested interest (i.e. certain affiliations). It would be useful to search for related or alternative studies to see how their findings compare. Is this study an anomaly?

CHAPTER

9

Writing an Argument – Making It Persuasive

Critical thinking and writing a convincing argument

We have talked a lot about the role of critical thinking in assessing and evaluating information and the claims that other people make. This is because in this ever-changing, complex world we want to ensure that our beliefs and practices are based on recent, reliable information. We want that information to be as close to the truth as we can get. As a foundation, we need to understand the process of knowledge formation and what makes something an acceptable knowledge claim. To assess that information or to reflect on what has informed our own beliefs, we need the right tools. We need to know how to question claims and evaluate the evidence and the reasoning. We need to understand the argument. That is what critical thinking is all about. It provides us with the techniques required to check our thinking and the knowledge base that informs our thinking and the thinking of others.

The 4 Rs of critical thinking – read, reflect, write, reason, reflect, read, write....

Just as we evaluate the quality of other people's claims, we can evaluate the quality of our own. A good critical thinker will apply the same techniques and tools to their own reasoning and writing.

Understanding what makes a strong argument will help you to write one

At university, you will have to write – a lot. And it won't be just describing a process or identifying factors. Instead, you will be expected to put forward your own ideas and points of view on a topic. Most of the time, you will be asked to respond to statements or questions that require you to conduct research and then come to a conclusion informed by that research. More often than not, the essay topic or question will require you to take a position. That position needs to be defended; it needs to be argued for and justified. You will be **writing an argument.** It is, therefore, doubly important that you understand what an argument is and what makes a good/sound/strong argument, to enable you to both critique what you read and to develop and present your own ideas effectively. These skills are useful anywhere and in any position or role that requires thinking and writing.

Remember: the same criteria we use to judge the quality of someone else's written work (strong argument, well supported and well-reasoned conclusion, addressing counter claims) will be used to judge the quality of our own.

EXAMPLE 1

Is this an argument?

The global institutions that were supposed to herald in an age of peace and prosperity for all have become tools whereby the rich nations have consolidated their economic position. The rich design these institutions to serve the interests of the rich. Although the rhetoric of the Atlantic Treaty is full of noble sentiments, the International Monetary Fund, the World Bank and the World Trade Organization have structured their rules in the interests of the developed world.

This passage does not contain an argument. It is passionate and perhaps persuasive but it is just a series of related claims about global institutions. These claims may be true. There is, however, no evidence presented to support the claims and there is no one particular claim we can identify that is the one being argued for. Each of the three sentences say the same thing in slightly different ways. When reading or writing critically, we need to first ensure there is an argument – a clear position or claim that is justified. Ask yourself – what is it the author is claiming? What is it **I** want to claim?

What makes a good/strong argument?

When critiquing other people's writing, we are critiquing the claims they make to see if we should accept them or not. The acceptability of a claim will depend on the strength of the evidence presented to support it and the relevance of that evidence to the claim. It will depend on the strength of their argument. We need to understand what makes a good argument (or a bad argument) in order to critique information effectively to evaluate its worth, and to assess whether or not that information can be used to justify our own claims.

An argument will be strong if it has the following:

- The premises are acceptable (they make sense)
- The reasons given to support the claim are reliable
- The reasons given to support the claim are relevant
- The reasons provide sufficient grounds for the claim
- The premises are connected semantically (meaning)
- The premises are connected syntactically (in a logical way)

A strong argument should be convincing. You should find yourself believing the claim or hypothesis that is being put forward, or at least finding the claim/conclusion reasonable or plausible. Think what makes an argument persuasive. It is not just having strong or reliable evidence; the evidence has to be shown to be relevant tothe claim such that it justifies that claim.

EXAMPLE 2A

Is this an argument?

According to Gruetzner (1992), people with dementia have problems with judgement, language, communication skills, concentration, new learning, abstract thinking, making an intended movement, recognising objects, remembering, the control of emotional reactions, and functioning in employment and social settings. In their 2005 study, Ferri et al. (2005) suggest that the number of people being diagnosed with dementia in developed nations is predicted to rise by 100% between 2001 and 2040, but by over 300% in China, India, South Asia and their Western Pacific neighbours.

This passage does not contain an argument. Unlike Exercise 1, however, this passage does contain some information. But it does not count as *evidence* unless it is related to a claim for which it counts as support. While the first sentence states what the symptoms of dementia are, there is no link from this to something else (it needs an opening topic sentence like '*Dementia has a debilitating effect on people's lives*', or an inference/implication like, '*this indicates that people with dementia need a lot of support*'). If the statistics referred to in the second sentence are important, we need to know why. What are the authors suggesting? As it stands, the passage is just making descriptive statements about dementia. The authors need to clarify their intention and state why those 'facts' are there. First they need to explain what the facts show – i.e. '*the incidence of dementia is increasing – and even more so in Eastern countries*' and then what this means, – *People with dementia need lots of support.* It is likely that the authors intended to argue that something should be done, like provision of services. However, it should not be up to the reader to try to interpret what an author may have intended (even though we do this with fictional texts, plays and poems). This should be clear. Facts alone don't argue for anything.

Evidence alone does not make a persuasive argument; it is **the way the evidence** is related to the claim that makes it an argument.

EXAMPLE 2B

Making it an argument (with a possible conclusion)

Dementia is a degenerative condition that has a debilitating effect on all aspects of a person's life. According to Gruetzner (1992), people with dementia have problems *with a range of normal cognitive tasks from* ~~judgement,~~ language and communication skills, ~~concentration, new learning, abstract thinking, making an intended movement,~~ *to* recognising objects, remembering, and controlling emotional reactions. *The loss of these skills drastically impacts on their* functioning in employment and social settings. *Of concern is evidence that the rates of dementia appear to be increasing.* In their 2005 study, Ferri et al. (2005) suggest that the number of people being diagnosed with dementia in developed nations is predicted to rise by 100% between 2001 and 2040, but by over 300% in China, India, South Asia and their Western Pacific neighbours. *If their predictions are correct, dementia will pose a major problem to existing health services worldwide. Asian countries in particular will find it hard to cope with the increased demand on their medical resources unless strategies are put in place now to plan for this emergency. This may be the time for a re-appraisal of current treatment options to see if dementia can be managed more effectively.*

How do I write a persuasive argument?

Think about what it is you want to claim. Once you have decided on a position, work out how you will put forward your point of view in a well-reasoned and objective way. Writing a draft structure or plan is helpful. Ideally, we want the reader to find our arguments persuasive. Start by thinking backwards. Ask yourself,

- What made me come to this particular position or conclusion?
- What information did I find convincing or persuasive? Why?
- What information did I find problematic?
- Why did I reject the alternatives?
- Why is this/my conclusion better than the alternative positions?

The answers to these questions will be the reasons that justify your claim or conclusion. If *you* found the reasons convincing, then so should the person reading your essay. But you need to include them. The person reading your work only has your text by which to judge your ideas. Make sure you have explained yourself clearly and included all relevant information, such as the reasons why you found an argument convincing (or not). Remember to acknowledge all the sources you accessed to get your information.

Writing an argument is writing a **record of the process** you used to come to your conclusion. This includes your reasoning as well as the evidence.

To present a strong argument, you need plenty of supporting evidence for your claim and minimal counter evidence; i.e. evidence that could argue **against your position.** If you don't have a lot of evidence to support your claim, then it is likely there is something wrong with the claim. Maybe it is not a defensible position and you will need to change it. The same holds if there are a lot of arguments against your position. This means your position is likely to be weak. Do not argue for something for which you don't have a lot of evidence.

It is easier to write **a strong argument** when you are clear why you hold your position.

Caution: Being convinced of the correctness of our position is not the same thing as having a strong argument. Remember we are prone to mistakes and biases so we need to be careful. The certainty of our belief in our position should be proportional to the strength of the evidence supporting it.

Indicate how relevant the evidence is in supporting the claim and show why any arguments against it are weak or irrelevant. Remember the **Straw Man fallacy** and address opposing positions fairly. If you can demonstrate why other positions are not acceptable, it strengthens your own position, assuming you can defend it with a strong argument. Acknowledging any relevant views or evidence that contradict or weaken your position also demonstrates your objectivity.

Do not ignore **counter evidence.** Include it and argue against it to show why it doesn't counter your claim. If it can't be dismissed, qualify your conclusion to accommodate it.

It might be the case that you are putting forward a claim that is still new and the research evidence is limited. It may be controversial. You will need to make this clear and perhaps adjust your position to make it more acceptable, and therefore, more defensible. If you have strong grounds for your claim and you structure your essay logically to show the relevance of those grounds to the claim, then it should be a persuasive argument.

A persuasive argument

- is written clearly
- has enough evidence to support the position (facts, references)
- explains why the evidence is relevant and reliable (language choice)
- has a logical structure that is easy to follow (sequence of ideas)
- acknowledges other opposing views and addresses them (balance, objectivity),
- summarises why the claim is the best one, given what has been shown (what is known).

What counts as enough evidence?

The first step in writing a persuasive argument is knowing that we have enough evidence to support our claim or conclusion and that the claim we are putting forward is the best conclusion to come to based on that evidence. It is, however, not always easy to know if this is the case. There may be counter evidence or other facts that we do not have access to, which would point to a different conclusion. We may be coming to our conclusion too soon based on limited evidence, or we may not be dealing with the evidence as objectively as we should. We may be ignoring other possible conclusions.

Exercise 1

What counts as enough evidence?

When researching decreasing cognitive capacities in the elderly, Carzine found a study by the National Institute for Aging (NIA) that claimed social, verbal and personal judgements improved with age. Her other research had indicated that old age led to a loss of cognitive skills. In this NIA study, older people were better at judging individuals as dishonest or bright and were better at storytelling than other age groups. Carzine decided to rewrite her thesis and argue that there needed to be a complete re-think about older people's cognitive capacities. *How reasonable is her conclusion, given the evidence?*

What can we infer?

Sometimes it is not a problem of enough evidence but whether or not we are drawing the right inference. What is the evidence showing us? What is it evidence of?

Exercise 2

Evidence of what?

Can we claim there is evidence of collusion or obstruction of justice? What more evidence would we need to form a reliable conclusion?

U.S. intelligence agencies in January 2017 concluded that the Russian Government interfered in the American election by hacking into the computer servers of the Democratic National Committee (DNC) and the personal Gmail account of Clinton campaign chairman John Podesta and forwarding their contents to WikiLeaks, and by disseminating fake news promoted on social media. Because the interference favoured Trump's campaign, the FBI investigated the possibility of collusion between the Trump campaign and Russia. *The New York Times* reported on February 14, 2017, that phone records and communications intercepts showed that Trump associates – including members of the Trump campaign – had 'repeated contacts' with senior Russian intelligence officials during the 2016 campaign. The Trump team issued multiple denials of any contacts between Trump associates and Russia, but many of those denials turned out to be false. A December 2018 Government sentencing memo for Flynn showed that members of the Trump campaign had discussed whether to contact WikiLeaks about the release of DNC emails, indicating they were aware and supportive of the release. President Trump said he dismissed FBI Director James Comey because of 'the Russian thing', raising concerns of obstruction of justice. President Trump has repeatedly made attempts to block the Mueller investigation, calling it illegal and a 'witch hunt'. The White House refused to share information or allow access to emails.

It is now known that Steve Bannon used Cambridge Analytica and Facebook to manipulate voters in America prior to 2016. It is also known that Russia interfered in the 2016 elections. Both events favoured the election of Trump over Clinton. However, that does not mean that the Trump campaign colluded with Russia or that Donald Trump was aware of and supported or promoted these activities. While the evidence might cast doubt on their ignorance, that doesn't prove the campaign was complicit. This means we would need to be cautious what conclusions we draw from the evidence (see answer).

EXAMPLE 3A

Think what would be a reasonable conclusion to draw (which ones could you defend based on the evidence presented in Exercise 2?).

1. President Trump was guilty of collusion with Russia.
2. The Trump campaign was guilty of collusion with Russia.
3. The Trump campaign knew of Russia's interference in the American election.
4. President Trump knew of Russia's interference in the American election.
5. It is likely that the Trump campaign knew of Russia's interference in the American election.

6. The Trump campaign supported Russia's interference in the American election.
7. It is likely that the Trump campaign supported Russia's interference in the American election.
8. There is a possibility that the Trump campaign supported Russia's interference in the American election.
9. President Trump is guilty of obstructing justice.
10. It is likely that President Trump is guilty of obstructing justice.
11. There is a possibility that President Trump is guilty of obstructing justice.
12. President Trump is not guilty of obstructing justice.
13. It is likely that President Trump is not guilty of obstructing justice.
14. The Trump campaign knew nothing of Russia's interference in the American election.
15. The Trump campaign did not support Russia's interference in the American election.
16. It is likely that the Trump campaign knew nothing of Russia's interference in the American election.
17. It is likely that the Trump campaign did not support Russia's interference in the American election.

As you can see, there is a broad range of different inferences or conclusions one could draw from the evidence presented, based around the two hypotheses behind the Mueller investigation – that there might be collusion, and that President Trump might be guilty of obstruction. Conclusions can range from a clear yes (1 and 2) to a clear denial (12 and 14). Note also that there are different aspects to this case. Knowledge of something is not the same as complicity. Knowledge does not necessarily imply support. Language choice is important. Note how the language of the suggested inferences goes from strong to less strong. This is called *qualifying* one's claim. One must always be careful not to claim more or less than the evidence supports. It will be easier to put forward a more convincing argument for a qualified claim than for one which is unequivocal (yes or no).

The **strength of the inference** or conclusion should be proportional to the strength of the evidence presented.

A Trump advocate would (is likely to) support statements 12 and 14, and possibly 15. An anti-Trump advocate would (is likely to) support statements 1 and 2, and possibly 9. However, the evidence presented here does not support *any* of those statements. They claim too much and are too strong. It would be easy for someone to argue against such unequivocal claims based just on the evidence presented here. Arguing for one of the other **qualified** claims would make your argument more convincing or persuasive than arguing for a yes/no claim, no matter which side you chose to defend.

Qualifying our claims

As people with opinions, we may reach different conclusions to each other despite having access to the same evidence. Depending on our political persuasion, we may need very little evidence to jump to a negative conclusion (1) or a positive one (12). This is why we need to be careful. From the evidence presented, and as discussed above, there is not enough evidence here to draw a straight yes/no conclusion either about collusion or obstruction to justice. Also, as Trump was not interviewed, we cannot determine how much he knew about Russia's involvement. However, it cannot be claimed that the *Trump campaign* knew nothing, as the evidence indicates they did, so it would be wrong to say no conclusions can be drawn at all.

EXAMPLE 3B

Here are three conclusions that *could* be defended, based on the evidence given in Exercise 2.

3. The Trump campaign knew of Russia's interference in the American election.

7. It is likely that the Trump campaign supported Russia's interference in the American election.

10 It is likely that President Trump is guilty of obstructing justice. [We may feel more comfortable supporting the weaker claim 11 (There is a possibility that President Trump is guilty of obstructing justice). However, Trump's publicly documented resistance to sharing information, emails and transcripts indicate a likelihood more than a possibility.]

We cannot say definitely that 12 (The Trump campaign supported Russia's interference in the American election) only that it is likely. We may also want to support 5 (It is likely that the Trump campaign knew of Russia's interference in the America election) rather than 3. However, there is enough evidence to show that they knew of Russia's interference.

We do need to be careful when qualifying, as qualifying too much can mean we say nothing or can even imply the opposite to what we want. Look at these two statements.

There <u>is a possibility</u> that the Trump campaign <u>may</u> have known of Russia's interference in the American election.
There <u>is a possibility</u> that President Trump is <u>not</u> guilty of obstructing justice.

Both statements have been qualified so much they seem to indicate the opposite is true. The first statement intimates that the Trump campaign's awareness of Russian interference is *highly unlikely*. The second statement implies that Trump's innocence is *highly unlikely*, the opposite of what a Trump supporter would want. It is important to choose the right qualifier for what you want to claim and for what you can claim.

Exercise 3

Assess this argument. Is the conclusion warranted?

Mouthwash exercise fear

A study led by the University of Plymouth has found using anti-bacterial mouthwash could reduce the benefits of exercise. Physical exertion is known to lower blood pressure, but the effects are significantly reduced when people use mouthwash instead of water. A team of international scientists said the results showed the importance of oral bacteria in cardiovascular health.

Using inference indicators

Using words like *may, might be, possible* are useful in writing our arguments as they indicate the level of conviction or support we have in our evidence. Using these words weakens our claim but makes what we say more acceptable or persuasive to a reader, if the evidence warrants it.

Sometimes we believe we have enough evidence to make a strong claim.

- The evidence indicates that this is not the case.
- Events in the Middle East show we have to act now to make a difference.
- It is clear that there is a serious problem with the new system.
- The government should increase its support for the elderly.
- We must be hygienic to reduce the spread of infections.

There are other times when the evidence only indicates a likelihood, a probability or a possibility. We need to judge our evidence appropriately and only claim what is justified.

- It may be that...
- There is a likelihood that...
- While it cannot be proven, it is highly likely that...
- The company might choose to take that path but it is less likely given its goals.
- This is a possible outcome.
- We could adopt their method.

Other useful discourse markers

There is a range of different words you can use that indicate the logical connections between your ideas, your attitude to the research you have included and the relationship between the evidence and what you are claiming. These are called logical connectives (and, but, or, either/or, if...then, therefore) and discourse markers. They let the reader know what your position is in relation to the evidence or claims you are presenting.

It is important for your readers to know how you relate the information or evidence you include in your argument to the position you want to argue for. The discourse markers make that relationship clear. Below are some useful examples.

Discourse markers for use in arguments

Citing evidence	Showing disagreement
According to Smith...	In contrast...
Smith claims that...	But...
Smith states that...	On the contrary...
As Smith claims/shows/illustrates,	On the other hand...
This is supported by...	However...
Research findings indicate/ show that...	Contrary to....
This indicates that...	
There is evidence to show that...	
Showing agreement	**Showing disjunction (qualifying)**
Consequently	Despite this...
At the same time...	Although...
As argued...	In spite of this...
As Smith argues...	While...
Further to...	Nevertheless...
In support...	Whereas...
As a consequence...	Regardless of...
Moreover...	Yet...
Furthermore...	Even if, even though...
	By comparison...

Exercise 4

What is the author's position?

Determine what the author's point of view might be, based on their use of language. Can you tell which side they might agree with and how they view the evidence?

1. On one hand, it could be argued that, in this particular case, the facts simply did not meet the requisite threshold to attract protection under section 18C. On the other hand, this case highlights that the law can be a blunt instrument when seeking to set and uphold standards of behaviour.
2. As Norris clearly demonstrates (1985), there is little evidence of the long-term impact of instruction in critical thinking, despite the fact that the vision of such impact is central to the justification of critical thinking instruction.
3. There is some evidence that lacking a language does have an impact on one's capacity to think. However, the extent to which language deficiency stunts cognitive capacities is hard to determine.
4. If there is no deep difference between what can be achieved by a biological brain and what can be achieved by a computer, then it follows that computers can, in theory, emulate human intelligence – and exceed it.
5. Even if all the coal mines and factories using fossil fuels were to shut down by the end of the year, it will still be too late to stop their impact on global warming.

Providing balance and avoiding contradictions

It is important to be aware of the many mistakes we can make, and do make, in our reasoning and, therefore, in our writing. When you critique someone else's written work, whether it is a newspaper article, a web page or an academic paper, you are looking for flaws, oversights or misrepresentations in the writing. You are trying to see if it stands the test of comparison against the critical standard you are measuring it against. This may vary depending on the text. We don't expect the same level of rigour in a newspaper article that we do in an academic paper. Nevertheless, we may still critique it for misrepresenting the evidence or for being biased or for putting forward a flawed argument.

We need to be equally rigorous with our own writing. Having enough evidence is a beginning but it is not the end. It is what we say about that evidence, what we infer from that evidence and the strength of the claims we can make based on that evidence that matters. It is not ignoring evidence that might contradict our ideas but showing how we can accommodate that counter-evidence.

For a balanced position, it is not enough just to say – here is a different opinion or here is some contradictory evidence. When we include an alternative view or piece of contrary information, we have to say something about it to show if we are taking it into account or if we are dismissing it as not important.

To avoid **contradicting** ourselves, any alternative view we include has to be adequately addressed or accommodated.

Look at this concluding passage from a student. The topic was animal vivisection, which can be an emotional and divisive issue. The students were told to make sure they included both sides of an argument to demonstrate their objectivity and to be fair to opposing views.

EXAMPLE 4

Animals for medical research

Using animals for the purposes of medical advancement is inhumane and is not worth the lives of animals. However, medical research is important to the survival of humanity and the use of animals has provided countless positive results. Therefore, the use of animals for medical research is acceptable.

The student has summarised both sides of the argument for and against vivisection. While this might appear to represent a balanced or objective point of view, it has resulted in a *contradiction*. The first sentence says it is inhumane and not worth the lives of the animals; the last sentence says it is acceptable. But you can't have it both ways. You need to reconcile the differences or show why one position outweighs the other or it won't be a persuasive argument.

The problem is that the student has, in their effort to be objective, written the first sentence *as a fact that they agree with.* This makes it hard to deny or critique. Yet their last sentence shows that they want to support the opposite view, the use of vivisection. One way out of this kind of dilemma is to distance oneself from the initial statement. You acknowledge that it is a value statement by saying it is a view held by *some* people (but not necessarily by me, the author).

EXAMPLE 4A

Adjusted vivisection argument

1. *Some people argue that/ It is often claimed that* using animals for the purposes of medical advancement is inhumane and is not worth the lives of animals. 2. Using animals for the purposes of medical advancement is *considered inhumane by animal rights groups and not* worth the lives of animals.

However, medical research is important to the survival of humanity and the use of animals has provided countless positive results. *While it is unfortunate that animals have to suffer, and we should do all we can to minimise that suffering, the results have saved countless lives*. Therefore, the use of animals for medical research is acceptable.

Note how we have inserted an additional sentence to justify the claim and to address the alternative point of view. This is necessary to make the argument more persuasive and less open to criticism. If we argue that a product should be used because it is better for the environment, but it is clear it would cost a lot more, we cannot ignore that point. We would have to justify the additional cost somehow, either by pointing to long-term gains or by showing it is feasible to manage within our budget.

Logical structure of ideas

Interestingly, we can use the same information in Example 3 above to argue for the opposite point of view. This is because evidence itself is not the argument but how we rate or weight that evidence in relation to the claims we make. Note the order the evidence is presented. It starts with the counter claim and then moves to explain why it is wrong. This reversal or change in the logical sequence lets the reader know what your position is in relation to the topic.

EXAMPLE 4B

1. *Many prominent academics argue that* medical research is important to the survival of humanity and *that* the use of animals has provided countless positive results. 2. Medical research is *considered* important to the survival of *humanity and the countless positive results are supposed to justify* the use of animals. *However*, using animals for the purposes of medical advancement is inhumane and is not worth the lives of animals. *No amount of cures can justify their unnecessary suffering*. Therefore, the use of animals for medical research is not acceptable.

EXAMPLE 5

Sequence of ideas

Now look at the ideas as they are set out in the passage below. See how each step builds on the next in a logical sequence that is easy to follow, making the conclusion persuasive and hard to argue against.

We know that the brain is the engine or powerhouse that takes care of all our bodily functions. And we know from comparisons with other animals that it is our distinctively human brain that gives us the special capacities that we have – such as language, art, music, science. This means explanations of our cognitive capacities will be found within the complex neural structures of the brain. All we need to do is identify and isolate those particular systems or neural structures that are responsible for performing those specific cognitive tasks. Once we have identified how they function, it should be theoretically possible to duplicate those functions in a functionally equivalent medium, such as a computer, creating machine cognition (AI). We can begin to see the success of this in our modern computers and programs like Deep Blue, which were modelled on human cognition.

Exercise 5

Try re-organising the sentences below to make a persuasive argument.

What does the evidence support, if anything? Add a conclusion and any other words to demonstrate the relationships between the sentences (ideas).

Many children in Bhutan do not learn or speak English until they attend school.
They do not have an English supporting environment as most families tend to speak only their local dialects at home.
Most teachers lack competent English skills and are unable to teach their lessons effectively. It is a mandate to teach in English in Bhutan.
The usage of English is confined to the classroom for pedagogical reasons only.
The inability by both teachers and students to express themselves comfortably in English seems to hinder meaningful academic learning for students.
The introduction of English as the medium of instruction in schools in Bhutan has had a negative impact on student academic learning.

____
____
____
____
____
____
____
____
____

Chapter summary

- Understanding what makes a strong argument will help you to write one
- An argument will be strong if:
  - The reasons given to support the claim are reliable and relevant
  - The reasons provide sufficient grounds for the claim
  - The premises are connected semantically (meaning) and syntactically (in a logical way).
- Evidence alone does not make a persuasive argument; it is the way the evidence is related to the claim that makes it an argument.
- Writing an argument is writing a record of the process you used to come to your conclusion. This includes your reasoning.
- Do not ignore counter-evidence. Include it and argue against it to show why it doesn't count.
- Choose the appropriate language to indicate your position in relation to your evidence or counter evidence.

Answers to Exercises 1–7

Exercise 1

When researching decreasing cognitive capacities in the elderly, Carzine found a study that claimed social, verbal and personal judgements improved with age... She decided to... argue that there needed to be a complete re-think about older people's cognitive capacities.

Carzine needs to be careful about coming to a hasty conclusion based on limited evidence (one study). First, the study she refers to may have a vested interest in putting forward positive views on aging. It is also contrary to other research on aging, which is cause for alarm. The capacities displayed (judging individuals as dishonest or bright, better at storytelling than other age groups) are not just difficult to measure objectively but are odd measures of cognition. They fall outside the standard tests for diminishing cognition (memory, attention, problem-solving, decision making). She does not have enough evidence to come to her conclusion.

Exercise 2

Summary of the Mueller report, redacted version – 'the investigation "identified numerous links between the Russian Government and the Trump campaign", found that Russia "perceived it would benefit from a Trump presidency" and that the 2016 Trump presidential campaign "expected it would benefit electorally" from Russian hacking efforts. However, ultimately "the investigation did not establish that members of the Trump campaign conspired or coordinated with the Russian Government in its election interference activities". The evidence was not necessarily complete due to encrypted, deleted, or unsaved communications as well as false, incomplete, or declined testimony. The report "does not conclude that the president committed a crime", but specifically did not exonerate Trump on obstruction of justice, because investigators were not confident that Trump was innocent after examining his intent and actions'.

Exercise 3

In this newspaper article, the claim (anti-bacterial mouthwash could reduce the benefits of exercise) is too strong. The evidence provided indicates that mouthwash counteracts the reduction of blood pressure resulting from exercise. A reduction in blood pressure, however, is only one of the benefits of exercise, so the claim is misleading. This is quite typical of the way newspapers report on research findings. The important finding is the role of oral bacteria in maintaining health.

Exercise 4

Can we work out what position the author might hold, based on their use of language?

- Although the author puts forward two positions in relation to 18C, the language choice indicates that the first one is only a potential position (it *could* be argued), indicating the author is not convinced; the second, however, has a more definite tone (this case *highlights*) and that the law *can be* a blunt instrument. The author favours the second view.
- When an author says 'as x argues' or 'as Norris…demonstrates', they are agreeing with that author's position, even though (*despite the fact* that) there may be other evidence to the contrary that they acknowledge.
- Here the author is acknowledging an alternative view or counter evidence, although note the use of 'some' which shows the reader that the author does not find it sufficient. The use of 'however' makes it clear that they take a different view and may disagree.
- This is a conditional or hypothetical 'if…then' statement. If the first part is true, then so is the second as it is a consequence of the first. Given the author then adds 'and exceed it', it is likely they agree with the consequence but they may not. The statement is not necessarily the author's view.
- This statement is also hypothetical as it is about a possibility, but the outcome is not conditional. The 'even if' is a clear indicator that the author discounts the effect of any action on the outcome. The choice of 'will' shows the author believes that global warming is inevitable regardless of our actions.

Exercise 5

There will not be just one way to organise these sentences as the order will depend on what you will be arguing for.

In Bhutan there is a mandate to teach in English. *There is evidence that* the introduction of English as the medium of instruction in schools in Bhutan has had a negative impact on student academic learning. Many children in Bhutan do not learn or speak English until they attend school. They do not have an English supporting environment as most families tend to speak only their local dialects at home. *At the same time*, the usage of English is confined to the classroom for pedagogical reasons only. *Because* most teachers lack competent English skills, they are unable to teach their lessons effectively. *This* inability by both teachers and students to express themselves comfortably in English seems to hinder meaningful academic learning for students. *In light of this, Bhutan should reconsider its mandate for teaching to be in English only. If, however, Bhutan wants to continue its mandate, it will need to look at ways to improve the English competence of both staff and students.*

CHAPTER

10

Writing (Critical) Literature Reviews

Addressing 'the literature'

There are a lot of bogus claims out in the world that we need to be aware of and know how to argue against. It is not good for any society to base their policies and practices on false beliefs. At the same time, legitimate cutting-edge research is being conducted all around us in all fields of expertise, and some of the findings will contradict current established beliefs. It is our job, as critical thinkers, to sort the wheat from the chaff. We do this by making sure claims are well supported by reliable evidence and that research is conducted properly such that the claims drawn from that research stand up to scrutiny. Literature reviews play a critical part in this process.

In Chapter 7 we discussed how to critique a piece of writing by focusing on how to critique or review a single (academic) article. The emphasis was on how well the article did what it said it would do, considering what we know about what makes a good argument and a good piece of research. In Chapter 8, we explored how research is conducted and what mistakes to look out for to ensure the findings are reliable. As well as understanding and evaluating a single article on its own merits, in terms of how well or not it puts forward a convincing, well-supported argument that contributes to knowledge, we are also likely to examine that single article in light of what we already know about the topic. We would evaluate it against other similar articles we had read on the same topic and then critically review it according to its contribution to that broader field of study.

Critical questions to evaluate an article's contribution to the field

- Did the article add to your knowledge of the topic?
- Did it give a thorough background to or discussion of the issues?
- Did it discuss something new or present a new perspective?
- Did it solve the problem it set out to?
- Did it clarify a point of view or perspective on an issue?
- Did it make you think differently about something?
- Did it confirm a previous approach?
- Did it make you question a previous idea or approach?

Any single article on a given topic is actually part of a much bigger **body of literature** in that field of research. What we call 'the literature' represents what other people have to say about a topic of research. It not only incorporates the body of accepted knowledge and the current state of research in the field, but it represents the current debates: it identifies the issues and existing problems, and it points to new directions.

The **literature** in a field represents what researchers believe to be the case, based on their own research and the research of others, past and present.

The literature as a tapestry telling a story

It is useful to think of the literature as a rich tapestry (rather like the Bayeux Tapestry, which depicts the events leading to the French invasion of England in 1066). All the events and key players that were part of the story are woven together to depict the story, from the beginning to the end. Similarly, all the research in any given field tells the story of what we used to think and why, and how that thinking or knowledge has evolved to the present position or story today. Each piece of research, each finding, fact, theory, idea, dispute and discussion has its place in the tapestry, big or small. There will be the mainstream views (main picture) which represent the consensus of opinion and research findings, past research (background events) that has informed current thinking, ideas (activities) around the peripheries of the main topic and new directions or challenges (foreground) that are starting to change the way we see or understand phenomena in the field. Major and minor disputes can also be depicted as part of the overall state of research at any given point.

When reviewing or critiquing the literature on any topic, it is necessary to understand how all the pieces fit together to form the tapestry, the story. Think where an idea fits; which camp it is in and how many supporters it has. Think who the revolutionaries are and what they are doing; think about why some ideas have won and others have lost or are no longer relevant.

A literature review is an overview and critical review of a body of work (the literature) on the same topic or field of study. It identifies the prevailing theories and hypotheses, what questions are being asked and why, and what possible answers have been suggested.

The main players

Unlike a review of a single article, a literature review requires you to understand who the key authors or **seminal writers** are and to understand their contribution to the development of ideas in that field. Why are they important? Why does everyone else refer to them, even if their work is outdated? What did they, or do they, contribute to our understanding of the phenomena under discussion? What battles have been fought and won, or lost?

You also need to be aware of current authors' affiliations with particular writers and their theories. Authors who contribute to the body of literature under review will often locate themselves in a place in that field by identifying what positions or other authors they agree with (or disagree with), what **theoretical framework** they identify with or are using and whether they are confirming current practice, critiquing the mainstream, exploring the peripheries or trying something new. When you write your review, you need to show that you are aware of their influence and position within the field. Where in the story or tapestry do they locate themselves? Where do *you* locate them?

The role of any literature review is to:

- Recognise and acknowledge the work and achievements of others (key theorists, researchers, scholars)
- Demonstrate that you understand what is known in a particular field
- Demonstrate that you have conducted thorough research on a topic, including addressing different views
- Describe and explain how knowledge in the field has developed and accumulated over time
- Clarify how different pieces of the research fit together
- Explain how your own research (topic) is connected to what is already known
- Explain how your own research is justified as needing to be done

Types of literature reviews

You cannot do successful or fruitful research unless you understand the literature and what others have done in the field. The literature review is the foundation for good research; the more thorough the review the more successful the research will be. First, identify what your aim is. Why are you writing the review? What is its purpose?

- ***Is it an introduction to an article or essay?***
  If the review is to introduce an issue or topic under discussion, then it will have a clear purpose. It should be structured to tell a particular story. This will make it narrower than a general informative review. You choose your literature carefully to convey specific points. This will be the context or background to the issue, why it is a problem, what has been done and what you intend to do to address the problem. You relate your intention to what has been done elsewhere as conveyed in the literature and justify your approach using the literature. You will point out whether or not you have any issues with the literature in relation to your topic, such as the researchers' approaches, their findings or interpretations, their limitations or any biases.
- ***Is it a standalone exercise?***
  Sometimes we write a review to give a thorough overview of a topic to understand what has happened, what issues have changed and where we now are in relation to our understanding of an issue. This kind of review will be quite broad and general. It may identify contrasting positions and what the source of disagreement is but will not necessarily resolve them. It should indicate where major gaps are and what research needs to be conducted to address them. It should evaluate and critique the literature it presents.

- ***Is it part of a thesis?***
  This is a special kind of literature review, which is used to showcase the breadth and depth of your research, as well as the breadth and depth of your understanding of the topic you are researching. Your review will both identify the gaps in the literature and how your research will fill one or some of those gaps. It should also be clear why the research is being done (significance) and why you choose the methods you do to conduct your research. It should give a comprehensive evaluation and critique of the literature, outlining what you see as limitations, controversies, disagreements, mis-directions.

Make sure the focus is on the literature (or an author) and not just the topic. Have a look at the examples below to see the contrast between a purely descriptive piece and a literature review. In Example 1, the focus is on the content or topic. Even though it refers to the work of several authors on the same topic, it is not a review of the literature. Example 2, however, focuses on what the *literature* is discussing about the topic, rather than the topic itself. Note the change in language and referencing. Note also an evaluative or critical approach in Example 2.

EXAMPLE 1

Topic-focussed, descriptive writing

The brain is the most complex structure that we know of (Chalmers 1996). It contains approximately 100 billion neurons, each with some 3000 synaptic connections with other neurons (some have 100,000, some a lot less) making a possible 100 trillion synaptic connections (10^{14})· Neurons are also constantly firing at different levels of activation. If each connection can realise one of a possible ten different activation levels at any one time, this adds up to a possible $10^{100,000,000,000,000}$ distinct neural states (Dennett 2003). The picture is further complicated by the intricate layering of neural banks and the presence of neural chemicals in the nervous system which can affect the activation levels of groups of neurons (O'Brien 2010).

EXAMPLE 2

Literature-focussed critical writing

The literature on critical thinking makes much of the fact that there are a multitude of definitions. Moore (2011) gives a comprehensive overview of the definitional issues and the key players in the field. Four writers in particular have shaped the discourse on critical thinking. Facione's broad definition is the most cited (1990), followed by the continually evolving Paul and Elder framework (2016). Ennis' work (2015) has also been influential, particularly in the workplace. More recent players, however, have been critical of some of the earlier frameworks, claiming their definitions are too narrow (Thayer-Bacon 2015). Thayer-Bacon's critique is supported by Gurin et al. (2012), who see critical thinking as a social practice rather than just cognitive.

Writing a literature review

The hardest task in any literature review is choosing what literature you include. There is so much, and you cannot include it all, so you must make choices. Your choices will be driven by what it is you want your literature review to say. What aspect of the literature on your topic are you writing about? What is the story you want to tell? What do you need to include such that your story makes sense and your research approach is justified?

Never just describe the literature (such as Jones said this, Nuygen claimed that). Make it clear why each piece of literature has been included and what it demonstrates.

Choosing the right text

Ask yourself, what role does this article play in the review? What is the point I want to make and which article or articles make that point?

- Does it provide historical or background information?
- Does it set the context of the study?
- Does it represent the current state of research in the field?
- Is it a seminal text?
- Does it identify the problem?
- Does it justify your methodology or approach?
- Does it indicate disagreement with your thesis statement?

Structuring the review

- Make it clear what the literature is demonstrating
  - Who are the main theorists/researchers?
  - What are the critical issues? The debates?
  - How have they been resolved/not resolved?
- Make it clear what you are arguing for in the review
  - What is your research question?
  - How does it fit within the field of research?
  - What/who supports your approach?
  - Why is it significant? Unique? Novel?
  - Is your review organised to demonstrate this convincingly and logically?

The literature review should have a logical structure – articles are **sorted and synthesised** around themes, **analysed** in relation to issues and approaches, and **evaluated and critiqued** for contribution and quality.

When we apply critical thinking to the literature in a field, we do more than just critique, even though that is an important part of our analysis. We think about and evaluate all aspects of the literature deeply so that we can do the following:

- Pick out and identify the main themes, trends, movements (sort and synthesise)
- Show the state of research at this time (summarise, synthesise)
- Identify current issues (analyse, evaluate)
- Identify and explain current debates (analyse, evaluate)
- Point out any relevant issues arising from the literature and their impact on the topic (critique)
- Evaluate other approaches to the issues, discuss pros/cons (critique)
- Explain and justify connection to your own research (evaluate)
- Argue for your position in relation to the literature (critique)

EXAMPLE 3

Overview or synthesis

What counts as Postcolonialism is hotly debated within the literature in topics like critical cultural studies, sociology and social geography. Social theorists such as Smith et al. (2004) claim South Africa and Algeria are typical examples of postcolonial countries, while others (Hodge 1998; Jones 2004) include settler countries such as Australia. Hoge (2003), on the other hand, argues that the term postcolonial should only be used in reference to *indigenous* struggles in countries such as Australia, Canada and New Zealand.

EXAMPLE 4

Comparing and contrasting the literature

However, while the studies of Ostrom et al (1993) and Fisman and Gatti (2000) show strong evidence of an overall positive effect of decentralisation on the reduction of corruption, many questions and issues remain. For instance, the analysis in Fisman and Gatti does not distinguish among the types of decentralisation that may be undertaken by governments. This means the correlation between decentralisation and corruption will vary from country to country. Prud Homme (1995, p. 214) observed that 'most discussions of decentralization... ignore geography', while in fact geography can be an important factor in the decentralisation process.

EXAMPLE 5

Analysing the literature

Although Dennett (1993) does not directly address the debate on what constitutes personal identity, his claims about the self reflect the central concerns of that debate. This means a parallel can be drawn between what he says about identity and what Parfit says (1996). Both argue that identity is strongly related to memory.

EXAMPLE 6

Critiquing the literature

One shortcoming of the research on reducing obesity is its assumption of individual choice. According to Hamish (2007), this leads to treatments that focus on changing individual behaviours, rather than societal factors. This may explain why such programs have only limited, short-term success. For example, the program cited in Jones (2009) did manage to reduce the weight of four students but it did not result in an overall weight loss for the group.

Most common complaints from lecturers and thesis examiners

- ***'I couldn't tell which ideas were yours and which belonged to other people'.***

  When we write, we refer to what other people have said and done to support our point of view (the literature). This is where our evidence comes from to justify our claims. Sometimes it is hard to know how we can write our own ideas when all our information is coming from other people's work. How do we include our own voice? How do we show what we think? This is done through our *choice of language* (refer also to Chapter 9). In particular, it is demonstrated by how we discuss the literature, what we say about it and by making it clear what our evaluation is. It should be evident to the reader that you have read the literature, processed it and produced your own ideas about it. You should have value added to the literature by including your understanding and critique.
- ***It is just a list of articles reviews (descriptive with no synthesis, no analysis and no critique).***

  Your lecturers will know the literature better than you, so they don't want a regurgitation of the text; make sure you are not just describing what someone has already said but that you are saying something interesting about it. Identify and summarise the themes running through the literature and acknowledge the emergence of new trends. Ensure you say what kind of contribution a research article makes or how it differs from or is similar to someone else's position. Note what position the author is writing from and how this may have impacted on their interpretation or viewpoint. Acknowledge whether or not the views are problematic, interesting or significant. Most of all, make it clear why you have chosen these particular texts and explain how they relate to your research or topic. All of this will demonstrate that you are thinking critically about the literature. It also demonstrates your voice.

You demonstrate critical thinking by how you **evaluate and discuss** the literature. Comment on the literature as you go, making it clear what you think about it and why.

Choosing the right critical language

There are several ways we can refer to the literature (but always by quoting, paraphrasing or summarising from a given text):

- We can write it as fact where the author is referred to indirectly.
- We can write it as fact where the author is referred to directly.
- We can write it as a finding where the author is referred to indirectly.
- We can write it as a finding where the author is referred to directly.
- We can write it as an opinion or point of view where the author is referred to directly.

EXAMPLE 7

The verbs used here show you support the author's findings.

- Research shows that... (Deng 2012; Woolcott 2010; Hazam et al. 2007)
- Another study (Deng and Huan 2015) found that...
- A comprehensive study by Deng (2012), demonstrated that...
- As Deng (2012) indicates...

Be careful how you refer to the findings in the literature. If you write something as fact, then you are indicating your support or agreement. It is hard to then critique it or evaluate it in some way. As in Example 7, if you say *'research shows...'* then you are telling the reader you accept this claim as fact or knowledge. If you say *'as Deng suggests...'* then you are telling the reader that you agree with Deng (refer to Chapter 9).

Referring to authors *directly* can create a distance between their statements and our own views which allows **space for critique.**

If you want space to critique or comment on the research or views of authors, then you need to pay attention to how you refer to their work. Choose the right form and language to suit your purpose. The examples below allow space for comment.

EXAMPLE 8

Directly referring to authors' work does not commit you to accepting their claims

- According to Deng (2012)..., However...
- Deng claims that..., but another study...
- An early study found that... These findings have not been replicated.
- While Deng's study seems to indicate..., there is evidence that...

Exercise 1

Can you tell what the author thinks?

1. As of February 2015, Uniqlo had 842 Japanese domestic stores and 716 international stores outside Japan in 15 countries (Tateyama 2016).
2. A study into sweatshop practices in Bangladesh (Cooper 2013) found evidence of widespread abuse and unhealthy working conditions.
3. Uniqlo's business model is attractive to Asian consumers but not to Westerners (Kimura 2014).
4. According to Brasar (2011), the primary role of Uniqlo stores in the West is image making to Asian consumers.
5. Albareda (2013) argues that workers' rights tend to be ignored in many developing countries, which raises ethical issues for the fashion industry.

Sample review

Note the choice of language in the review below. The author has synthesised, analysed and evaluated writers on evolutionary epistemology, grouping them according to their position or their critique of a position. The author critiques and evaluates the current status of the debate in the literature and offers a possible way out.

A short literature review with critique

Evolutionary epistemology has become bound up with **a complex knot of disputes**. Amongst **those who favour the Darwinian paradigm**, **some have argued** that the claims of a Lamarckian component in sociocultural change rest on a distorted understanding of Lamarck's ideas (Hull 1982, 1988). **Others have accepted** that some aspects are Lamarckian – or at least non-Darwinian – but **have not seen this as vitally important** (Popper 1975, 1979; Toulmin 1972; Campbell 1979), while **their critics consider that this admission undermines** the whole enterprise (Cohen 1973, 1974; Losee 1977). Several theorists have offered generalised versions of Darwinian theory (Popper 1975; Toulmin 1972; Hull 1988); **a move which plunges us into** the problems surrounding the nature of the 'evolutionary units' involved. This sketch of **the tangle of issues suggests that**, if they are to be resolved, we need to stand back and **examine the fundamental concepts of change** in general and evolutionary change, followed by an investigation of the kinds of process or mechanism that can produce them.

Synthesising

Analysing

Analysing

Evaluating

Critiquing

Chapter summary

- The literature in a field represents what researchers believe to be the case, based on their own research and the research of others, past and present.
- A literature review is an overview and critical review of a body of work (the literature) on the same topic or field of study. It identifies the prevailing theories and hypotheses, what questions are being asked and why, and what possible answers have been suggested.
- You demonstrate critical thinking by evaluating the literature. Comment on the literature as you go, making it clear what you think about it and why.
- Never just describe the literature (such as Jones said this, Nuygen claimed that). Make it clear why each piece of literature is there.

Answers to Exercise 1

1. *As of February 2015, Uniqlo had 842 Japanese domestic stores and 716 international stores outside Japan in 15 countries (Tateyama 2016).* This is a statement of fact. The indirect reference tells us the author accepts this statement at face value. We use facts to make a point but this is not referring to the literature.
2. *A study into sweatshop practices in Bangladesh (Cooper 2013) found evidence of widespread abuse and unhealthy working conditions.* This is referring to research findings, not the literature. The author appears to accept this study as it is written as fact.
3. *Uniqlo's business model is attractive to Asian consumers but not to Westerners (Kimura 2014).* This statement is written as if it were fact (author is referred to *indirectly*), which indicates the author agrees with it. However, it expresses an opinion or value judgement that would need to be argued for. It does not refer to the literature.
4. *According to Brasar (2011), the primary role of Uniqlo stores in the West is image making to Asian consumers.* This expresses an opinion, which would need argument. The author may or may not agree with it.
5. *Albareda (2013) argues that workers' rights tend to be ignored in many developing countries, which raises ethical issues for the fashion industry.* Although this is an opinion, it may be justified (argued). It is not definite that the author agrees with it but the second part of the sentence suggests that they may accept the truth of the claim (i.e. if true, then...).

CHAPTER

11

Critical Thinking as Critical Self-Reflection

Thinking critically about oneself

Developing critical thinking skills is not easy. It requires hard work and paying attention to one's thinking. As well as being aware of what makes a statement a sound claim and why, one has to also be aware of one's own reasoning skills and their limitations. The prior chapters in this book have presented a range of techniques you can use to make yourself a better critical thinker. Many of those techniques are about understanding how we think, why we judge situations the way we do and how these influences can be moderated and our critical thinking capacity improved. Being aware of the barriers to good critical thinking can help us overcome them.

- Think about how knowledge is constructed and why we accept some claims rather than others.
- Be aware of the physical/perceptual limitations we have as humans and their impact on how things may appear.
- Be aware of the cognitive limitations we have and their impact on how we reason.
- Be conscious of the role our own experiences and biases play in how we see and judge the world around us.

Critical thinking is **purposeful**. It has an outcome. It is about coming to the best decision we can in any given set of circumstances, and knowing **why** it was the best decision.

Very few of us are aware of how much our beliefs and values influence how we see the world and the way we judge or interpret information. Our beliefs can prevent us from seeing what is really there (or make us see things that aren't there!) and our values can influence what we judge as important or inessential, right or wrong (refer to Chapter 2).

At the same time, we cannot ignore the influence of our past experiences in shaping our particular perspectives. We judge current situations based on those experiences. We jump to conclusions and generalise too quickly. We are prone to stereotyping. We impose our value systems and beliefs on others and judge their behaviour from within that framework.

While we may not be able to view the world completely objectively, given our singular perspective, we can strive to have a more open and balanced view. This requires us to acknowledge that we *have* a perspective and that it may be playing a bigger role in our cognitive processing than we think (refer to Chapter 3).

Engaging in **critical self-reflection** is the single most important strategy we can apply if we want to become a critical thinker.

Having a critical thinking disposition

Some people argue that applying a few rules in the right place won't make someone a critical thinker. They argue that no amount of skill will make someone a critical thinker if they don't have the **right disposition** (Ennis, 1987; Abrami et al, 2008).

There is some truth to this belief. If we just want to prove a point or get our own way, then we will never be good critical thinkers. Our thinking will be biased towards a fixed outcome, irrespective of the evidence. What we need to do is be as objective and as rigorous in our thinking as possible. We don't have complete knowledge and we cannot always see the consequences of our decisions. No one is right 100% of the time. And sometimes **there is no right or wrong**, just difference. To be a critical thinker we must genuinely want to seek out the truth, regardless of its consequences to ourselves.

Critical thinking requires us to sometimes **override self interest** in the name of truth and honesty. Always be truthful to yourself and don't be afraid to be wrong.

Critical thinking is not just about assessing information sources or critiquing claims and arguments to see how reliable they might be. While it is essential to be able to tease our thinking apart to examine it, we also need to be able to evaluate the quality of our thinking, by ensuring we minimise potentially negative tendencies.

Ideal critical thinkers embody intellectual empathy, humility, perseverance, integrity and responsibility.

This is why critical thinking and **critical self-reflection** go hand-in-hand. We have to pay attention to our thinking and decision making to ensure we are not being misled by past events or personal bias. In order to become critical thinkers, we need to consciously evaluate the potential impact our cognitive limitations and biases have on how we judge or react to a situation. We need to be **self-aware**.

Do you have a critical thinking disposition? A self-reflective exercise

Exercise 1

Questions to ask yourself (honestly!)

- Do you tend to take the leadership role in your circle?
- Are you the one who has read the text and knows the answers?
- Do people listen to you?
- Do you feel you know more than others in your circle?
- Do you readily give your opinion?
- Do you feel you are right most of the time?
- Do you argue the point without conceding ground?
- Do you find it hard to accept you might be wrong?
- Do you wait impatiently for someone else to finish talking?
- Do you interrupt frequently?
- Do you have to be asked to share your opinion?
- Are you easily persuaded that you might be wrong?
- Do you feel others know more than you?
- Do you listen carefully to what others say?
- Do you acknowledge when someone has made a legitimate point?
- Do you concede that others may have a different point of view?
- Do you carefully consider both sides of a debate before expressing a view?

This exercise (or something similar) is good to do in a group. It can help group dynamics and discussion. Each member rates both themselves and each other person in the group with simple **yes/no/sometimes** responses on separately named sheets. Each person then collects all the responses that are about themselves. Responses are anonymous but the results should be open and shared. This can be challenging but does throw some light on how others see us compared to how we might see ourselves. If, for example, you answered the same as the group to most of these questions, then this shows you are self-aware and are more likely to be able to critically self-reflect. If others answered 'yes' or 'no' to most of these questions on your behalf, and you didn't, then this may indicate your image of yourself differs widely from how others see you. This is cause for some targeted self-reflection and group discussion.

It should be clear that the traits in the exercise are neither all negative or all positive. They are mixed and some are neutral. As part of the exercise, the group needs to discuss what they feel about some of the traits. Which traits do they see as positive and which as negative? Are there other questions they feel should be added? This kind of discussion is beneficial for group dynamics so that everyone's expectations are met.

Importantly, any major group-versus-individual differences need to be discussed. Self-reflective questions to consider are:

- What is it about my behaviour that led the group to think this about me?
- Why did I respond differently?
- Why do I think I know more than others?
- Why do I think others know more than me?
- Why do I think my opinion is not important or as legitimate as someone else's?
- How could I change my behaviour to accommodate their feedback?
- What could I do to make others feel differently about me?

The need for critical self-reflection

Critical self-reflection is an important component of critical thinking. It has become an essential tool in some disciplines of study, in particular those disciplines that lead to professional qualifications in the human sciences/human services – i.e. social work; education; nursing and midwifery. These areas of study will often have a work-related placement requirement as part of the qualification. Self-reflective reporting on that placement experience is an essential part of the assessment. There are two key aspects to this critically self-reflective process:

- Critically reflecting on the relevance and application of discipline knowledge to practice
- Critically reflecting on our own performance and application of knowledge to practice

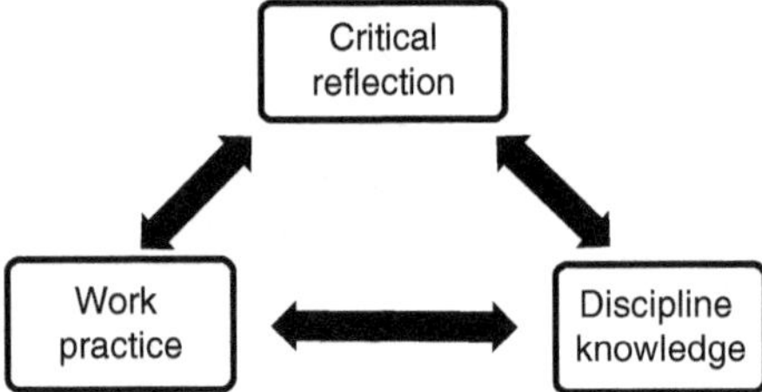

Importance of understanding epistemology and its relation to practice

To be able to reflect on and apply our knowledge effectively in the workplace, we need an understanding of the process of knowledge creation – how we know what we know, and how/why we know that we know it – epistemology (refer back to Chapters 1–4). It is essential we understand why we believe certain things or engage in certain practices now, and why we no longer believe in or engage in other practices anymore. Understanding *why* those knowledge claims either stand or change over time enables us to understand the link between that knowledge and its application in and to practice.

As practitioners, we need to understand the relationship between knowledge, theory and practice. We need to know **why** we do x rather than y.

Knowledge has changed over time and this has had implications in a wide range of practical areas. There are past practices in all the human services that we no longer engage in and other newer practices we have adopted and incorporated as standard current practice. Think of the changes to medical practice over the last 100 years. Practice has changed in line with changes to our knowledge and the subsequent development of supportive technologies. As practitioners, we need to know **and understand** why things are as they are now.

EXAMPLE 1

Changes to practice over time

1. The use of corporal punishment in educational practice.
2. The awareness of social determinants to health in social work practice.
3. The acknowledgement and acceptance of mental health as a medical health issue in psychology.
4. The acknowledgement of postpartum depression and its consequences in midwifery practice.
5. The impact of trust and quality care on healing in nursing practice.
6. The acknowledgement of legitimate alternative gender categories (LGBTQ) in all areas of practice.
7. The right to equal treatment and access to mainstream services of people with disabilities.

Exercise 2

Try to think of two (other) changes to our knowledge or understanding in your field of study that have had an impact on how we practice in that field. What are they? What was the reason for the change? Why is it considered better than before?

Caution: some changes are purely economic so make sure there is a justifiable epistemological rationale for the change.

The examples above are just a selection of changes that have had a major impact on accepted practice in various fields of the human services professions. There are many more. One can see that practice changes in line with our increase in knowledge and understanding. Knowing why practice has changed, why we engage in one practice rather than another, will enable us to justify that practice should we need to. We should also know why it works and **why it works better** than past practice.

A *non-reflective* practitioner only enacts a practice because they have rote-learnt what to do and how to do it. They do not know why they do it. They will not understand that a particular intervention or practice may solve a problem most of the time, but not all of the time. Simply applying a set of problem-solving heuristics or tried-and-true methods to any and all situations without reflection will not always be successful. When dealing with humans in dynamic real-world contexts, it is unlikely that two situations will be completely identical. Each will require a different solution.

If we understand why a practice works, we can think critically about its application in a particular context and decide whether it might work more effectively if applied differently or to a different but related problem. It will help us understand why it may not work as well, or at all, in another related situation. We can improvise or adapt to suit the context.

Thinking critically and reflectively helps reduce our mistakes and the probability of doing something wrong. We don't just do what we do because that is what we have always done; past practice or tradition is not necessarily best practice. As humans, we can (and do) make mistakes; we can be, and have been, wrong.

We need to **be flexible** in our practice and in our beliefs so that we can change practice in light of new convincing evidence.

Current practice is not fixed and may also change in the future. Our knowledge is finite, not infinite. Just as in the past, some of what we currently accept as true may turn out to be false. Consequently, it is important to continually check and question our practice. We cannot be rigid or closed-minded. Having **an open mind** is a positive critical thinking trait.

We should **keep up-to-date** with current research to ensure our beliefs and the claims we make within our professional field still hold.

Critically reflective thinkers apply their knowledge through their practice, critically observe the results of their actions, and reflect on the effectiveness of that practice (and their experience) as they go. They analyse and question. They don't always accept a situation or solution at face value or because someone says this is what should be done. They want to know why or why not.

Reflecting on our knowledge, practice and cultural differences

Our practices have not just changed because of new research findings, new drugs or technology. They have also been influenced by our changing social/cultural context. Natural disasters and political upheaval around the world, globalisation, the internationalisation of universities, skills-based immigration policies and an influx of refugees have led to large numbers of culturally, religiously and linguistically diverse people being thrown together.

People from different cultures have different values, beliefs and practices. They bring different information and ideas, they use different approaches and treatments, and they have different understandings and attitudes towards work, education, health and family (Parker and Egege, 2019).

Critical self-reflection is essential in assessing our reactions to challenging situations, culturally diverse groups and **alternative practices** or social norms.

While cultural diversity enriches our society, it can lead to conflict *because* of the diversity of beliefs and values. We need to be aware of and be prepared for this diversity and what it may mean for our practice, any practice. Confronting social or cultural diversity unprepared or **unreflectively** can increase the risk of misunderstandings and mistakes. As practicing critical thinkers and members of a diverse society, we should all,

- Be aware of and reflect on our own cultural and social beliefs and values and know how these can impact on our work practice. A lack of such reflection can lead to ill-informed actions and inappropriate interventions through misunderstandings and cultural/social stereotyping.
- Be aware of the cultural and social values and beliefs of our clients/students/colleagues and how these may impact on *their* practices and *their* understanding of our practices. Acknowledging difference can help understanding and prevent problems arising through misunderstandings or miscommunication.
- Be cognisant of our epistemic beliefs and practices to see how these impact on what is considered good practice in our field. Our reactions to or judgements of our clients/students/colleagues should be epistemically rather than culturally/socially informed. This makes an understanding of our own epistemological framework and knowledge of the evidence that grounds our practice highly relevant.

Exercise 3

Is a belief in the virtue of cleanliness cultural or scientific? Assess in light of the statements below.

- There is scientific evidence that *washing our hands* properly with soap can prevent the spread of germs, such as colds, influenza and gastric infections (as well as viruses such as COVID19).
- There is evidence that living in squalor with rotting food and animal faeces encourages vermin and bacteria that spread disease.
- Cleanliness has been aligned to purity of mind and good character (*cleanliness is next to godliness*) in many cultures. Dirt or dirtiness is aligned to lack of self-respect and poor moral values (having a clean or dirty mind). Think of the contrasting virtues attached to the colours white and black.
- Cleanliness is culturally associated with higher class and status. The working class had dirty jobs and often 'smelt'. The poor were always dirty.
- Cleanliness was used as a sign of the superior Western civilisation. Some African and Asian cultures were denigrated as 'uncivilised' for not using soap, for living in 'dirt' houses, for washing infrequently, or for using dirt, cow dung or urine to clean themselves.

- Recent scientific evidence shows that washing too much (every day) can make us vulnerable to skin problems because it removes the colonies of good bacteria that prevent infections and skin irritations. Washing hair too often gets rid of the natural oils.
- Overuse of household cleansers prevents exposure to germs, preventing children's immune systems from functioning properly, and making them prone to allergies.
- Exposure to dirt (even eating dirt) encourages our immune systems to develop and build antibodies, reducing the risk of allergies.

Exercise 4

Cultural difference and nutrition

A student from China was studying nutrition and dietetics and was asked to design a healthy breakfast for an aged care facility. At home, a typical breakfast might be a chicken congee (rice porridge), dumplings and fried dough sticks with green tea. Or it could be savoury tofu crepes, soy milk and a range of fruit and vegetables that are not easily accessible outside China. Dairy products are not common in China but the student knew dairy was important in the Western diet. She decided to substitute cinnamon doughnuts for the fried dough sticks, added pork dumplings and put in an iced coffee for the dairy. She failed her assignment.

What are the cultural issues here for the student? Can you think of any cultural assumptions the lecturer may have made? How could the matter have been dealt with differently?

As critical thinkers and critical self-reflectors, we should all be aware of our own cultural and social biases and how these might influence how we react to others who have different biases. These beliefs and biases become critically important when we are dealing with a **diverse clientele** in our work practice or profession. If our colleagues are also from diverse backgrounds then we need to be aware of any potential conflicts or misunderstandings that could result from those differences. As a self-reflective native speaker, we should also pay attention to and reflect on our use of language. Not everyone will have the same competence.

- Don't assume parallel linguistic competence in non-native speakers
- Pay attention to your use of acronyms and explain them if necessary
- Reflect on your use of culturally-specific metaphors and analogies
- Watch your pronunciation and use of colloquial expressions
- Speak clearly and at a sensible speed

The above reflective guidelines apply to all workplaces, practices and professions, including studying at university. Many of the classrooms and forums we participate in will be composed of people from culturally and linguistically diverse (CALD) social and educational backgrounds. We need to reflect on how those differences can impact on communication and understanding of ideas. Some professional study areas focus explicitly on critical self-reflection as an assessable part of the course, particularly as part of a compulsory placement.

Self-reflective practice in nursing

Nursing education is one of the key disciplinary areas that demand critical self-reflection. Nurses are considered more than functionaries and nursing is not just a matter of applying facts to processes. Nurses are responsible for patient care in the broadest sense. This takes into account the mental, social and physical health and well-being of their patients. Nursing practice draws on epistemological knowledge, personal experience, close observations, and intuitions which develop over time through self-reflective practice.

> Self-reflection enables the nurse practitioner to identify health and illness problems; to learn the skills and strategies needed to assess the unique circumstances of each situation; to select the **best choice of interventions**; and to develop the ability to evaluate the effectiveness of the interventions chosen.

More importantly, self-reflection helps the nurse practitioner improve the standard of their care. The nurse practitioner does this by asking critical questions of themselves, often retrospectively.

- What did I identify as the main issue with patient x?
- Was I right? What influenced my thinking? Was there another issue I should have noticed?
- How was my assessment related to what I had been told of patient x's health problem? Would my assessment have changed if I had examined the patient myself and applied my own knowledge?
- Did I make any assumptions about patient x that may have impacted on my treatment or assessment?
- Were these assumptions correct or justified?
- How did my behaviour impact on patient x?
- Was my treatment appropriate in the circumstances?
- On reflection, could I have acted differently? What would I have changed?
- For the future, what do I need to be aware of with my own thinking and behaviour that may have an impact on patients in my care?

Nursing is a profession that deals with a diverse and problematic clientele. As nurse practitioners we need to be aware of our own cultural and social values and how these may come into conflict with those of our clients. Our clients are vulnerable, stressed and anxious; they may be facing a period of disability or even a terminal illness. They may not speak the language or be familiar with the practices of a hospital. It is our role to put the patient's well-being first. This means dealing with families and friends of patients appropriately and sensitively, and relevant to the context. Applying critical thinking, thoughtful communication and self-reflection to our practice will help minimise inappropriate actions.

EXAMPLE 2

A cultural clash. What would you do?

A midwife was assisting during the labour of a woman from the Sudan. The patient had limited English but had a relative with her to translate. The midwife knew the woman had an 'infibulation', a cultural practice which removes parts of the labia and then sews the remaining tissue together, leaving only a small hole for the passage of urine and menstrual blood. It makes childbirth difficult and necessitates an episiotomy. After the birth, her translator said that the woman wanted to be re-stitched as before. The midwife did not approve of female circumcision and was reluctant to comply.

Exercise 5

On reflection, what should the nurse have done differently? What are the issues? What assumptions are being made?

A 55 year old Middle Eastern man has had a stroke which has affected his speech and mobility. The morning nurse (a young female) comes in to help him and starts to feed him breakfast. The man tries to interrupt but cannot make himself understood. The nurse speaks loudly to him that he should just relax and let her do the work; she will look after him. She finishes feeding him and then, despite his resistance, proceeds to bathe him, clean his teeth and dress him. She doesn't understand why he seems so unhappy and thinks it is because of the stroke. She tells him not to worry, he will get better, and then she leaves.

Self-reflective practice in social work

Social work is another profession which expects and encourages self-reflective practice. Social work theory itself is critically self-reflective. It seeks to be objective and neutral by critically examining accepted norms and practices to reveal their underlying assumptions. Social workers aim to maximise the development of human potential and the fulfilment of human needs, through an equal commitment to:

- Working with and enabling people to achieve the best possible levels of personal and social well-being.
- Working to achieve social justice through social development and social change.

Because the targets of social work practice are frequently people with various levels of social disadvantage, critical social and political analysis of what causes that disadvantage is essential. This analysis may uncover social inequities due to race, gender, ethnicity, income, intellect, disability, age, health or even location. Any and all of these factors can contribute to social inequities and social injustice.

Again, as with nursing, the social workers' clientele will be diverse and challenging. Often there is physical and/or emotional trauma. Social work intervention itself could create trauma for the client, depending on the context. Social workers make decisions that profoundly affect the lives of individuals. As social workers, we need to be sensitive to our clients' needs and situations. We need to ensure we do not judge only from within our own perspective of what constitutes appropriate behaviour, but try to reflect on the knowledge, values, beliefs and experiences of our clients. What is it like for them? Why do they believe this? Why do they feel like that? What do they think will work?

Practitioners must ask more than 'what works?' They need to ask 'what will work in **this situation** with this particular client or community at this time?'

Self-reflection can improve personal and professional awareness and therapeutic competence. Self-reflection is a process of self-inquiry – it involves self-analysis, self-evaluation, self-dialogue and self-observation. It is only through this process of critical reflection that we can identify those values and personal assumptions that may impede our ability to make the best decision in the circumstances or which prevent us from improving our practical competence. Too much compassion or too little understanding can both lead to **poor judgements,** leading to poor outcomes.

EXAMPLE 3

How expectations can influence what we see

A 26-year-old Indigenous patient was brought into the Alice Springs hospital with her sick 1-year old baby. After being examined by the paediatrician, the patient and her baby were taken to their ward and settled in bed. A social worker on the ward noticed the baby was becoming increasingly distressed and crying loudly while the mother just sat in the chair near the child's cot impassive and totally ignoring the child's distress. The social worker was surprised and a little shocked by the mother's lack of concern for her baby and mentioned it to the paediatrician who was doing her rounds. She suggested that the social worker look a little closer at the woman. The mother was trembling, had rapid breathing and looked extremely anxious and quite unwell. She was manifesting classic symptoms of shock. The paediatrician explained that the mother and baby had travelled a long way from a remote part of Australia to the hospital; it was apparently the first time the mother had been in a Western hospital (or a city or seen a lift). She didn't speak the language, she had met very few Westerners, and she was away from her own 'country and people' for the first time. The woman was incapable of responding to her child's needs at that time. The judgement that this was an uncaring mother was based on a hasty assessment, a cultural assumption of appropriate maternal behaviour and a lack of understanding of the patient's context.

Exercise 6

A cultural misunderstanding. What are the issues? Could it have been handled differently?

A 74-year-old Caucasian man based in in his own home was receiving services from an agency to support his independent living. A social worker originally from Ethiopia was assigned to work with him three times a week, but after only one week the client rang the agency and demanded she be removed from his weekly roster. When contacted by the agency, he stated 'she doesn't care about me. I told her I almost died last night but she showed no interest, just wandered into the kitchen and then kept cleaning and left'. Her line manager immediately filed a complaint against the social worker, suggesting to the cultural consultant that the she might have some 'residual mental health problems' from being a refugee. When questioned by the cultural consultant, the social worker stated the client hadn't said anything about almost dying the night before. All he said was he had 'almost kicked the bucket' but the social worker couldn't find any bucket in the kitchen and assumed the client was playing about. He often made jokes she couldn't understand.

Self-reflective practice in education

Critical self-reflection allows us to examine what we have done, why we have done it and whether or not we could have done something else, something that may have been better or more successful, or something that may have been just different.

In education, the ultimate goal of self-reflection is to **improve** the way we teach.

Teaching practice is challenging, not least because any classroom is full of diverse individuals with different skills and competencies, and various levels of engagement. Once again, we need to reflect on that diversity and what it means for our teaching practice.

- How do we manage a diverse cohort in a single setting?
- How do we acknowledge and teach to that difference?
- How might the values and experiences of the students differ from our own?
- What impact does that have, or could that have, on how we teach?
- What impact will it have on how students respond to our teaching and teaching material?
- How could we factor the diversity into our teaching pedagogy and utilise it?

As teachers, we need to reflect on our epistemological framework and our understanding of learning. We need to try and think from a student perspective – how did they respond, what did they learn, were they engaged? Do I need to revise my learning outcomes in line with student needs and abilities? Who are in my cohort and where are they from?

EXAMPLE 4

Being aware of a student's perspective

A teacher notices that a girl from China tends not to raise her hand to participate in discussions. The teacher knows the girl is not fluent in English and takes a moment to talk quietly to her to see if this might be an issue. The girl is worried that others will laugh at her and make fun of her accent. The teacher divides the class into small groups to do collaborative research so that the girl can practice speaking English in a less threatening environment. The teacher also takes it as an opportunity to discuss tolerance and difference to increase cross-cultural understanding.

In culturally and linguistically diverse classrooms, teachers can promote critical thinking by making the rules of the classroom culture explicit. Students can compare and contrast the rules with those from other cultures present in the classroom. This provides an opportunity for them to develop cross-cultural awareness. For such learning to take place, however, teachers must have the attitudes, knowledge, and skills to make their classrooms effective learning environments for all students. Teachers also need to have a clear sense of their own ethnic and cultural identities.

Effective instruction explicitly acknowledges students' gender differences and reaffirms their cultural, ethnic, and linguistic heritages.

Good teaching practice is synonymous with **teaching critical thinking skills.** It is practice which encourages students to identify and solve problems, explore issues from multiple perspectives, analyse and evaluate text and generally develop autonomous and independent thinking. So not only is critical thinking essential for us as teachers but is also part of what we should be encouraging in our students.

By reflecting on our teaching, we can ask ourselves whether or not we are engaged in good teaching practice that encourages the development of critical thinking in our students.

- Do we expect rote-learning of facts and processes and test them accordingly?
- Do we have a set of right answers we expect students to learn?
- Do we lecture at our students rather than facilitate their learning?
- Do we expect certain students not to do as well as others and, as a consequence, don't challenge them to do better?

As reflective practitioners, we should want to do the best by our students. We should:

- Have high expectations of/for them and their ability to succeed
- Encourage them by giving them challenging and demanding activities
- Involve them in collaborative and novel problem-solving activities

- Ask open-ended questions requiring students to use their judgement and form opinions
- Choose activities where students must use analytic skills, evaluate, and make connections.

Exercise 7

Reflecting on the teacher's practice, what do you think went wrong? How might the outcome be improved?

A new teacher has been sent to an inner city high school with a mixed ethnic and socioeconomic student cohort. To find out about his students and their neighbourhood, the teacher gives each student a questionnaire for them to fill out at home with their parents. He also asks them to interview 10 more adults in their street and bring the results back on Monday to share. The questionnaire asks for standard demographics such as income, profession, education levels, religion, number of people in the house, diet, most frequent holidays abroad, number of cars, as well as some general questions about political beliefs. He is disappointed when very few questionnaires are returned on Monday, and these were mostly from the middle-class, English students. When he queries the low response, he is met by shrugs and an overall lack of interest in complying.

Critical thinking and the role of a self-reflective journal

Critical thinking has practical applications. It has a purpose. It helps us to improve our thinking and improve our practice. However, we cannot achieve either of those aims without examining or **reflecting on** both our thinking and our practice.

Self-reflection is a form of self-correction. By reflecting on what we did or said, we can think about what we *could have* done or said and what the consequences of those changes might have been. Would changes in my behaviour have improved the outcomes? Will I change my practice or my approach as a result of my reflections? Were there things that I did which were just right or which worked well? Have I learnt something new? Has my understanding (of myself and my professional practice) increased?

A self-reflective journal is a **record of our journey** as a practitioner. It documents our growth into a professional.

Keeping a journal allows us to reflect on our performance without judgement. It provides a safe space to document what we do or did, how we felt about it and what we could do better. It shows how we take our discipline knowledge from theory into practice. It demonstrates how we reflect on our professional knowledge and how we learn to adapt and apply it to real life situations. Over time, it will reveal how much we have changed and learnt and how much more experienced we have become.

EXAMPLE 5

A sample reflection (general)

24/6 – I tried to make my client feel comfortable and offered her a cup of tea. On reflection, that wasn't the best idea as it took me some time to find a kettle and there was no sugar! A glass of water would have worked as well. We did start chatting comfortably and I asked if it was okay to record the interview. My client was okay to start with but as we talked more she became uncomfortable and asked me to turn off the tape. I could see she was a bit emotional so I suggested we stop for a bit. When we resumed, she was more at ease and said it was okay to record again. Next time I will discuss the interview process in more detail before we start so we can establish boundaries. I think this would increase my client's confidence in me.

Ideally, a reflective journal should show how your practice is developing in light of your knowledge and expertise. Reflective writing is not the same as essay or report writing. It shows:

- Your response to your experiences as they relate to your practice
- Your response to your reactions to your experiences
- Reasons why you responded as you did (both in your thinking and in your actions)
- Reflections on if those responses were justified, appropriate, productive, counter-productive
- How you are learning and exploring new knowledge
- How you are making sense of your experiences
- How you are developing your understanding and growing in your practice

Critical thinking and self-reflection are ways we can improve what we do. It is not about being right or wrong but whether or not we could do better. It is recognising that we still have a lot to learn and experience, all of which will add to our expertise – if we are open to change.

Chapter summary

- Engaging in critical self-reflection is the single most important strategy we can apply if we want to become a critical thinker.
- Critical thinking requires us to sometimes override self interest in the name of truth and honesty. Always be truthful to yourself and don't be afraid to be wrong.
- Ideal critical thinkers embody intellectual empathy, humility, perseverance, integrity and responsibility.
- Self-reflection is essential in assessing our reactions to challenging situations, culturally diverse groups and alternative practices or social norms.
- We need to be flexible in our practice and in our beliefs so that we can change practice in light of new convincing evidence.
- We should keep up to date with current research to ensure our beliefs and the claims we make within our professional field still hold.

Answers to Exercises 1–7

Exercises 1–2

Exercises 1 and 2 have no general answers. They will depend on how students respond or what students suggest.

Exercise 3

Is the belief that cleanliness is beneficial cultural or scientific?

There is some very reliable evidence indicating that certain types of personal hygiene practices (such as washing hands regularly or avoiding contamination from faeces or rotten foods) reduce the risk of contracting infections or spreading infections to others. Having clean water, clean utensils and fresh food are part of that hygienic practice. There is some evidence that we can be 'too clean' by excessive washing using soaps and detergents which kill the good bacteria that aid our immune systems. Dirt per se is not a health risk and some of our reactions to dirt and alternative cleaning practices have a cultural or class bias. In fact, dirt-play for children is being encouraged to help reduce the instance of allergies. While washing will be restricted in countries and areas where there is limited access to clean water, this does not always connote with unclean practices. Smells can also be a culturally acquired taste. Commercial companies can also make us paranoid about 'germs' to sell their cleaning products. We do have to reflect on whether or not our attitudes towards cleanliness (or dirt) are driven by class or culture, and to what extent they are health driven.

Exercise 4

Cultural difference and nutrition. What are the cultural issues here for the student? Can you think of any cultural assumptions the lecturer may have made?

The student from China needed more information about nutritional balance but also about Western food and their cultural place. While in the West the breakfast food is quite distinct and would not be served for lunch or dinner, many other cultures eat similar foods for breakfast and lunch. In the East, bread is not a staple nor is dairy. The lecturer may have limited cross-cultural knowledge and assumed that a good breakfast is a Western-style breakfast. This is why we need to reflect on our practices, as people in the aged-care facility are likely to have a multicultural background too.

Exercise 5

On reflection, what should the nurse have done differently? What are the issues? What assumptions are being made?

Shouting is often used when it is assumed someone is not a native speaker. The patient is not deaf and his English may be fine. The nurse should have tried to talk to the man first to ascertain what his needs were, what he could manage by himself, and what he was comfortable allowing the nurse to do. This could be managed despite his difficulty speaking and would have given him some autonomy, reducing his stress and frustration. As a 55-year-old Middle Eastern man, he may not be comfortable with a young female dressing him. This may be cultural but could also be gender-related. The nurse needs to show some sensitivity to the vulnerability of his situation and his loss of control over his life and decision-making. Her wrong assumption about why he was unhappy highlights a lack of effective communication and disregard for the patient as a person. She needs to reflect on her behaviour and how it impacted on his well-being.

Exercise 6

A cultural misunderstanding. What are the issues? Could it have been handled differently?

There is an obvious cross-cultural misunderstanding in this example. A non-native speaker of English will not always understand colloquial expressions like 'kick the bucket.' In this instance, it has caused a major problem. However, the line manager should not have accepted the client's story without careful investigation, nor should they have assumed fault on the side of the social worker. The line manager has quickly accepted the claim that the social worker lacks competence or compassion. This haste may indicate an underlying problem between the line manager and the worker. Given the comment about the state of the worker's mental health in relation to her Ethiopian background, there may be some underlying cultural or racial issues that need to be addressed. All assumptions made by the line manager could be false. The line manager needs to reflect on her own attitudes and beliefs.

Exercise 7

Reflecting on the teacher's practice, what do you think went wrong? How might the outcome be improved?

The new teacher has not reflected on his cohort nor on how he can best engage them. There will be many reasons for their lack of compliance – the lack of sensitivity of the questions, potential embarrassment/shame, non-English speaking parents, community tensions, religious tensions, cultural differences (some female students not allowed to go knocking on doors), safety/security issues, literacy issues, respect, student status – this is an inner city high school with a mixed ethnic and socioeconomic student cohort. Questions may have been better if structured around 'safe' topics like music taste, interests, clothes, food, etc. The students won't see the point of the exercise. What will they learn, get out of it? He made a lot of assumptions about their engagement and willingness to do as he asks. He needed to engage them in the exercise, maybe get them to design something, a questionnaire around what they are interested in, or an artwork. There was no learning outcome and it failed as a PR exercise. He now looks silly and has lost authority. He will need to reflect on how he can get credibility back.

CHAPTER

12

Critical Thinking in the Workplace

The complexity of work-life in the contemporary world

We live in a world which is vastly different from the one our parents and grandparents inhabited. The advent of satellite technology, multi-media platforms, personal computers and the Internet enable immediate information checks and constant coverage of current affairs as they happen anywhere in the world, with Facebook and cell phones giving us immediate visual access to remote places and events that we have never had before. Immigration, both legal and illegal, has led to an influx of diverse ethnic groups moving into what were once monocultural, monolingual spaces. The world has become physically much smaller but socially more complex. Old problems and solutions are unlikely to be relevant in this new environment.

To deal successfully with the new environment of the future, and to keep pace with the globally connected world, we need to develop the **right skill set** to suit it.

Not only is this new world becoming increasingly complex with an over-abundance of information to deal with and digest, but technology is continuing to advance at a rapid rate. Some people suggest we are entering the *Fourth Industrial Revolution*. Advanced robotics and artificial intelligence, driverless cars, increased automation, biotechnology and genetic engineering will change the future in radically different ways that are hard to predict.

On top of these changes, we cannot ignore the impact of diminishing resources, increasing non-recyclable waste, and climate change on the planet and, hence, on our lifestyle and future choices. We need to think clearly and deeply about what kind of world we will be living in, and what kind of world **we want** to be living in.

We need to invest our time in developing the analytical thinking skills we will need to come up with the **right decisions and solutions** for the future.

Critical thinking as a future skill-set

Think about the issues that are facing the world at this time and their relevance to you as a future worker, as employee or employer, as a citizen and as an active participant in a representative democracy. Think about how the world is now and how it could be. Think about the kind of world you want to live in. Ask yourself,

- What skills can I acquire that will be most useful to me now?
- What skills will be applicable in a broad range of diverse situations?
- What skills will help me critically assess opportunities and evaluate options?
- What skills will I need to help me come to the best decisions I can for my future self?
- What skills will I need to contribute positively to future societal/world outcomes?
- What skills will help me to thrive in an uncertain future?

While developing a sound knowledge base, professional expertise and job-relevant skills are useful, we do not know what the future will bring. We do not know what jobs will still be available, what new areas will be developed, and which old ones will go or be replaced by automated machines. If resources become limited, certain trades may be unsustainable. The job market is volatile and unpredictable, as COVID19 has demonstrated. It is suggested that today's students will have more than 15 jobs in their lifetime, many of which do not yet exist.

Having a well-developed critical thinking capacity will go a long way to **future-proofing** your university education and your life skills.

We will all need to be more strategic, efficient, adaptable and resilient in the work-place than our predecessors were. The skills of the past will not be enough to guarantee flourishing in that future, given we will need to operate in ever more complex and changeable situations. Having the ability to think critically and rationally about what we will deal with in our future life and career will not just be a bonus but a necessity.

EXAMPLE 1

Employable skills

A recent study on future work states that more than 30% of at least 60% of today's jobs have activities that are technically automatable. However, there are some attributes or skills that are not easily automated. Social intelligence skills such as understanding or predicting people's reactions within special contexts can't yet be mastered by machine intelligence, nor can caring for others. Creative intelligence, such as innovating, imagining or coming up with original ideas is proving hard to automate. Finally, automatons are presently incapable of working on tasks focused on unstructured work or in complex situations.

From ANU McKell Institute Study, 2019

Changes to our economies, use of new technology and automation are transforming the ways we live and work. The jobs that are important to us today are disappearing and jobs that we can't even think of today are expected to become standard in workplaces in the near future. We will need to develop the right skill set to survive and thrive.

Solving societal problems was once just the domain of governments but the landscape has changed dramatically. The world has become much more complex (think of the impact COVID 19 has had). There is a growing demand for innovators and creative thinkers to look at new ways of addressing the issues we will face. The old solutions and models of governance are no longer as effective as they were.

Critical thinking is not specific to a particular discipline or profession even if the ways it is implemented differ in different fields (Egege and Vered Orr, 2019). Critical thinking encompasses what are called **generic** or generalist skills. These are skills that are applicable and adaptable for use in any field of enquiry and that can be applied fruitfully in every profession. They include the ability to:

- Assess what is relevant to (or in) a given situation
- Know what questions to ask to get more information
- Draw inferences about what the issue or problem might be and why it is an issue
- Analyse the situation, problem or issue to gain a fuller understanding
- Apply appropriate knowledge to the situation, identify any gaps and know-how to fill them
- Know when and how to draw on others' expertise as you need it
- Critically examine and evaluate different or novel approaches to the issue or problem
- Problem-solve by trialling solutions and drawing out potential implications of different approaches
- Reflect on one's own thinking to ascertain any biases, false assumptions or possible mistakes in reasoning
- Judge what is the best solution or approach, based on sound reasoning and examination of alternatives
- Be strategic

We need to spend time developing this skill set and the requisite critical thinking dispositions if we want to be ready and able to meet the challenges of the future. Over time, applying this skill set will become automatic or habitual. The skills of critical thinking become embodied, a part of how we think and act. Questioning, reasoning, correcting and re-evaluating become the norm. We become critical thinkers.

Having a critical thinking mindset and being able to **articulate and demonstrate its value** will give you an employability edge.

Revisiting a critical thinking disposition

Most of the chapters in this book have looked at how we can develop a critical mindset by applying critical thinking skills to the claims *other people* make about the world we live in. Challenging those claims using a set of reliable criteria helps us to understand how and why we believe what we do, and whether or not we should continue to believe what we do. Acknowledging and seeking ways to overcome the barriers to our understanding will help us find the most viable solutions we can to the problems facing the world.

Chapter 11 introduced the idea of a *critical thinking disposition* and the role that **self-reflection** plays in becoming a critical thinker. Reflecting on our thinking and the processes we follow to reach solutions are core attributes for becoming a critical thinker. To reflect effectively requires **honesty and integrity**. These are generic attributes that are expected in the human services professions and valued in all workplaces.

In addition, there are certain traits that form part of what is known as the critical thinking disposition suite of attributes. Having these traits or attributes makes it more likely we will be *disposed* towards a critical thinking mindset. They can be developed over time. **Becoming a critical thinker is a process**. It is not a static set of criteria or heuristics one applies to a situation in the hope for a better outcome. It takes time and effort and a desire to improve our thinking. Fortunately, we do get better with practice.

Exercise 1

Critical thinking dispositions

Rank yourself on the items below from 1 to 5 (where 1 is never and 5 is always). Be as honest as you can.

- I seek the truth regardless of self-interest or prior beliefs 1 2 3 4 5
- I recognise and acknowledge my limitations 1 2 3 4 5
- I am open to alternative views and outcomes 1 2 3 4 5
- I am not afraid to question 1 2 3 4 5
- I am rigorous and systematic in my thinking 1 2 3 4 5
- I am logical and analytic 1 2 3 4 5
- I always bear in mind the possibility that I might be wrong 1 2 3 4 5

Exercise 2

Critical thinking obstacles

Rank yourself on the items below from 1 to 5 (where 1 is never and 5 is always). Be as honest as you can.

1. I get defensive when my opinion is challenged 1 2 3 4 5
2. I try to avoid conflict when I can 1 2 3 4 5
3. I find it difficult to back down from an argument 1 2 3 4 5
4. I target evidence that supports my position 1 2 3 4 5
5. I don't like to be wrong 1 2 3 4 5
6. I struggle to justify my position when questioned 1 2 3 4 5
7. I find it hard to justify my ideas when asked 1 2 3 4 5
8. I change my opinion all the time 1 2 3 4 5
9. I tend to believe what I read 1 2 3 4 5
10. I like clear instructions to follow 1 2 3 4 5
11. I always want to know what the right answer is 1 2 3 4 5

What employers want now

Employers have been talking for a long time about the need for graduates to have a well-developed critical thinking capacity. They want their graduate employees to be able to think innovatively about industry-related problems and for them to come up with innovative solutions. Often, they talk of employees needing to 'think outside the box.' That capacity requires thinking about an issue or problem from different angles or points of view, a basic critical thinking trait.

According to a worldwide report by Pearson North America (2017), employers across the globe agreed that good decision-making requires an ability to assess relevant information, ask the correct questions and pick out reliable facts, which are the basics of critical thinking. Almost 70% of the employers surveyed acknowledged that they try to assess candidates' critical thinking skills during the selection process. Around 49% of employers evaluated their *current* employees' critical thinking skills as **average or below average.**

Employers frequently complain that the graduates they get often do not have a critical thinking capacity and have poor reasoning skills, even though they have high grades. This supports evidence from studies that show high school and university students are not being taught to think critically and they are graduating without a well-developed critical thinking capacity. A 2017 study of students from 200 American Colleges indicated that their critical thinking skills were below what should be expected from college graduates (Belkin, 2017). At more than half of the schools tested, at least a third of seniors were unable to make a cohesive argument, assess the quality of evidence in a document or interpret data in a table.

EXAMPLE 2

A 2018 survey by PayScale Inc., an online pay and benefits researcher, listed the following 10 graduate attributes that employers are looking for in order of importance.

1. **Interpersonal and communication skills (written and oral)**
2. Drive and commitment/industry knowledge
3. **Critical reasoning and analytical skills/technical skills**
4. Calibre of academic results
5. Cultural alignment/values fit
6. Work experience
7. Teamwork skills
8. Emotional intelligence (including self-awareness, confidence, motivation)
9. Leadership skill
10. Activities (including intra and extracurricular)

The PayScale survey identified communication and critical thinking skills as **numbers 1 and 3** in terms of priority. Communicating effectively, both verbally and in writing, is a requisite skill in all fields of employment. Good critical thinking skills develop logic and clear thinking which encourages a more systematic communication of ideas. Understanding what constitutes strong evidence and knowing how to construct a convincing argument will help you put your ideas forward or help promote the company's case, an asset to any employer. Critical and analytic skills should aid with problem identification, analysis and the pursuit of viable solutions (Ventura et al, 2017).

To be employable, graduates must develop the analytical reasoning and **problem-solving** skills they need to thrive in a fast-changing, increasingly global job market.

Relevance to employment

Critical thinking skills are essential in every industry at every career level, from entry-level associates to top executives. Good critical thinkers will work both independently and with groups to solve problems or to generate ideas for new projects.

EXAMPLE 3

Problem-solvers

Good problem solvers gather relevant information about a problem, analyse the data or information, and begin to generate possible solutions. Employees who solve more problems, small or large, are more valuable to employers. Things will go wrong at work and require solutions. Problem solvers can figure out where things have broken down and come to an understanding of the root cause. This is a very important skill because finding the real problem is critical to solving it.

Teamwork and critical thinking

Employers value employees who are problem solvers, because they are able and willing to take on challenges by thinking critically and creatively. But research also shows that people come to better decisions when working in a group where they have to take other points of view into account.

Employers know that rational decision-making can be improved by group participation. Teams outperform individuals, as they represent multiple perspectives related to a given problem and can generate more possible solutions. The team forces individual thinkers to think differently and to be more accountable for their own ideas. There are many decision-making points embedded in team problem solving, and the team needs to be able to use a variety of proven group decision-making strategies.

Good critical thinkers are **good problem solvers.** They seek input from others, and consider a number of solutions. By applying their critical thinking skills, they help everyone be more productive and effective in the workplace.

Public/civil service and government

Many students or graduates end up working in the government sector in some capacity where there is a demand for literate critical thinkers. As an employee you may be asked to produce a report on a specific issue that includes suggestions or recommendations to, for example, review current programs and policies, improve outcomes, solve a funding issue or deliver a service in a different way. You will be asked to generate ideas or come up with novel solutions. This is exciting as you have the potential to have an input into government policy and practice. You need to bear in mind, however, that there will be institutional and political boundaries that constrain what can be contemplated and achieved. Declining resources and public funds translate into having to be more efficient with less.

Exercise 3

An ethical challenge

You are a graduate recently employed by the public/civil service as a policy officer. There has been a policy decision (actioned by your department and sanctioned by the appropriate government minister) to move a homeless facility from the inner city to a less central area. There is intense opposition in Parliament/the Senate to this move and public outcries from all the major welfare, health and medical organisations. You are asked by your supervisor to write a defence of the policy and a rebuttal to the criticism for the minister to read out at the next sitting of Parliament/Senate. The prevailing culture is to 'cut and paste' a response from previous ministerials and to 'cherry-pick' supportive research to justify the shift. Politically, you do not agree with the policy change and believe it was designed to please business interests. What do you do?

To apply critical thinking successfully in the workplace, you need to be **aware of your constraints** and those of your office. Query how far you can go.

Avoid the 'cut and paste' mentality

People wonder why real change takes so long, is difficult or is only superficial. While most organisations, including the public or civil service do want critical thinkers, and there is a genuine desire to apply critical thinking to service provision, there are institutional impediments to being able to think critically in situ.

- Time-frame – Often government or other reports have fixed and narrow deadlines. This limits the amount of time that you can spend on thorough research and genuine exploration of alternative solutions or approaches. It is easier to adapt a previous or existing practice than to come up with something new.
- Inadequate resources – There may be limited funding or resources available to develop something new or different. There will be competing demands on your

time. There may be an expectation that the change be 'cost neutral', which means there are little or no funds to spend on implementation of something genuinely new or different.

- Inexperience – As a new person in the field, you will be nervous and unsure of what is required and expected. You are likely to model your submission on past submissions and/or take the advice of a more experienced colleague. While taking advice is good, this can perpetuate old thinking models.
- Conformity – You want to fit in, impress and not create waves. You are likely to be influenced and guided by what has received approval before and be inclined to copy or adapt that model or approach.
- Compartmentalisation – You are likely to have been given only one aspect of an issue that exists in a much bigger framework. You may be unaware of where or how your proposed solution will fit in the overall framework. And changing just one part of a system is unlikely to result in any real change.
- Culture – The 'culture' of an organisation has an impact on how well it operates. Changing the culture to make it more productive requires changing staff behaviour, some of which may be entrenched. Staff often resist change, especially if they have been with an organisation for a long time.

Real change requires moving away from old models, looking at an issue with fresh eyes, and seeing it from different angles.

We tend to look to government to solve all of society's problems. But government has less capacity to solve our problems now than it did in the past. There is an aging population worldwide, there is less public income from taxes, more demands on the public purse, and the problems we face are much bigger and more complex. The solutions of the past will not solve the problems of the future. The onus will be on the **critical thinkers employed in the workplace** to devise novel real-time solutions.

Exercise 4

Think about climate change

Let's assume that the climate is changing and the planet is getting warmer. Let's also assume that there are human practices and lifestyle choices that have contributed, and still are contributing, to this change. It follows from this that if we continue with these practices, the warming of the planet and the changes to climate patterns will continue, and our current lifestyle will not be sustainable.

What do we do? How do we deal with this global problem? What are some possible realistic solutions? If we are to **think critically** about the situation, how might our thinking change? Is there a best approach to take?

Industry and business

Like government, industry and business need to do things differently in order to survive. The average life cycle of a corporation has reduced from 95 years to 27 years since the 1930s. Companies face the challenge of keeping current with rapidly changing technology and software, as well as utilising new marketing channels. Accessing big data and benefiting from data analytics is becoming critical for companies to keep on top. Predicting customer and product trends requires **innovation and rapid learning**; hence the continued demand for critical thinking skills in employees. Business needs new ideas and ways to solve problems.

No one could have imagined the worldwide crisis of the corona virus pandemic (COVID 19) and the impact it has had on business. Many businesses struggled to survive during isolation and those that did had to be innovative. It is predicted that pandemics and other disasters will become more frequent because of the ways we have changed the environment and our interaction with other species.

Ambidextrous organisations

Ambidexterity is the ability to **exploit** present conditions by optimising the current business model's operations while **exploring** opportunities to redefine that business model by taking pioneering risks – risks on creating new value (higher margin business) while simultaneously squeezing out operational inefficiencies (higher margins, lower costs) in the existing model. It is achieved by balancing exploration (developing new ideas and approaches) with exploitation (improving existing practice).

While businesses need to innovate to survive and thrive, they have additional pressures from their shareholders and customers to also behave in a socially responsible manner. There is a demand for businesses to demonstrate both **a social conscience and ethical practice**. These days, it is better to be green and clean, and sensitive to the values of one's customers.

QANTAS has recently come out as LGBTQI (lesbian, gay, bisexual, transgender, queer or questioning, and intersex) supportive, and a lot of companies now display the rainbow flag on their websites. Some companies publicly state their ethics on animal cruelty or child exploitation. Several supermarket chains have committed to reducing plastic waste. Being socially responsible and taking an ethical stance can help a business survive.

Applying critical thinking creatively in the workplace, to develop new ideas or improve old practices, can save a company time and money and produce a better outcome.

EXAMPLE 4

Applied critical thinking in different workplace situations

- A manager trying to be as objective as possible when settling a dispute with fairness to all parties by summarising the different perspectives, identifying the causes of friction or disagreement, and exploring viable solutions.
- A team of scientists working with precision through a complex experiment in an effort to gather reliable data, control the variables and analyse the results.
- A person running a small business trying to anticipate the possible changed economic and human consequences of switching to more contemporary business software systems to ensure a competitive edge over their rivals.
- A master sergeant and a captain working out the tactical plans for a dangerous military mission.
- A football coach working during halftime on new tactics to maximise their team's strengths and to attack the weaknesses of the other team for when the match resumes.
- A student explaining to his or her peers why and how a certain methodology or standard of proof was applied to an issue and why a particular conclusion was reached.
- An educator using clever questioning to guide a student to new insights.
- Police detectives, crime scene analysts, lawyers, judges and juries systematically investigating, interrogating, examining and evaluating the evidence as they seek justice.
- A policy analyst reviewing alternative drafts of product safety legislation while determining how to frame the law to benefit the most people at the least cost.

Critical thinking skills are hard to develop. It does take effort to **become a critical thinker**. The benefits to our own lives and to the world, however, make it worthwhile. Through thinking carefully and rigorously about our ideas and beliefs, we can help reduce misunderstandings, increase tolerance of difference and, hopefully, come to better, more effective solutions to the problems we face in the world.

Chapter summary

- To deal successfully with the new environment of the future, we need to develop the right skill set to suit it.
- We need to invest our time in developing the analytical thinking skills we will need to come up with the right decisions and solutions for the future.
- Having a well-developed critical thinking capacity will go a long way to future-proofing your university education and your life skills.
- Having a critical thinking mindset and being able to articulate and demonstrate its value will give you an employability edge.
- Applying critical thinking creatively in the workplace, to develop new ideas or improve old practices, can save a company time and money and produce a better outcome.

Answers to Exercises 1–4

Exercises 1–2

Exercises 1–2 have no right or wrong answers

Exercise 3

Ethical challenge

The problem in this situation is the pressure you will be under to comply with the request from the minister, which will mean selecting facts to suit a pre-determined outcome – supporting a policy that is not in the best interests of the clientele and which you have ethical concerns about. This would go against any critical thinking disposition you may have.

Issues to deal with – prevailing 'cut and paste' culture, lack of open mindedness, lack of honesty, conflict of interests, no real desire to come to the best decision. You should discuss with your supervisor and express your concerns.

Possible solution – put forward the best case you can to raise doubts about the advantages of the policy change, along with any counter evidence. Make it as well researched and as balanced as you can so that it raises issues of concern rather than just criticising the change. A good critique can reverse policy decisions, especially given the opposition that exists. The minister may decide to reconsider. While the land is prime real estate and would sell for a good price, this should not be the only driver.

Exercise 4

Climate change

We should stop expecting our governments to have the capacity to solve complex, multi-causal problems like climate change. No government agency or institution can solve the massive global problems we are facing on their own and in isolation. They are too big to be resolved by one solution. That doesn't excuse them from doing something but we need to be realistic. As critical thinkers, we need to ensure our facts are well-researched and supported and we have the latest, most reliable data from which to determine causes and generate any solutions. Greenhouse gases are a prime contributor, so reducing these would seem a priority. However, we need to understand the consequences of that and the potential impact on lifestyle and business. This is why solutions need to be holistic and have national or even worldwide support and cooperation. Industry has to be onboard as does the public. Goals need to be achievable and within our scope. Devise goals for industry and government and different ones for the general public. Work on multilevels and multifronts. While the extinction rebellion has raised awareness of the public's feeling towards climate change, their solutions are not clearly defined. Political pressure works but the goals need to be ones that can be reached and that make a difference. How do we reduce plastic use but preserve trees? There needs to be sustainable solutions and these will impact on all levels (i.e. reduced use of personal devices like iPhones; less use of private cars). It is worth spending time identifying possible changes to our current lifestyles that would make a difference.

References

Abrami, P. C., Bernard, R. M., Borokhovski, E., Wade, A., Surkes, M. A., Tamim, R., & Zhang, D. (2008). Instructional Interventions Affecting Critical Thinking Skills and Dispositions: A Stage 1 Meta-Analysis. *Review of Educational Research*, 78(4), 1102–1134. doi:https://doi.org/10.3102/0034654308326084

Bean, J. C. (2011). *Engaging Ideas: The Professor's Guide to Integrating Writing, Critical Thinking, and Active Learning in the Classroom* (2nd ed.). San Francisco: Jossey-Bass.

Belkin, D. (2017). *Exclusive Test Data: Many Colleges Fail to Improve Critical-Thinking Skills*. Retrieved October 5, 2018, from https://www.wsj.com/articles/exclusive-test-data-many-colleges-fail-to-improve-critical-thinking-skills-1496686662

Egege, S., & Kutieleh, S. (2013). *What Is Critical Thinking? A University Guide to Critical Thinking*. Bedford Park: Flinders University, Flinders Press.

Egege, S., & Vered Orr, K. (2019). Using Shared Inquiry to Develop Students' Reading, Reasoning, and Writing in the Disciplines. *Across the Disciplines*, 16(3). https://wac.colostate.edu/docs/atd/australasia/egege_vered2019.pdf

Ennis, R. (1987). A Taxonomy of Critical Thinking Abilities and Dispositions. In J. Baron & R. Sternberg (Eds.), *Teaching Thinking Skills* (pp. 9–26). New York: W. H. Freeman.

Facione, P. (1990). *Critical Thinking: A Statement of Expert Consensus for Purposes of Educational Assessment and Instruction*. Millbrae: The California Academic Press.

Facione, N., Facione, P., Giancarlo (Sánchez), C. (1994). Critical Thinking Disposition as a Measure of Competent Clinical Judgment: The Development of the California Critical Thinking Disposition Inventory. *Journal of Nursing Education*, 33(8), 345–350.

Fine, C. (2008). *A Mind of Its Own: How Your Brain Distorts and Deceives*. New York: W.W. Norton and Company.

Govier, T. (2010). *A Practical Study of Argument* (7th ed.). Wadsworth: Cengage Learning.

Halpern, D. H. (1997). *Critical Thinking Across the Curriculum*. Mahwah: Lawrence Erlbaum Associates.

Horning, A. S. (2007). Reading Across the Curriculum as the Key to Student Success. *Across the Disciplines*, 4. Retrieved from https://wac.colostate.edu/atd/articles/horning2007.cfm

National Graduate Attributes Project. (2009, May 17). *Introduction to Mapped Universities' Statements of Graduate Attributes*. Retrieved from http://hdl.voced.edu.au/10707/327383

Parker, S., & Egege, S. (2019). Think Well, Practice Well: Teaching Nurse Students to Think Critically. In S. Dyson & M. MacCallister (Eds.), *Handbook of Nurse Education*. London: Routledge. https://www.routledge.com/Routledge-International-Handbook-of-Nurse-Education/Dyson-McAllister/p/book/9780815358862

Paul, R., & Elder, L. (2001). *Instructor's Manual for Critical Thinking: Tools for Taking Charge of Our Learning and Your Life*. Upper Saddle River: Prentice Hall.

Paul, R., & Elder, L. (2010). *Universal Intellectual Standards*. Retrieved September 28, 2018, from http://www.criticalthinking.org/pages/universal-intellectual-standards/527

Sievers, K. (2001). How Do You Know That...?. In *Critical Reasoning Handbook*. Bedford Park: Philosophy Department, Flinders University.

Van Gelder T. (2005). 'Teaching critical thinking: some lessons from cognitive science,) *College Teaching*, 53:1.

Ventura, M., Lai, E., & DiCerbo, K. (2017). *Skills for Today: What We Know About Teaching and Assessing Critical Thinking*. London: Pearson.

Additional Resources

Abrami, P. C., Bernard, R. M., Borokhovski, E., Waddington, D. I., Wade, C. A., & Persson, T. (2015). Strategies for teaching students to think critically: A meta-analysis. *Review of Educational Research, 85*(2), 275–314. https://doi.org/10.3102/0034654314551063

BBC Learning English (2017) *Study Skills – How to think critically.* https://www.youtube.com/watch?v=FMt_RIR_JHo (accessed 9/20).

Cottrell, S. 2017. *Critical Thinking Skills,* Macmillan Study Skills series, London: Red Globe Press.

National Graduate Attributes Project. (2011, May 17). *Introduction to mapped universities' statements of graduate attributes.* Retrieved from http://www.itl.usyd.edu.au/projects/nationalgap/resources/gamap/introduction.htm

Nurse Killam (2015). Ontology, Epistemology, *Methodology and Methods in Research Simplified*! https://www.youtube.com/watch?v=hCOsY5rkRs8 (accessed 9/20).

The Foundation For Critical Thinking (2020) http://www.criticalthinking.org/pages/online-courses-for-your-students/1384

van Gelder, T. J. (2015). Using argument mapping to improve critical thinking skills. In M. Davies & R. Barnett (Eds.), *The Palgrave Handbook of Critical Thinking in Higher Education* (pp. 183–192). Basingstoke U.K.: Palgrave Macmillan.

van Gelder, T.J. *Critical Thinking: Some Lessons Learned.* Adult Learning Australia Adult Learning Commentary Number 12, 30 May 2001

van Gelder, T. J. (2016). *Argument mapping with word smartart.* https://timvangelder.com/2016/07/16/argument-mapping-with-word-smartart/

Wolcott, S. & Lynch, C. (2020). *Steps for better thinking;* http://www.wolcottlynch.com/educator-resources.html

Index

www.ingramcontent.com/pod-product-compliance
Lightning Source LLC
LaVergne TN
LVHW010901110826
845149LV00005B/1439